NIKE

BETTER IS TEMPORARY

SAM GRAWE

CONTENTS

Sports have always been more than a game to me. I have been shaped by sports for my entire life. In high school and college, I played basketball. We weren't always the most talented of teams. But we had teamwork. We had each other. And so we won some games. I realized then the incredible power of the team.

When I entered the business world, sports remained. In my first job, my boss saw that I was dealing with a fear of failure as I transitioned into new and greater responsibilities. One day he pulled me aside and offered me a baseball analogy. He said that it was easy to bat .900 in Little League, to rarely miss a pitch. But in Major League Baseball, that success rate is impossible. At best, you'll hit .350. You'll strike out two out of three times. And yet despite these odds, the world's best players wake up every day ready to swing. They understand that if you want to become world-class in anything, failure is a necessary by-product.

Nike's history proves this point. Our journey is often portrayed as the ultimate success story, and it is—because it shows how setbacks can lead to truly great accomplishments. Success, it turns out, is a messy process. It requires hard work, tough decisions, sacrifices, risks, and failures. I've learned this as a CEO and in my own life, and it's evidenced by the innovations charted in this book. It's why Nike time and again invests in experimental concepts and technologies. Not all will immediately succeed; far from it. But each will teach us an unknown lesson— and it is these lessons that will lead us to something unexpected that transforms our reality.

Like life, innovation is an imperfect journey. Positive outcomes are easy to package as linear successes, but we know the path to innovation is riddled with doubt, missteps, and stress. Never in my thirty-plus-year career have I stood in the middle of anything and been certain I was doing the right thing. It's my commitment to the course and my faith in the process that lets me try new things, solve problems, and, ultimately, succeed. In the end, success comes down to who capitalizes on opportunities— or failures—better. Take any World Cup match: usually the difference between claiming the title and being the team no one remembers is one goal, waiting for that one opportunity to put boot to ball. At its best, sports offer us a reminder that winning is about having faith that you can prevail but not knowing until the last minute whether you will.

Our athletes, from LeBron James to Sarah Reinertsen, have demonstrated this over and over, not by always winning but by facing adversity head-on, eyes open. Since day one—when Bill Bowerman and Phil Knight saw the market potential of a curiously new kind of running shoe—Nike has done the same, fearlessly confronting challenges and seizing opportunities by innovating. It's a spectacular story.

But any champion knows what worked yesterday won't tomorrow. The game is always evolving. Never has this been a more apt description of our world. The rapid pace of change brought on by the digital age demands new, immediate innovation—as do the massive societal, cultural, and environmental issues facing our world. This is precisely why I view Nike's next chapter with great optimism, because through adversity comes progress.

Nike's focus will always be to deliver performance innovation that lets athletes do their very best. But serving the world of sport has never meant more opportunity than it does today. We're rapidly expanding and accelerating our digital platforms to reach more athletes worldwide. We're empowering our communities to break down more barriers. And we're strengthening our deep relationship with consumers all around the globe. This all serves not only to improve sport outcomes—it serves to elevate sport itself. Our goal is to further democratize sport, to do the seemingly impossible and allow everyone to win.

So as we pursue progress over perfection, we will continue to redefine what's possible by giving ourselves permission to try the counterintuitive, to refrain from making assumptions, to occasionally fail, and to keep on failing until we succeed. We will recommit daily to the complicated journey—the messy process—celebrated in the following pages.

Over the years I've been asked, "What's the difference between innovation and design?" To me, innovation solves real problems and makes an experience better. Design has the power to bring humanity to an object—it creates a connection emotionally or even spiritually. I've always believed the foundation for doing both well is strong relationships—true partnerships that lead to an exchange of experiences and expertise.

At Nike the heart of the creative process is the chemistry across our own teams. Designers, makers, coders, engineers, and scientists all work together to pour dozens of ideas into one product or platform. Our process is rarely a linear one. We're constantly curious. Ideas sit on the corners of a desk, maybe for years, waiting for their moment. All it takes is for the right conversation to take them somewhere new or the right tool to make them possible. The key is we stay open and flexible. That can happen organically, but it's also important to actively create opportunities for diverse points of view to collide. We see it in our creative workspaces, our research labs, and in the field with our athletes every day. There's no question that Nike is a place where exploration is best done together.

We're lucky, too, that our muse is often restless. As designers in sport, we'll never be without inspiration because the problems we solve for continually change. Athletes get faster. They get stronger. They train differently. And our technology advances. Sport is constantly progressing, which creates new needs, giving us new insights that ultimately lead to new products. It's a virtuous cycle.

History has proven when Nike and the world's best athletes put our faith in one another, great things happen. What makes our teams special is not only how we translate an athlete's feedback into innovation but also how we share a bit of their soul with the world. Because the true personality of a product is revealed when we get to know the people behind the achievements. Who are the biggest influences in their lives? What are their pregame rituals and internal pep talks? What are they drawn to creatively? And do they have a bigger platform outside of sport? Uncovering all of it takes time. And, more importantly, trust.

This book is filled with stories of athletes who have shared in that process with Nike. Sometimes those collaborations are born from relationships that were built over years. Or sometimes inspiration can strike like a bolt of lightning.

Of all the athletes I have been privileged to work with, perhaps none came to the table with a clearer point of view than Kobe Bryant. He was always prepared with thoughtful questions and strong opinions, pushing us into new territory with every project. One of the best examples of that conviction was demonstrated through the process of designing a revolutionary low-cut basketball shoe with the Kobe IV. Having lived in Europe as a child, Kobe was a student of the beautiful game of football, or soccer. He wondered out loud to his longtime Nike design collaborator, Eric Avar, why football players, who stopped and started as abruptly as basketball players, were not asking for high-top shoes. In fact, some of the world's greatest goal scorers opted for the most minimal boots possible. "I want to prove that you don't need all this crap around your ankle . . . that you can play at the highest level in a low-top," he told Avar. "I think the market needs a shift too." The project had all the elements of Nike at its best. "Here's an insight. This is what I'm feeling. This is what I want to try." We backed it up with science from our research labs. And then we drove it forward with Kobe, who was passionate and creative. The low-top design changed convention forever, offering a fresh aesthetic and bringing natural motion to basketball shoes.

The relationship between Kobe and our design team, and me personally, deepened over the years. He was always demanding. One thing was certain, though: rising to meet the expectations of Kobe made everyone better. He was a gift. And we miss him dearly.

In the following pages, you'll also see the value of mutually beneficial relationships through collaboration with artists, musicians, and subcultures at large. I've always believed being open and curious to the world is a way to nourish and inspire our own creative culture. As others interpret our brand, we learn from it.

Over the years, a person who excelled at building communities for Nike relationship by relationship was Sandy Bodecker. In the mid-1990s he took on the challenge of making Nike authentic in football. He took us from outsider to leader one victory at a time, earning respect by being genuine with everyone he met, content to keep his head down until he conquered the ultimate goal. A few years later, he took the same approach with the skateboarding community. Sandy and the Nike SB team built the trust of shop owners and athletes. He could make a believer out of anyone because he himself believed that both Nike and skateboarding would be better if they worked together. He was right. Sandy later joined a Special Projects team within our Innovation team to create product that was all about making athletes measurably better—significantly better—which turned into the epic Breaking2 project. It was one of his and Nike's most ambitious and inspiring works ever.

With heavy hearts, we lost both Sandy and Kobe within fifteen months of one another in late 2018 and early 2020, respectively. Both had a sincere passion for learning and approached life through the lens of constant improvement. And both paid that forward as teachers and mentors— focused on unleashing the potential in others. They treasured working with their teams and were generous collaborators.

I hope this book serves as a reminder of just how human sport is, after all. It's full of stories about personal relationships; of working together to overcome obstacles. Because, in the end, it's people and the strength of their connections that set off a chain reaction of ideas at Nike. If the ingredients are right, it leads to something better. Until, of course, we meet again to talk about the next challenge.

BREAKING2

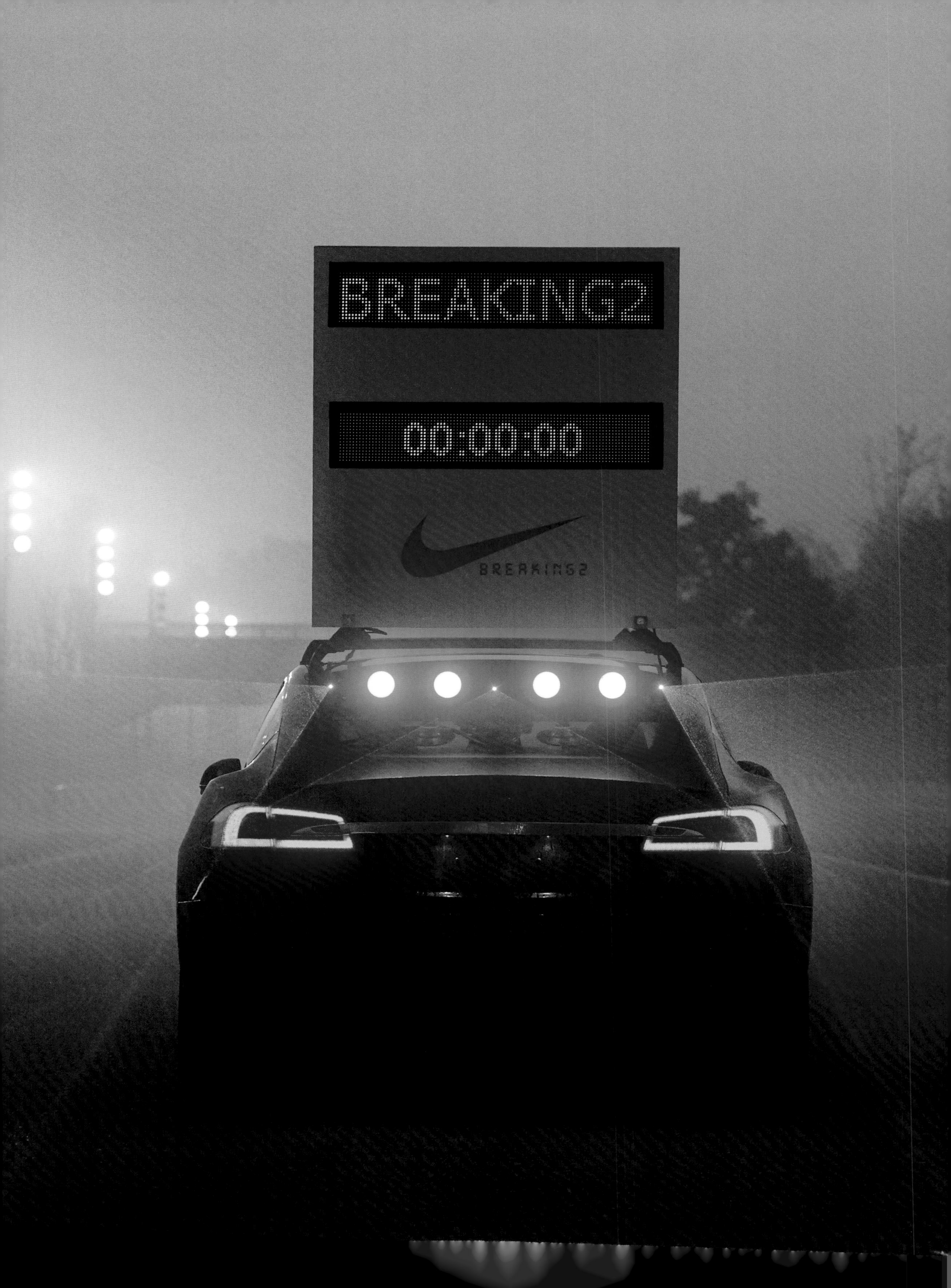
BREAKING2
00:00:00
BREAKING2

The air is cool but not cold. A blanket of low clouds hovers over the flat plain at the foot of the Italian Alps north of Milan in the stillness of the predawn hours. A small trapezoidal section of white asphalt on the Autodromo Nazionale Monza—one of the world's fastest Formula One courses—is illuminated by a ghostly green array of lasers emanating from a pace car. Windbreaker-clad staffers scuttle to and fro, busily monitoring their radio channels while a small crowd looks on from the sidelines. There is a palpable prerace tension in the air, though there are no engines idling and no crews in the pits. At exactly 5:45 a.m., an air horn sounds, signaling the start of one of the most audacious experiments in modern sport, and the culmination of more than four years of behind-the-scenes research, development, and design conducted by the world's leading sportswear manufacturer.

It is May 6, 2017, and three of the world's best long-distance runners are making a bold attempt to run a marathon in less than two hours. That Nike, a multibillion-dollar company with a corporate agenda to fulfill, has brought them to the track at Monza (not coincidentally sixty-three years to the day after Roger Bannister ran the first sub-four-minute mile) might let the effort be dismissed out of hand as a publicity stunt. But scratch beneath the surface—all the way back to 2014, when the moonshot idea of breaking the two-hour barrier first emerged—and it becomes clear that the entire endeavor is a clear-eyed expression of Nike's stated mission: "to bring inspiration and innovation to every athlete* in the world (*if you have a body, you are an athlete)." Moreover, proving the impossible possible is a challenge few—if any—organizations would take upon themselves to try.

Large companies are, by their nature, difficult to grasp. To the outside world they avail themselves as monolithic entities, known singularly for providing *X*, servicing *Y*, and being *Z*. These tendencies are only exacerbated in today's world of brand-savvy consumers and 24-7 digital communications, because of which everything a company says and does instantly emerges into a highly pressurized environment, and the slightest potential misstep could set off a chain of rippling repercussions. Staying "on brand" is paramount. But pass through the corporate bubble that keeps the outside world at bay, and you find a familiar sight: human beings doing human things. In this respect, Nike is no different from its competition. People come to work there. They bring their unique experiences, networks, ideas, creativity, and passions. The uncommon alchemy is in how a company marshals its collective human resources into something more than the sum of its parts. And it's here that through the years—and on that spring morning in Monza—Nike has managed to achieve something beyond the scope of what any org chart could tell you.

With twelve million Internet viewers live-streaming the event (dubbed Breaking2) and the resources of a major sporting occasion on the ground in Italy, it seems almost inconceivable that Nike's entire effort to break the two-hour marathon mark could be traced back to the vision and determination of a single person within a company of more than seventy thousand

employees. But in 2014 Sandy Bodecker, a thirty-five-year veteran executive with a storied career of firsts, championed the efforts of a small
team of researchers and innovators within the Nike Sport Research Lab
(NSRL) that had been looking at new footwear solutions for long-distance
running but wanted to take a bigger, riskier leap. Employing research
and data-gathering techniques honed over decades, the NSRL contributes key metrics and insights to drive the company's innovation engine.
With Bodecker's encouragement, and budgetary path clearing, the group
realigned its approach to focus squarely on the two-hour barrier. "The
sub-two-hour marathon barrier is one of those rare ones that, if broken,
can transform a sport," Bodecker said. "It will impact the way runners
view distance running and human potential forever." With "1:59:59"
tattooed on the inside of his wrist, Bodecker literally embodied the
mission, but shaving nearly three minutes off the then-current world
record (2:02:57) would mean achieving a 4:34-mile pace to drop seven
seconds off each of the marathon's 26.2 miles (42.2 kilometers).
Academic physiologists had long since broken down the math in ways
that hypothesized a sub-two-hour time was achievable, but the team
quickly understood that turning that possibility into a reality would take
a lot more than number crunching and new shoes.

In the 1972 Eames Office film *Design Q&A*, famed mid-century designer
Charles Eames defines design simply "as a plan for arranging elements
to accomplish a particular purpose." The team at Nike took a similarly
wide-angle approach—thoroughly examining and extrapolating every
single element that goes into a marathon attempt to design the perfect
race. They developed a broad framework for holistic problem-solving that
included athlete selection, product, training, nutrition, and race optimiza-
tion. The outcome was still far from given, but by looking at it in this way,
the team started to believe that chalking up a diverse array of marginal
gains could conceivably make the impossible possible.

The first order of business was to find the right runners. The NSRL scientists
leading the project, physiologist Dr. Brad Wilkins, and Dr. Brett Kirby, the
lab's principle researcher, starting poring over all of Nike's sponsored
runners—from 5Kers up to marathoners—for the right mix of speed and
stamina and invited eighteen top prospects to come to the lab for intensive physiological testing. There were three main factors to assess: oxygen
consumption (or in automotive terms, the size of their engines), running
economy (average gas mileage), and sustained velocity (ability to keep
the engine revving). Working from a model that predicted the necessary
thresholds in each of these areas to achieve a sub-two-hour marathon,
the team plotted the statistical viability of each runner. However, even with
the extensive data sets informing their selection, they also understood
that the psychological barrier to running a perfect race was as great as the
physical one. The team zeroed in on athletes with the mental capacity and
drive believed necessary to win and eventually whittled the field down to
three of the world's most elite distance runners. Ethiopia's Lelisa Desisa,
the youngest of the bunch, was famous for winning the 2013 Boston
Marathon and returning his medal to the city of Boston after the tragic

events that unfolded that day. Although his race times weren't as fast as those of the other runners being considered, the testing showed he had a huge oxygen consumption capacity. Eritrea's Zersenay Tadese became that country's first Olympic medalist with a bronze in the 10,000-meter race at the 2004 Summer Olympics in Athens and held the half marathon world record at 58:23. His tests revealed a particularly strong running economy. Kenya's Eliud Kipchoge was rapidly becoming the most dominant long-distance runner in the world, having won marathons in Chicago, Berlin, and London, and received multiple Olympic medals dating back to 2004. His test scores weren't particularly revealing (in part because he despises running on treadmills), but nonetheless the team knew he had what it would take to win.

With the runners selected, Wilkins and Kirby dug further into their systemic approach for designing the perfect race. To calculate personalized hydration programs, they had the athletes exercise in a climate chamber to model their sweat loss. They also developed individual nutrition programs to determine the right type and dosage of carbohydrate to administer to best get them through the 26.2 miles. Even with the runners back home training in their native countries, they were able to share detailed real-time biometric feedback and insights to enable Wilkins and Kirby to tailor their regimes up until race day.

Meanwhile work continued apace on developing the shoes that would get the runners to the finish line on time. While the operating thesis for long-distance running had been developing as lightweight a solution as possible, the group led by Tony Bignell, vice president of Footwear Innovation, and Dr. Geng Luo, former NSRL biomechanist, made a breakthrough when they asked themselves what the "right weight" would be instead. Over the course of a marathon, a runner makes roughly twenty thousand foot strikes with forces greater than three times their body weight. The footwear research team started looking at a special, highly resilient lightweight foam developed for the medical industry that was capable of returning 80 to 90 percent of that energy when placed underfoot. The shoes took a new turn, incorporating large stacks of what the team called ZoomX foam to offer runners superior cushioning and comfort with only a modicum of additional weight. Another breakthrough came when the team started to explore embedding a scoop-shaped carbon-fiber plate within the foam. It not only served to stiffen the shoe but also helped to return more of the runner's expended energy with each foot strike. When they sent the prototypes out for external testing, the Nike researchers found a consistent 4 percent improvement across speed ranges and different types of runners. Real-world tests yielded equally impressive results—athletes wearing prototypes of the new design won all three medals in the 2016 Summer Olympics marathon in Rio, including Kipchoge's gold.

A quantifiable boost in performance was the holy grail researchers and innovators within the NSRL had been aiming for, with implications for far more than the Breaking2 effort. "We now are confident that just by opening an orange box and putting the shoe on, you're instantly better," said Matthew Nurse, PhD, vice president of the NSRL. "You may not want to be 4 percent faster, but you're going to be 4 percent more efficient. If you only have half an hour to do a run, you can feel 4 percent less fatigue, or you can run 4 percent farther. That's up to you. And you'll have 12 percent less muscle damage, so tomorrow, you're gonna feel better."

Through computational design, the final shoe, known as the Zoom Vaporfly Elite, was further tuned to the distinctive profile of each athlete; based on extensive lab test results, the embedded carbon-fiber plates were given a customized stiffness profile. To create an optimal fit with unique regional support and breathability, the stitching patterns of the shoes' Flyknit uppers were tweaked based on three-dimensional scans of the athletes' feet.

Alongside the footwear, the apparel research team also developed a ground-up, head-to-toe running kit that aimed to mollify a range of known issues, from thermal regulation to aerodynamics, and further enhance each runner's performance. With the express goal of creating a garment that wouldn't cling to the body and pick up excess weight from perspiration, the team developed a sleeveless shirt made from lightweight yarn that featured a computationally designed open-hole structure to allow for greater breathability where the body runs hot and insulation where it needs warmth. Body scans from the runners allowed the designers to further remove distracting excess fabric and cut back on wind resistance. An independent knitted sleeve—snug at the ends and flexible around the elbow—offered adjustable coverage and comfort. Dozens of prototype shorts were produced before arriving at the half-tight, a garment engineered to offer compression through the hamstrings and quadriceps and maximum freedom of movement through the hips. The team also developed a five-piece construction sock that locked to the foot to prevent slippage in the shoe while offering more ventilation on the upper. Each item of apparel was individually tailored to the runners' preference and fit.

Even with all the work put into readying the athletes and their gear, some of the biggest problems involved in designing the perfect race remained unsolved. Perhaps no factor would be greater in determining the overall success of the venture than the conditions for the race itself. While the team at Nike decided early on that they wouldn't seek ratification from the International Association of Athletics Federations (IAAF) to make it an official world record attempt, they also decided not to pursue ideas that detracted from the idea of human achievement, such as pushing the runners with a giant fan or blocking the wind with large sheets of plexiglass. The team also knew they needed to find a flat course that would offer low temperatures, low winds, and low humidity. The Junior circuit at Monza fit the bill to a tee. Moreover, unlike a conventional marathon course, the 1.5-mile (2.4-kilometer) loop allowed the team to develop and implement pacing and support strategies that would prove critical to the effort.

While the pacesetters' normal role is to help keep the runners moving at a desired speed, with Breaking2 they served an even more important function—blocking the wind. Though wind resistance makes little difference in most amateur racing conditions, eliminating a headwind over the course of a fast marathon can translate into more than a minute of saved time. Nike's pacesetting strategy was also a critical consideration in its decision not to seek IAAF certification. The association's rules stipulate that all runners on the course must start from the beginning of the race— after which they typically break off once the desired pace is established. The Breaking2 strategy instead called for a sequence of pace runners to enter and exit with each lap.

At a wind tunnel designed for runners and cyclists at the University of New Hampshire, Durham, Wilkins and Kirby experimented with countless arrangements before determining that an arrowhead-shape formation of six pacesetters yields the optimum result. For the event itself, Nike recruited thirty pacers comprising some of the world's best runners— including Sam Chelanga, Aron Kifle, Bernard Lagat, and Lopez Lomong— to each contribute two laps. The highly choreographed strategy called for the three runners to exit the race at the end of each lap, the runners in the rear to pull in front, and new runners to join from behind while maintaining the arrowhead ahead of Desisa, Tadese, and Kipchoge. Pacers were selected for their ability to run calmly and seamlessly in tight proximity to one another. Lasers pointed from the rear of an electric car driving at exactly 13.1 miles (21.1 kilometers) per hour helped to keep them in exact formation ahead of the marathoners.

In the early morning hours at Monza, with the race underway, everything is playing out according to plan. For nearly an hour, as the opaque sky slowly illuminates, the pacers seamlessly glide in and out of position while behind them Desisa, Tadese, and Kipchoge maintain their blistering velocity. The first signs of trouble arrive around the 11-mile (17.7-kilometer) mark—Desisa can no longer hold on. At the halfway point, Tadese too has fallen off. It is all on Kipchoge now. With a relaxed, monastic stoicism on his face, for the next forty minutes he shows no signs of relenting. There are now only two laps left, but the split times have begun to waver, and Kipchoge's legs have drifted—almost imperceptibly— from their once-metronomic tempo. The final lap arrives, and to make the 1:59:59 barrier, he must deliver a 4:17 mile. Four years of banked belief still hang in the air, but even for the greatest long-distance runner on earth, it is too great a task. He crosses the line at 2:00:25, 2:32 faster than the then-current world record. Moments later Kipchoge lies across the track, a gleaming smile spread across his face.

While Breaking2 may have come up short on the scoreboard, it was by no means a failure. Although the team that had rallied around their moonshot was devastated in the moment, Kipchoge still shaved 2:40 off his fastest time (2:03:05)—a remarkable accomplishment by any standard. As he crossed the finish line and broke into a broad smile, Kipchoge was far from downtrodden; instead he realized the dream of a sub-two-hour race was closer than ever. "It was hard for me to shed all those minutes," he said, "but I think it will be easy for another human being to shed twenty-five seconds." A little more than two years later, that human being turned out to be him. On October 12, 2019, in an event held in Vienna, Austria, Kipchoge ran a 1:59:40 marathon outfitted in the fourth generation of Vaporfly Elites, the Air Zoom Alphafly NEXT%, and an apparel kit built off the Breaking2 platform. As for Nike, Breaking2 modeled a new approach to holistic problem-solving that could be applied in any number of directions going forward. For a company that thrives on the idea of "What's next?" Breaking2 offered no shortage of what-ifs. "The amount of data and insights we are able to collect and the experience gained from these efforts," said Bodecker, "will provide us with years of innovation territories to explore and invent around, which ultimately leads to better products and services for athletes of all abilities."

With that statement, Bodecker may well have spoken for nearly five decades of innovation and design at Nike. Breaking2 was perhaps one of the more extraordinary endeavors in the company's history, but the foundation upon which it was built is the same as that found in so much of what Nike does. There is the relentless drive toward improved performance, the deep listening and collaboration with athletes, the restless search for new problems to solve, an underlying foundation of sustainable practices, and the spirited expression of the Nike brand through product and communications.

For Nike, Breaking2 was a stop on the way. The corporate trajectory insists that the next frontier—whether it's something huge, such as the two-hour marathon, or something small, such as a better way to put on a pair of shoes—always lies ahead. "There's no such thing as peak athleticism," says chief design officer John Hoke. "I believe it gets harder and harder and harder, but that doesn't mean there's a peak; it means there's one more ingredient needed, one more set of training, one more advance that's gonna bring you a little bit higher." The more athletes push sport, the more Nike pushes too. In other words: better is temporary.

Breaking2 would not have been possible without the dedication of the thirty pacers:

Collis Birmingham, Australia	Selemon Barega Shirtaga, Ethiopia	Philemon Rono, Kenya
Nguse Tesfaldet Amlosom, Eritrea	Stephen Omiso Arita, Kenya	Stephen Sambu, Kenya
Aron Kifle, Eritrea	Victor Chumo, Kenya	Stephen Mokoka, Russia
Goitom Kifle, Eritrea	Stephen Kosgei Kibet, Kenya	Julien Wanders, Switzerland
Teklemariam Medhin Weldeslassie, Eritrea	Noah Kipkemboi, Kenya	Polat Kemboi Arikan, Turkey
Yitayal Atnafu, Ethiopia	Gideon Kipketer, Kenya	Andrew Bumbalough, USA
Abyneh Ayele, Ethiopia	Laban Korir, Kenya	Sam Chelanga, USA
Tadu Abate Deme, Ethiopia	Moses Kurong, Kenya	Christopher Derrick, USA
Dejene Debela Gonfa, Ethiopia	Abdi Nageeye, Kenya	Bernard Lagat, USA
Getaneh Tamire Molla, Ethiopia	Alex Korio Oloitiptip, Kenya	Lopez Lomong, USA

Breaking2 sub-two-hour marathon attempt, race day	Autodromo Nazionale Monza, Monza, Italy	May 6, 2017

In the predawn hours of May 6, 2017, the nocturnal mist blanketing Monza, Italy, was fractured by the ghostly glow of the Autodromo Nazionale Monza, where stadium lights silhouetted a pack of runners completing their warm-up. Just as the sky began to brighten, a cacophony of radios crackled and a single pace car's lights illuminated the Grand Prix racetrack. Seconds later, at precisely 5:45 a.m., an air horn blared and Eliud Kipchoge (in red), Zersenay Tadese (in light blue), and Lelisa Desisa (in white) shot off the starting line behind six black-clad pacers in triangular formation. The athletes were chasing the seemingly impossible—to run a marathon in less than two hours—as a handful of bystanders, vibrating with anticipation, issued their first cheer. Sandy Bodecker, distinguished on race day by a gold jacket, stood at the center of the small crowd.

The visionary behind Breaking2, Bodecker was Nike's vice president of Special Projects when the company broadcast its ambition to shatter the sub-two-hour marathon barrier. A then-thirty-five-year Nike veteran, whose tenure included a litany of formative firsts—he led Nike's first Global Football business, founded its Skateboarding business, and served as its first head of Global Design—Bodecker had long been obsessed with the record, as evidenced by the 1:59:59 tattoo on the inside of his left wrist. The way Bodecker saw it, a sub-two-hour marathon was a once-in-a-generation feat with the promise not only to redefine running but also to alter existing ideas of human potential. He tirelessly championed the moonshot project until his death in October 2018, just more than a year before Kipchoge made his second attempt—and succeeded—to "break two" in Vienna, Austria.

Breaking2 pacer training camp	Autodromo Nazionale Monza, Monza, Italy	May 1–5, 2017

During training for Breaking2 Eliud Kipchoge declared, "100 percent of me is nothing compared to 1 percent of the whole team." While Kipchoge, Tadese, and Desisa embodied the heart of Breaking2, the audacious quest epitomized teamwork. From the insights of bio-mechanists, nutritionists, sports psychologists, and physiologists to the creativity of designers, materials developers, and engineers to the dedication of coaches and entire training camps, it was the confluence of collective expertise and effort rather than individual brilliance that cemented Breaking2's promise. This communal culture visually manifested on race day in the form of thirty pacers: world-class distance runners selected for their speed and calm, steady temperaments. As their title indicates, pacers are traditionally used to maintain a consistent race pace. In Breaking2, however, their essential function was to mitigate headwinds, an advantage theoretically equivalent to running a marathon on a 2.5 percent downhill gradient and calculated

to save more than sixty seconds. To ensure peak performance, the pacers arrived in Monza five days prior to the race and began training daily to familiarize themselves with Breaking2's novel pacer formation and exchanges. Six pacers would run ahead of the three racers in a revolutionary triangle shape, with the lead pacer positioned 19.7 feet (6 meters) behind the pace car, as indicated by green laser beams the black Tesla Model S would project onto the asphalt. After two laps, pacers would cycle on and off in carefully choreographed groups of three, with thirty-minute breaks between cycles to mitigate pacer variation and fatigue. While the perfectly executed strategy maximized efficiency, as well as time and energy, it disqualified the race's results from IAAF certification—a consequence Nike dismissed. Breaking2 was about more than setting world records; it was about challenging and upending perceptions.

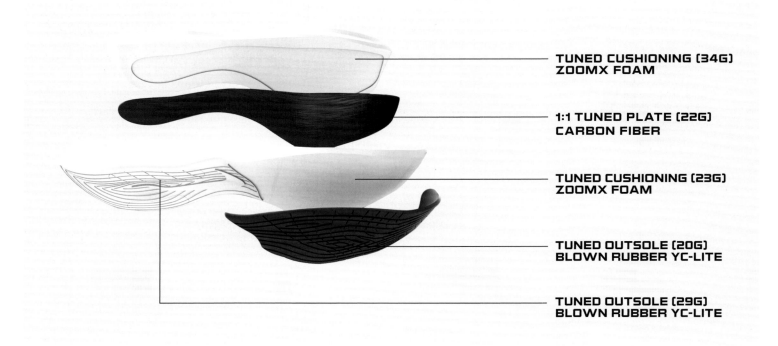

TUNED CUSHIONING (34G)
ZOOMX FOAM

1:1 TUNED PLATE (22G)
CARBON FIBER

TUNED CUSHIONING (23G)
ZOOMX FOAM

TUNED OUTSOLE (20G)
BLOWN RUBBER YC-LITE

TUNED OUTSOLE (29G)
BLOWN RUBBER YC-LITE

Zoom Vaporfly Elite 1:1 tuned tooling system	2017

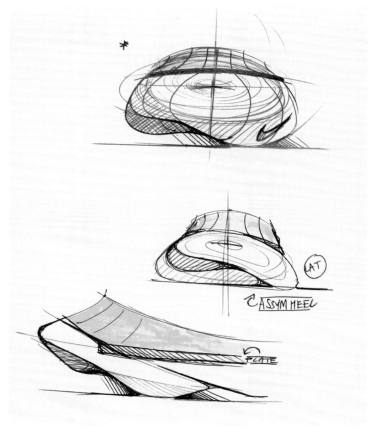

Computational aerodynamic form testing	2017

Aerodynamic midsole and carbon-fiber plate sketch	c.2015

Nike officially announced Breaking2 on December 12, 2016, with a public statement declaring that, although many considered the quest to shave nearly three minutes off the existing marathon world record impossible, it believed "the impossible is an opportunity to envision the future of sport." The future Nike's Breaking2 team conceived leveraged science and technology to analyze and radically rethink every aspect of athletic performance. Evolving a prototype four-layer tooling system—comprised of critical cushioning, propulsion, and outsole components—Nike designers took a form-must-follow-function approach to reimagining each element of a conventional long-distance running flat. To adapt the concept shoe to the three athletes' individual biomechanics, Nike analyzed 3-D scans and pressure maps of the runners' feet, plotted their foot strikes, and monitored their muscle attrition. The team translated the information into customized race-day shoes with personal stitching patterns combining zonal rigidity and breathability. Body-mapping technology—identifying airflow, mobility, support, warmth, and aerodynamic zones—also guided the creation of custom marathon apparel that focused on five critical areas of improvement: weight, fit, comfort, fatigue, and grip.

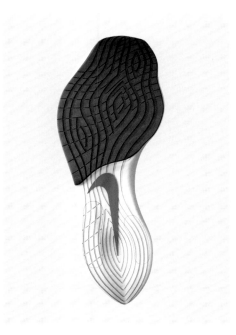

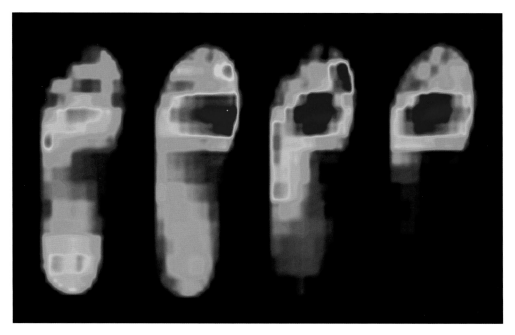

Zoom Vaporfly Elite outsole	2016

Pressure maps used to optimize the Zoom Vaporfly Elite insole	c.2015

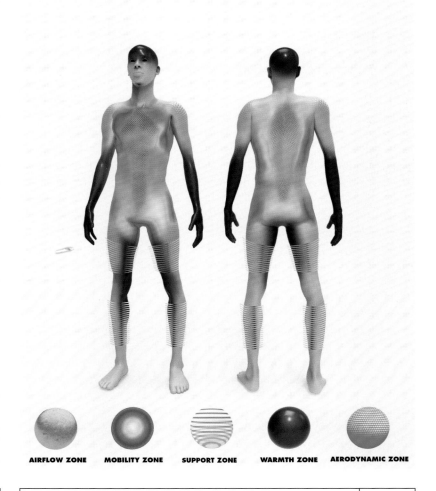

AIRFLOW ZONE   MOBILITY ZONE   SUPPORT ZONE   WARMTH ZONE   AERODYNAMIC ZONE

Breaking2 race-day apparel	c.2016

Zonal body map for Breaking2 race-day apparel creation	c.2015

Beyond optimizing Breaking2's performance product, science and technology played a vital role in priming the athletes for their ambitious undertaking. Principally, it informed their selection for the project. Physiological data of Nike's top eighteen long-distance runners identified Kipchoge, Tadese, and Desisa as the most promising Breaking2 prospects. From there Dr. Brad Wilkins, former Nike Sport Research Lab (NSRL) physiologist, and Dr. Brett Kirby, principle researcher for the NSRL, dialed into each runner's biometrics. The athletes were monitored for energy consumption and conversion, resulting in the creation of personal nutrition programs and custom carbohydrate blends that, testing data revealed, they should consume every 1.5 miles (2.4 kilometers), or at the completion of every loop of the Autodromo Nazionale Monza. This was a marked change from their previous fueling patterns, which included fewer than 2 ounces (60 grams) of carbohydrates per hour. Likewise, climate-chamber testing enabled the Nike team to model the athletes' sweat loss and establish targeted hydration plans.

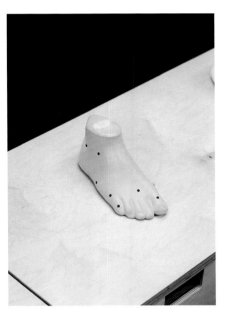

| Breaking2 racer analysis and biometric mapping at the NSRL | Nike World Headquarters, Beaverton, Oregon | c.2016 |

Key performance markers, such as maximum oxygen intake and critical velocity—the top speed a runner can maintain for a long period—were also monitored via NSRL lab evaluations, training camp visits, and GPS watches with heart-rate monitors and accompanying chest-strap transmitters that remotely reported real-time performance and progress figures. These analytics informed algorithms that comprised the center of continuously evolving, meticulously tailored training plans aimed at amplifying each athlete's unique strengths and diminishing his prospective weaknesses. For Desisa, this initially meant building endurance. Once he began logging up to 200 miles

(322 kilometers) a week, the team prescribed specific track workouts to foster speed. Tadese, conversely, first focused on speed training that familiarized him with the race pace. Later he was prescribed longer runs, between 20 and 25 miles (32 and 40 kilometers), that would enhance his endurance and cultivate speed over a longer distance. Kipchoge's data and performance uncovered little room for improvement, which led the team to craft a varied training plan—incorporating a balance of long endurance runs and detailed speed work—that closely aligned with his regular training.

| Kipchoge, Desisa, and Tadese's custom Zoom Vaporfly Elites | Ice Blue/Bright Crimson/University Red/Blue Fox | 2017 |

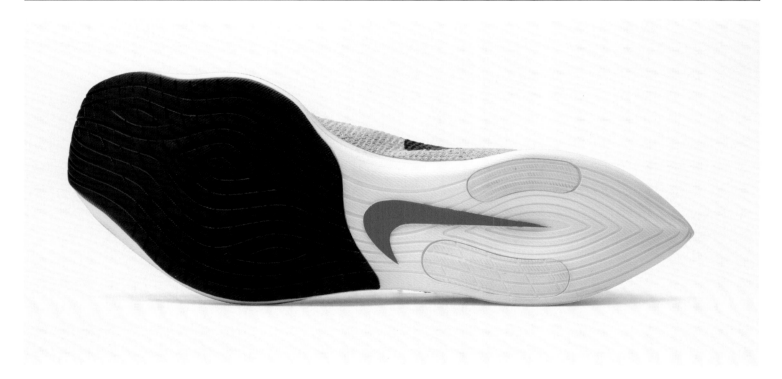

| Zoom Vaporfly Elite outsole | | 2017 |

The Zoom Vaporfly Elite—the official footwear of Breaking2—propelled Kipchoge, Tadese, and Desisa around the Autodromo Nazionale Monza 17.5 times. For the event, each athlete's ice-blue and bright crimson shoes were custom-crafted, incorporating the silhouette's defining innovation, its tooling system, and a personalized message: Kipchoge's read "Beyond the Limits," his personal mantra; Desisa's paid homage to his parents; while Tadese's featured his wife's name. In development since June 2013, the system comprised two fundamental technologies: ZoomX foam, an ultra-lightweight, soft foam capable of providing up to 85 percent energy return, and a full-length carbon-fiber plate.

Featuring a scooplike shape, the plate increased stiffness, provided a propulsive sensation, improved stride-by-stride efficiency, and minimized energy loss. An aerodynamic heel was also integrated to reduce drag, while a Flymesh upper with a dynamic midfoot arch band provided zero-distraction containment without adding weight. Holistically, these features delivered an average of 4 percent improvement in running economy and were found to reduce muscle damage by up to 12 percent when compared with Nike's previous fastest racing flat. Tony Bignell, vice president of Footwear Innovation, led the Zoom Vaporfly Elite's conception by continuously urging his team to question the accepted.

BREAKING2

05.06.2017
2:00:25

10.12.2019
1:59:40

Breaking2 race-day apparel, singlet and shorts as worn by Eliud Kipchoge	2017

While the Zoom Vaporfly Elite maximized the output of every foot strike, custom Breaking2 apparel kits minimized the wind resistance, sweat, and muscle fatigue that result from maintaining a tempo of 13.1 miles (21 kilometers) per hour for 26.2 miles (42.2 kilometers). To inform the groundbreaking apparel, Nike designers mined body scans of each athlete for biometric insights, then conflated the data with personal fit preferences and Nike's most progressive materials.

Lightweight yarn woven into a computationally designed open-hole structure formed a singlet that enhanced ventilation and reduced perspiration weight. Short tights were individually tailored, with targeted compression through the hamstrings and quadriceps, mobility through the hips, and AeroBlade texture for enhanced aerodynamics. Arm sleeves combatted cooler temperatures without adding surface friction, while AeroSwift tape diminished drag on the lower legs.

| Zoom Vaporfly 4% | Ice Blue/Bright Crimson/University Red/Blue Fox | 2017 |

| Zoom Vaporfly 4% | Blue Fox/Bright Crimson/University Red/Black | 2017 |

| Zoom Vaporfly 4% outsole | | 2017 |

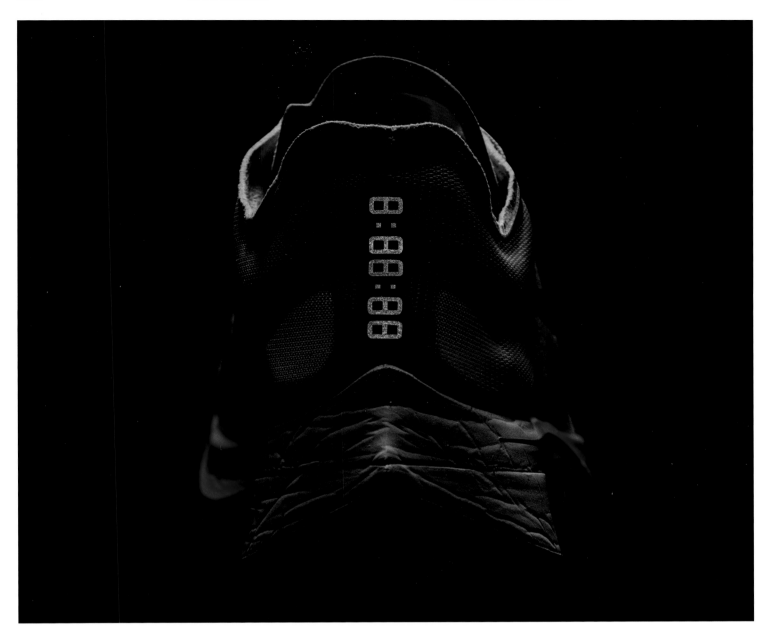

| Zoom Vaporfly 4% aerodynamic heel | 2017 |

| Zoom Vaporfly 4% aerodynamic heels | 2017 |

| Zoom Vaporfly 4% ZoomX foam midsole | 2017 |

Even before Kipchoge demonstrated the measurable merits of Breaking2 with his 2:00:25 finishing time, Bodecker lauded the project for its progressive process that toppled assumptions about both human potential and running product. Ultimately the quest provided Nike with crucial insights, technologies, and innovations to perpetually fuel the company's foundational mission: to bring inspiration and innovation to every athlete* in the world (*If you have a body, you're an athlete). Proof of the quest's trickle-down effect emerged just more than two months after the race, when Nike unveiled a trio of new training and running shoes—crowned by the celebrated Zoom Vaporfly 4%—that adapted the Zoom Vaporfly Elite's innovative geometry and technologies for athletes of all levels.

| Mo Farah training in the ZoomX Vaporfly NEXT% | Ethiopia | 2019 |

| ZoomX Vaporfly NEXT% | Electric Green/Guava Ice/Black | 2019 |

| ZoomX Vaporfly NEXT% carbon-fiber plate | 2019 |

| ZoomX Vaporfly NEXT% outsole | 2019 |

As a Nike advertisement once famously stated, "There is no finish line." The April 2019 debut of the ZoomX Vaporfly NEXT% showcased the legacy of this philosophy. A successor to the Zoom Vaporfly Elite, the third-generation running shoe incorporated 15 percent more ZoomX foam, an improved upper, a retooled midsole, and a redesigned traction pattern for better forefoot grip, with contoured treads for smoother turns. Its name nodded to the silhouette's ever-increasing speed potential, which Kipchoge validated when he wore an even newer edition of the design on October 12, 2019, while breaking the two-hour-marathon barrier in Vienna with a time of 1:59:40.

- ZOOMX / Returned midsole system
- Carbon Fiber plate @ more Zoom x foam in forefoot
= Added stability, energy conservation
= Propulsive Feel

- Anatomical tongue
  → avoid irritation
- Foam Pad = Heel fit
- Heel Collar = Engineered for stability

- Intelligent S...
- Reduce weight
- Zoomx foam
- Vaporweave

- Propulsive Feel
- Dense grooves

1 THE VOICE OF THE ATHLETE

Hyperdunk Lamar Odom House of Hoops
Hyperdunk Pau Gasol House of Hoops
Hyperdunk Supreme Lithuania
Zoom Kobe I
Zoom Kobe IV
Zoom Kobe V
Zoom Kobe IX Elite
Waffle Trainer
Blue Ribbon Sports Pre Montreal
Track spike made for Steve Prefontaine
Triumph
Vainqueur
Track spike made for Mary Decker
Track spike made for Sebastian Coe
Zoom Ultra II
Track spike made for Michael Johnson
Zoom Super Fly
Zoom Superfly R3
Zoom Matumbo 2

Zoom Superfly R4
Zoom Superfly Elite
Hyperdunk+ Sport Pack
LunarTrainer+
LunarFly+3
LunarMX+
Lunar Chukka Woven+ ND
React Hyperdunk 2017 Flyknit
Epic React Flyknit 2
Odyssey React
Joyride NSW Setter
Joyride CC3 Setter
Free 5.0
Free 4.0
Free 3.0
Free 3.0 V3
Free RN
Free RN 5.0
Free Train Force Flyknit

Free Trainer 7.0
Pegasus
Pegasus Racer
Air Zoom Pegasus 35
Zoom Pegasus Turbo 2
Zoom Pegasus 35 Turbo
Pegasus Turbo NEXT%
Air Zoom Alphafly NEXT%
Air Zoom Viperfly
Air Zoom Tempo NEXT% FE
Air Zoom BB NXT
Air Zoom Victory
USA Women's Flyknit Airborne Top
Germany Women's Dri-FIT AeroSwift
Athletics Unitard
USA Women's Dri-FIT AeroSwift
Athletics Unitard
HyperAdapt 1.0
Adapt BB

U.S. Route 26 climbs steeply out of Portland, Oregon's, western edge through Tanner Creek Canyon, snaking its way up through the primal evergreen forests of the Tualatin Mountains, where you half expect to spot the Pacific Northwest's fabled Sasquatch emerging from the lush ferns and pines at the side of the road. Once the grade crests, the vista expands across the Tualatin Valley and yields to a suburban milieu of strip malls, gas stations, fast food restaurants, and low-rise offices. It takes ten or fifteen more minutes traveling westward to reach Beaverton, Oregon, a place with seemingly little to distinguish itself from countless other American suburbs, save for the world-famous brand headquartered on a vast tract at its northwestern limits.

Set behind a large berm, and encircled by a running trail that glides through stands of pines and atop the oversized entrance gates, today's Nike World Headquarters (WHQ) consists of no fewer than 74 structures spread across its 286 acres (115.7 hectares). The company first set up shop here in 1990, occupying eight semi-anonymous Richard Meieresque buildings centered around a man-made lake. At the behest of cofounder Phil Knight, each building on campus takes its name from the athletic protagonists central to the brand's success: Dan Fouts, Mia Hamm, Bo Jackson, Michael Jordan, Steve Prefontaine, Nolan Ryan, Pete Sampras, Mike Schmidt, Tiger Woods, and so on. As the business has grown, so too has its real estate footprint. Today it seems as much office park as construction site. An unmissable assemblage of cranes, earth movers, cement trucks, and construction trailers is a testament to the company's astronomic growth. Nike's new construction scraps the anodyne corporatism of its past in favor of a muscular futurism—all slashing angles, textured cladding, and reflective surfaces, executed in deep matte tones with decisive pops of fluorescent orange. Two of the buildings now under construction are particularly significant to the company's future. Reflecting her outsize presence on the tennis court, the Serena Williams Building— designed by Portland-based Skylab Architecture—will be the largest and tallest on campus, and adds more than a million square feet to house a number of Nike's critical business functions. Just on the other side of the 2018 executive building, named after British middle-distance runner Sebastian Coe, lies the LeBron James Building. Designed by Tom Kundig of the firm Olson Kundig, based in Seattle, Washington, the building will provide expansive state-of-the-art facilities for Nike's Advanced Innovation teams. "These are all environments to try to stir connectivity and creativity—and have people riff on each other's ideas," says Nike chairman Mark Parker, who instigated the building boom during his tenure.

But at Nike's WHQ, much of the riffing takes place outside of typical conference rooms and cubicles. There is not one but three world-class gyms, replete with squash, racquetball, and basketball courts; a swimming pool; a climbing wall; yoga and spin studios; and every piece of workout equipment imaginable. Step outdoors and there are two full-size football fields; basketball, tennis, and beach volleyball courts; a turf field; a replica tee and green from Pebble Beach's 18th hole; and, in addition to the aforementioned trail, a five-lane, 400-meter track made from fifty thousand recycled athletic shoes. The facilities are not just there to encourage employees to "make sport a daily habit" but also as real-world wear-testing and practice facilities for the many professional and amateur athletes in the company's orbit. On any given day, you're just as likely to find a local youth team kicking around footballs as you are an NBA superstar shooting hoops. From the company's earliest days to the present, Nike's success has been inextricably linked to the goals and dreams of athletes.

"We're incredibly lucky, because we work with athletes who have big ambitions, and when you combine that with our passion and obsession, it creates the future," says chief design officer John Hoke. "We at Nike— and in design specifically—have a pretty healthy disrespect for the status quo, barriers, limits, and world records. Athletes push us there."

While this dynamic was made explicit with the Breaking2 effort to log a sub-two-hour marathon in 2017, it is also implicit with each successive design and innovation Nike produces. The drive for continuous improvement can be traced back to cofounder Bill Bowerman's experiments for his runners at the University of Oregon—a never-ending cycle of tinkering, testing, and refining. Both Bowerman and Knight understood that winning—both in sports and in business—requires an edge to stay ahead of the competition. For Nike, that's meant building an unparalleled pipeline for innovation, product development, and design. What was once a lone coach in a workshop under the grandstand at Hayward Field has evolved to encompass a highly sophisticated sports science laboratory, concept-creation center, and a large staff of innovators, engineers, developers, scientists, technologists, researchers, and designers in what's called the Nike Explore Team (NXT). Shoes, such as the Zoom Vaporfly Elite, are representative of the significant breakthroughs the organization is capable of when it puts these talents together. At the same time, stalwart lines, such as the Pegasus running shoe, have been successively upgraded for more than thirty-five years, with each new version offering a feature set that helps athletes to run faster, safer, and more comfortably. At the heart of all this activity is a simple motto, executed sculpturally in the lobby of the Mia Hamm Building—where the NXT group sits today—and echoed in conversation after conversation with the teams responsible for delivering the innovative technologies and designs that help Nike get ahead: "Always listen to the voice of the athlete."

"It's important to work with key athletes that have innovative and creative minds," says Eric Avar, vice president and creative director of Innovation. "It always starts with gaining their insights." Avar launched his career at Nike in 1991, working on the Air Flight Huarache under Tinker Hatfield before stepping out on his own with such classics as the Air Max Penny, Air Foamposite, and 2008's Hyperdunk. The latter, worn and made famous by the late Kobe Bryant as he led the USA team to a gold medal in the summer of 2008, would cement both Avar and Bryant's footwear legacies. Bryant—an NBA champion five times over, eighteen-time All-Star, two-time U.S. gold medalist, and Naismith Basketball Hall of Fame inductee, posthumously awarded in 2020—scored 33,643 points in his twenty-year career with the Los Angeles Lakers (and he was the youngest player in league history to reach the 30,000-point milestone). Undoubtedly his success was owed in some part to his exhaustive pre- and postgame routines—hours-long regimens of stretching, shooting, strengthening, massage, treatments, and mental preparation. In addition to his stardom, Bryant's rigorous attention to detail and an almost superhuman self-aware-ness of his physicality and athleticism made him the ideal candidate to collaborate with Nike on a signature line of shoes.

Having worked in close contact since 2003, Bryant and Avar teamed up once more in 2008 on the Zoom Kobe IV, cutting against the grain with a design that was significantly lower than other basketball shoes on the market at the time. Avar recounts, "[Kobe] kept saying, 'I want to enhance my range of motion, and I want to feel like I can be quick and explosive, so I want a low-top that gives me a good stance and a good base of support. Get all the rest of that stuff away from my ankle!'" Although there was resistance internally from those who felt the shift away from high-tops was too drastic, Bryant's insight and insistence set Nike Basketball on a new path, eventually going even lower for the Zoom Kobe V. "The unique thing about Kobe," says Avar, "is that he's . . . looking through the lens of what he wants and what he needs to play basketball at the highest level. . . . In this case, he proved you can play basketball in a low-top too." Nowadays players in the NBA and NCAA frequently choose low-tops, and research has shown there to be relatively little difference between the two in terms of risk of ankle injury.

One of the phrases that comes up repeatedly among the NXT team is to think about "zigging when people are zagging"—a maxim that originated with Tinker Hatfield but has now come to broadly represent another part of the Nike formula for staying ahead of the curve. After Bryant tore his Achilles tendon in a game against the Golden State Warriors on April 12, 2013, that's exactly what he and Avar did with the design of the Zoom Kobe IX Elite, which debuted in early 2014. Taking inspiration from boxing boots and utilizing Flyknit for the upper of a basketball shoe for the first time, the Kobe IX bucked trends by offering a higher-than-high high-top that still plays like a low-top. Adapting Flyknit from running to basketball shoes meant accounting for the variety of lateral movement and stop-start action required by the sport. Avar and his team pushed the technology to attain the necessary structure and support in the upper, augmenting it by incorporating Flywire into the lacing system to help lock down the foot, and included carbon-fiber "support wings" at the heel and midfoot to help increase stability. The socklike Flyknit collar was designed to create a protective feel without limiting any of the natural motion Bryant had become accustomed to while wearing his signature low-tops. "Kobe being Kobe," recounts Avar, "he wanted to mess things up—and mess people up—by going to a high-top."

A 2007 profile of Bryant in *Esquire* brought attention to the star's belief that minute differences in his equipment and game preparation—the

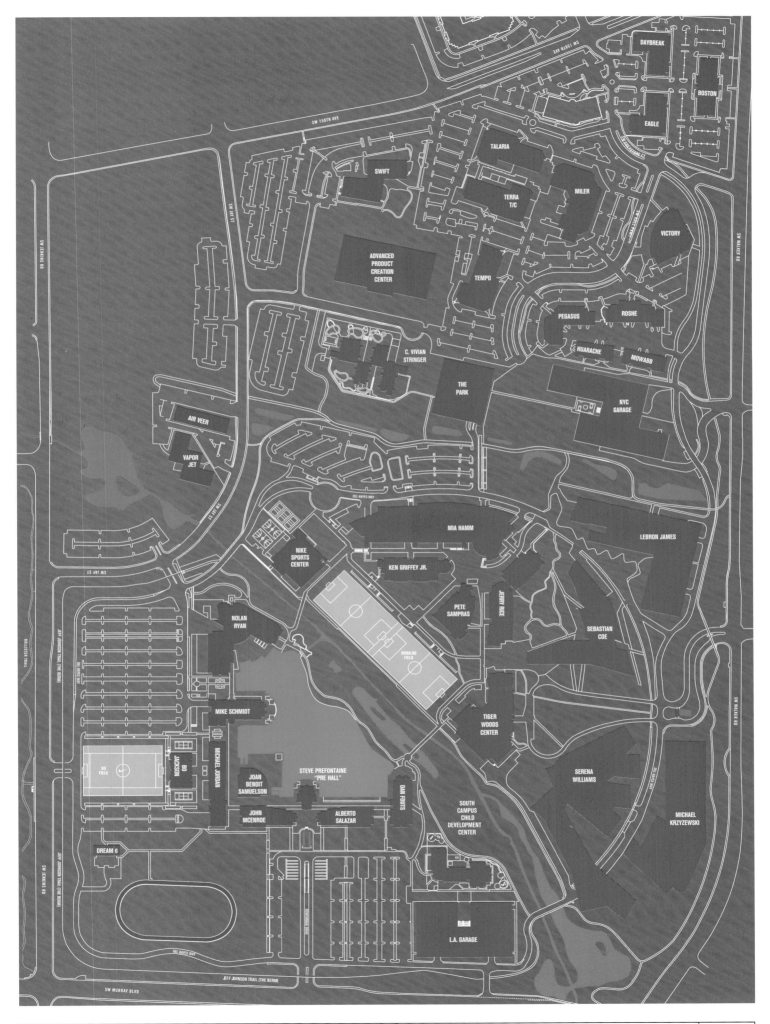

Nike World Headquarters map | Beaverton, Oregon | 2020

fraction of a second recovered from his sock not sliding inside his shoe, an alloy band in the heel to bolster reaction time, a warm-up specially designed to drive heat away from the knees in order to aid recovery— helped give him the edge he needed to topple opponents. But all these ideas do not come from Bryant alone. Certainly a long history of working with athletes of his caliber in a variety of sports has been critical to developing Nike's collective understanding of needs and wants, and of what works and what doesn't. But to deliver season after season of innovations that truly make athletes better, the company has organized around a sophisticated, interdependent engine of sports research, product development processes, design and manufacturing capabilities, and, increasingly, technology and data science. Today the NXT organization is composed of the Nike Sport Research Lab (NSRL), the group responsible for driving innovation through a scientific understanding of athletes and athletic performance; design and development teams dedicated to footwear, apparel, and materials; a Smart Systems team looking at technology and digital applications; the Advanced Product Creation Center (APCC), a maker's wonderland equipped with the most advanced manufacturing and design technologies; and the Space Kitchen, an unconventional group of multidisciplinary talents exploring the furthest reaches of where the business might go. "It's sort of the difference between hunting and farming cultures," muses Parker. "There's a pure, aggressive focus on innovation that is more free-form. It's creating a want that maybe isn't obvious in some cases. And then there's innovation that's more focused on addressing an obvious need, and is more prescriptive and directional in design. We try to create the right balance between the two."

The NXT group as it stands today started in earnest after cofounder Bill Bowerman passed away in 1999. For the design teams at Nike, the legendary coach remained a powerful influence up until the end. "He used to drive up from his workshop in Eugene," recounts Michael Donaghu, vice president of Innovation, "and pester us with all the reasons why he thought we'd become too superfluous. He'd bring a scale out of his briefcase, weigh whatever you were working on, and give you shit about why it had to be that heavy." Bowerman's passing was a wake-up call that made the group question if they were doing enough to spur innovation— and the answer was no. From those conversations, the Innovation Kitchen (the earliest incarnation of today's NXT team) was born.

One of the most impactful products to come out of those early years was the Free, developed by Tobie Hatfield in response to the trend of runners training barefoot to strengthen their feet. For Donaghu and the rest of the team, Free was part of a broader philosophical transition away from perfect motion—a kind of protective, hypothetical ideal—to a better understanding of natural motion, and enabling people to be more in touch with their movements and their bodies while playing sports. "Free completely changed the way that we think about footwear," says Kathy Gomez, vice president of Cushioning Innovation. "For thirty years we tried to protect the foot, and then there was a total mind-shift where we tried to unlock it and let the foot do what it does naturally."

Composed largely of highly technical engineers who work in close collaboration with the company's material scientists and manufacturing experts, the Cushioning Innovation team is responsible for everything that goes on under the foot on a pair of Nike shoes—and today, more than ever, there's a lot going on down there. "We build cushioning platforms on a spectrum of performance that goes from propulsive to comfortable—and everything in between," Gomez explains. Working with an array of technologies that includes proprietary Nike Air, which has become synonymous with the brand, energy-returning foams, such as ZoomX and React, and novel experiments, such as the beanbaglike Joyride, Gomez's team works in a way that is illustrative of the company's broader drive to innovate in service of the athlete. "We make systems, and we put those systems together," she says. "A foam will have an inherent characteristic that's different from the characteristics of an Air unit, and you can combine them in all kinds of ways where one plus one actually equals three."

While the math behind athletic performance may indeed be that fuzzy at times, with an ever-widening range of tests and data-collection techniques at their disposal, the NSRL keeps Nike's approach to innovation grounded in quantifiable science. Led by Matthew Nurse, PhD, vice president of the NSRL, the lab measures, records, and monitors thousands of athletes who pass through its doors each year, with the explicit aim of using science to improve performance and positively impact on human behavior. While some of this work helps the team to create tailor-made solutions for specific athlete requirements, it also informs the development of entirely new platforms and innovations. There are five baseline tests performed on every athlete: a three-dimensional laser scan of the feet to better understand the diversity of complex contours and foot shapes; a high-resolution pressure map of the feet to provide an assessment of function; a full measurement of ankle range of motion, from most extended to compacted, to optimize support and protection; countermovement jumps on force plates—forward and back, side to side, and vertically— to examine explosive movements as researchers look for opportunities to optimize cushioning and mechanics; and a body scan that creates a three-dimensional model of the athlete from a composite of hundreds of camera angles to help determine fit and sizing averages. In addition to tests on athletes, the NSRL is also responsible for applied product research—helping to model and quantify the performance of new designs and components as the innovation team works toward a solution. "I think people would be surprised by our ability to model performance and to digitally replicate how different parts of the product are going to respond," says Thomas Clarke, PhD, president of Innovation. "The ultimate goal is to have a digital file of an athlete—how the parts of their body move and other aspects of their physiology—and then you can translate that to the innovator or designer's desk so, in both footwear and apparel, they see how every decision they make impacts the performance of that athlete."

These digital design capabilities, including the use of computational design, have become a major focus within the Innovation team and now serve as a key ingredient in the design process—like materials or color—

across teams and product lines. One of the key architects of this development is Lysandre Follet, who joined the company nine years ago as an industrial designer—albeit one with a background in computer science and mathematics—and is now a director for the Computational Design group within the NXT. Upon his arrival he noted that Nike was sitting on an untapped trove of data that had the potential to be integrated into product creation. While computers were, of course, commonplace in Nike's design process, it was Follet and his team who began to build algorithms and harness machine learning to utilize the computer as a generative tool. Their work first came to the fore in the summer of 2016 with a track spike designed for sprinter Shelly-Ann Fraser-Pryce. The relatively contained parameters of a straight, short ten-second race in dry conditions offered an ideal springboard for exploration. That the diminutive Fraser-Pryce wears a U.S. size 5 shoe was another factor in pursuing the project. For years the typical approach to footwear design had been to create a men's size 10 and scale it up and down to create other sizes. In the process, without variation in the shoe's properties or materials, large sizes typically become too flexible and small sizes too stiff. The team believed that feeding the right data through the right computational design tools could wrestle with those parameters to achieve outcomes human designers would never think of. Data culled from Fraser-Pryce's foot strikes and foot shape was used to guide the placement of spikes, balance maximum coverage with weight elimination, and determine where the shoe's plate should offer flexibility versus stability. "The idea is to build an algorithm that has rules to describe the product, not a fixed outcome," Follet explains. "That allows us to explore a wide range of design solutions because the model recomputes every time we change the data. We quickly end up, in a matter of weeks, looking at hundreds of solutions you would never have envisioned." Thanks to the advanced manufacturing capabilities on campus at the APCC, these prototypes end up in real-world tests in a matter of days as opposed to after waiting for weeks on a sample from overseas. The data from those tests goes back into the system in a process of iterative learning and improvement.

"There's surprise and delight from seeing what the machine is doing," says Follet, "which is very exciting as a designer because you start to see the computer as a partner in creation." Instead of casting computational design as a replacement for human insight and design talent, Nike sees it as a process wherein both people and machines play to their strengths. "The machine informs the design process by creating near-to-perfect solutions and then, as the designer, you start to take on a role that is more of curation. You start to look at that and tune the system, a little bit like a conductor of an orchestra. . . . That's what we're really good at doing—connecting dots, curating, understanding the right mix between pure performance and aesthetics and sensibility."

After designing the Zoom Superfly Elite for the 100-meter sprint, Follet and the team began to introduce parameters of longer races—accounting for turns as well as optimizing cushioning as the duration increased—to their algorithm. Ultimately, Nike athletes, including Fraser-Pryce,

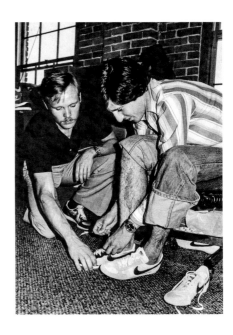

| The original Nike Sport Research Lab | Exeter, New Hampshire | c.1980 |

The first Nike Sport Research Lab (NSRL) was established in 1980, just six years after the iconic Waffle Trainer publicly debuted, turning the athletic footwear industry inside out and establishing Nike as a household name. The tiny facility's name was fittingly coined by the company's future CEO and chairman Mark Parker, and its goal was to better understand the needs of the burgeoning league of athletes who had been converted by the late 1970s running boom. Although the original lab was located in Exeter, New Hampshire—where Nike manufactured shoes from 1974 to 1984—its inspiration came directly from Eugene, Oregon, more than 3,000 miles (4,800 kilometers) away, where Nike cofounder Bill Bowerman formed the first chapter in the company's innovation legacy by translating athlete insights into radical performance products.

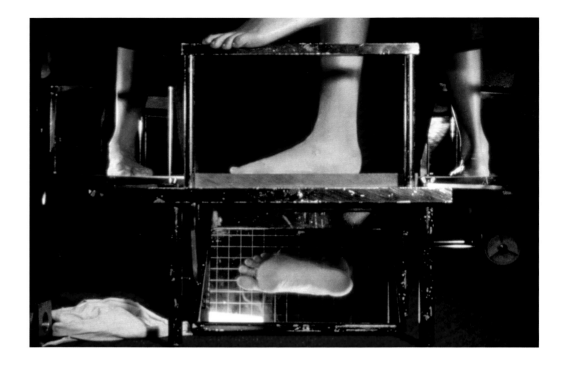

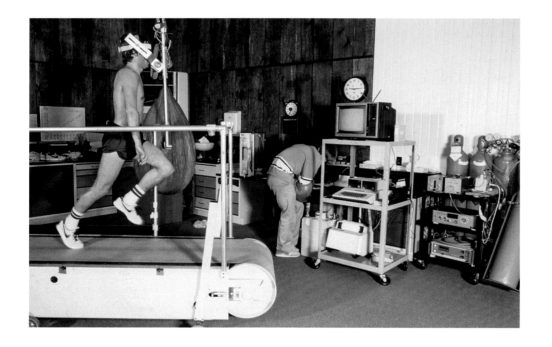

| Athlete testing at the NSRL and footwear manufacturing | Exeter, New Hampshire | c.1978–80 |

were awarded 166 Olympic medals in 2016, including 54 golds. With the validation of success, the group pointed their approach elsewhere within Nike, creating a computationally designed cleat for baseball slugger Mike Trout—the Force Zoom Trout 4—and for American football players, the Alpha Menace Elite. Today, with a growing team offering critical input on projects ranging from footwear to apparel, computational design serves as a core capability within Nike's innovation process.

Although the tools have changed significantly, it's not hard to see the connection between such work and that of Nike's original designer, Bill Bowerman. "He was doing customization for his athletes—drawing outlines of his runners' feet, shaving shoes by hand—but by a totally analog method," says Follet. "It's a beautiful story, because it's always been there in the DNA of Nike." Even as the company expands into new arenas and the staff grows by the hundreds, through the power of tribal lore, Bowerman's spirit continues to infuse the company's approach to innovation. "Bill was the creator, whether he was the sports scientist or the designer—he was the da Vinci of his time," says Nurse. "What he did fifty years ago in a small lab in Eugene is essentially the same as what we're doing. It's more sophisticated now, it's quicker, and we have more tools and more powerful insights, but we still have the same 'Don't talk about it; build it' mentality." And while Bowerman's priority may have been the runners on his team, he also was responsible for the oft-repeated Nike mantra, "If you have a body, you're an athlete." According to Donaghu and others on the Innovation team, the real power of Nike today isn't just in helping the best athletes in the world to become even better; it's in democratizing those insights, applying them broadly, and delivering them to millions of people around the world to make sport accessible.

No single product in Nike's history is more representative of this approach than the Pegasus—the company's longest-running and best-selling product line. Originally conceived by Mark Parker in his role as director of design concepts and engineering during the early 1980s (along with retired Nike designer Bruce Kilgore, then working on the Air Force 1), the Pegasus was designed as an accessible running shoe that would serve the broadest possible base of consumers. Improving upon quality and performance issues the company was facing with its first Air-cushioned shoe, the Tailwind, the Pegasus debuted in 1983 with the Air-Wedge, a small insert in the heel encapsulated in a polyurethane Air unit. While other shoes in the line may have offered greater stability or more cushioning, or have been more lightweight, the Pegasus came in just behind the leader in each category, making it the go-to selection for people just getting into sport or for serious runners in search of a practical training shoe.

Some thirty-seven years later, with dozens of variations and technological advances in the books, the Pegasus holds a similar place in Nike's running line—mining insights from the leading edge of the company's R&D and translating them into a shoe for everyday use. Launched on the heels of the Breaking2 effort in the spring of 2018, the Air Zoom Pegasus 35 offered an ideal snapshot of this strategy. While retaining the cut-and-sew mesh upper of previous Pegasus models, the shoe's most revolutionary new feature was a full-length articulated Zoom Air unit inspired by the curved carbon-fiber plate inside the Breaking2 shoe (the Zoom Vaporfly Elite). A spin-off dubbed the Pegasus Turbo went a step further to bridge the gap between the two models by cutting out another ounce of weight and incorporating the Vaporfly Elite's super-resilient, energy-returning ZoomX foam. Offering a veritable best-of of the company's latest innovations, the Air Zoom Pegasus 37 launched in May 2020.

Beyond the controlled environment of Nike's WHQ, global sporting events not only offer a stage for the best athletes in the world to compete but also for Nike to put its most advanced product developments to the test. In an era when enough news for a year fits into a week and Nike's release schedule includes new drops every few days, the gap between such events offers a veritable eternity in which to revolutionize footwear and apparel. There's nothing like the constraint of a hard deadline to push a creative team—and the designers at Nike savor these moments to unleash the torrent of innovations they have been busily working on behind closed doors for months. From highly breathable football uniforms with customized patterned weaves to marathon shoes that offer a quantifiable advantage, 2021's sporting calendar will see the release of some of the most advanced Nike performance products to date.

Evolving from insights and technical advances built during the Breaking2 experiment, a full slate of new running shoes will make its debut in races ranging from the 100-meter sprint to the marathon. The Air Zoom Victory is built for middle-distance races and features an articulated carbon-fiber plate sandwiched between ZoomX foam on top of spikes. Where typical racing shoes have been exercises in minimalism, shaving off layers and material to shed weight and provide direct contact with the track, during Breaking2 the Zoom Vaporfly Elite proved that bigger could be better. With the Victory, that approach is being challenged once more. Building directly off previous platforms, Nike's marathoners will wear the Air Zoom Alphafly NEXT%. Images of the shoe lit up the Internet in fall 2019 when Eliud Kipchoge wore a prototype pair to break the two-hour marathon barrier in a demonstration race in Vienna, Austria. Now fully tested and finalized, the Air Zoom Alphafly NEXT% adds a Zoom Air pod to the forefoot, additional ZoomX foam, and a redesigned carbon-fiber plate to improve running economy. Finally, evolving from the Pegasus Turbo, the Air Zoom Tempo NEXT% is built on a platform that combines React and ZoomX foam and will serve as many athletes' training shoe. Designed for daily use, the Tempo NEXT% follows a long line of performance footwear that takes insights from elite athlete testing and translates them into innovation that everyone can benefit from.

While Nike anticipates that the new shoe designs will give their athletes a firm footing for victory, television viewers are more apt to take note of the dazzling kits worn by the U.S. track-and-field athletes, which feature Nike's new Dri-FIT AeroSwift technology. Spearheaded by Janett Nichol, vice president of Apparel Innovation, the team synthesized their

Athlete testing at the NSRL	Nike World Headquarters, Beaverton, Oregon	2014

When it relocated to the Nike World Headquarters in Beaverton, Oregon, the NSRL blossomed from a rogue sidenote to an integral element of the company's creation process. Occupying 16,000 square feet (1,500 square meters), it houses multidisciplinary researchers and a catalog of cutting-edge data-capture technology, including 3-D foot and body scanners, environmental chambers, pressure maps, force plates, and a sensor-filled track. Every year thousands of athletes use this equipment to feed hundreds of thousands of figures into the company's data library, grounding Nike design in quantifiable science and fueling the process of iterative learning that propels the company's innovation. This capability will exponentially expand with the NSRL's move to the new LeBron James Building, where the lab will add ninety force plates, a half football field, a basketball court, a 200-meter track, and more.

| Athlete testing at the NSRL | Nike World Headquarters, Beaverton, Oregon | 2014 |

state-of-the-art approaches to computational design and knitting fabrication technology with a groundbreaking lenticular visual aesthetic to create
a uniform that performs and looks like nothing that came before it. The
U.S. women's 100-meter athletes, meanwhile, will be kitted out in an
equally impressive two-piece Flyknit uniform. "Try to picture what women
are wearing right now," says Carmen Zolman, senior design director of
Apparel Innovation and the lead designer on the project. "They've got one
to two bras for support up top, and a cover up with their country's logo.
In addition to shorts, they're wearing some sort of underwear, most likely a
very thin boy short. So you've got all these layers. We wanted to solve for
that." Marrying thermal atlas maps of the body with data derived from a full
motion capture of a sprinting sequence to show areas of tension and slack,
the designers began engineering garments that would respond to the
specific demands of the body in a race situation. Thanks to the hacked
knitting technology used extensively throughout Nike since the advent of
Flyknit, entire pieces of clothing can now be engineered at a pixel-by-
pixel level and fabricated in a single sequence to produce apparel with
few, if any, seams. Generating almost zero waste, the process also results
in a single-layer garment that is at once highly structural where support
is needed while remaining flexible and breathable. The ribbed bands that
give the clothing its distinctive performative qualities also enabled the
team to play with color so the fabric would appear to be as alive and in
motion as the runners themselves—an optical trick baked into the architecture of the weave. The superhero-like aspect of the effect isn't lost on
the designers. "Wearing this Nike uniform," says Nichol, "means you have
reached the point you were working . . . all those years to attain. There's
a connection between the inanimate object and the emotion and drive
and passion an athlete can have." While the U.S. sprinters will be wearing
the new garments on the field, the role of the Apparel Innovation team is
to demonstrate the viability of new capabilities and approaches that can
then be integrated into a variety of product lines going forward.

Once the entirety of the NXT group moves into their new home in the
LeBron James Building, quantifying performance will reach a whole new
level. Not only is the new building at the heart of Nike's expanded campus (putting innovation literally at the heart of the company), the design
puts athletes at the center of the innovation process. While the exterior
features a massive 15.63 percent concrete incline ramp, which extends
more then 500 feet (152.4 meters) and offers athletes a valuable opportunity for training on a campus without natural hills (included in the design,
purportedly, after vice president of Creative Concepts Tinker Hatfield said
to architect Tom Kundig and Mark Parker that the building didn't look fast
enough), the interior is perhaps even more impressive. Light pours in
through a sunlit four-story atrium that physically connects all of the NXT
teams' functions and departments, while the entire top floor, a cavernous
triple-height space larger than many collegiate stadiums, contains a
hugely expanded NSRL. Considering the weight, load, and sensitivity-
measuring equipment involved, the decision to place the NSRL at the top
of the structure was a bold one—but one that Nike's leadership and the
innovation team felt was important to (again, literally) elevate the role and

prominence of athletes in the design process. The expansive space, outfitted with state-of-the-art motion-capture equipment and no fewer than
ninety force plates, is large enough to house half a football field, a full
basketball court, and a 200-meter track, with variable partitions and hardware to allow for different events and uses. The opportunity for the NSRL
is not only to set a new gold standard for sports science but to unlock a
realm of insights that will come from, for instance, observing a basketball
game in real time versus a simulation of a single jump-shot motion. "Of
course, you want to think about cushioning and traction or ways to jump
higher," says Nurse, "but when you start observing entire games, it may
lead to thinking about how to change fatigue in the fourth quarter or at the
end of a season."

For the team involved with designing the building, creating the optimal
environment to nurture innovation over the coming decades was paramount. "Since we first put pen to paper on the new building, so much has
changed," says Nurse. "Prototyping today is so different than it was even
five years ago; there's hardware engineers, software engineers, and
electrical engineers. We're not just doing foams and uppers. We're going
to have all those capabilities in the new space, and be more effective,
with more interaction and the ability to play and feed off each other."
In the lab's future state, it will act like a centralized brain, collecting,
aggregating, processing, and making sense of data from all over the
world—ultimately harnessing and disseminating insights more efficiently
and effectively than ever before.

Initially born out of the idea for a self-lacing shoe, Nike's emergent Adapt
platform will serve as the vehicle for the company's most significant
future technological endeavors and "smart" products. While the company
has put semiconductors and microchips into Nike+ footwear since 2006,
explored wearables with the FuelBand, and built a connected community
through networked smartphone apps, such as Nike Run Club, the cutting
edge of innovation promises to integrate intelligence into products to
make them more personal, higher performing, and able to learn over time.
Ironically, the Adapt platform was originally inspired by the conceptual Nike
high-top Michael J. Fox wears in the 1989 movie *Back to the Future Part II*.
Hatfield conceived of the self-lacing shoe for the movie at the behest
of director Robert Zemeckis as a whimsical play on what a Nike shoe from
the year 2015 would be. As the actual date approached, Hatfield, former
Nike innovator Tiffany Beers, and a dedicated team within the Space
Kitchen began to make the fictional design a reality. Although pairs of the
shoes replicating those from the movie were eventually produced in only
a limited run to raise money for charity, the power-lacing, underfoot
mechanism the team developed was incorporated into a sportswear shoe
the following year—the HyperAdapt 1.0. Led by Avar, the Adapt team next
turned its attention to basketball—a sport in which the demands of the
game on the player's feet can cause them to expand as much as half a
size during play. "In a normal basketball game, the athlete's foot changes,"
says Avar, "and the ability to quickly change your fit by loosening your
shoe to increase blood flow and then tighten again for performance

is a key element that we believe will improve the athlete's experience." Within the Nike Adapt app, a player can set his or her preferred tightness for gameplay and time-outs (and even warm-ups) and then quickly shift between settings to alleviate swelling and maintain an optimum fit.

Combining footwear with firmware and a user-controlled app, the Adapt platform may be in its infancy but is evolving rapidly to enhance the athletic experience—and Nike's business model—in exciting new ways. "For most footwear out there, buying the shoe is the end of a transaction. But here, buying the shoe is just the beginning," says Donaghu. "Imagine a cycle where opting in creates data about your activity to inform personalized guidance from Nike. And as your performance improves, we can connect you to new products and services for your new goals—and the cycle continues." As the Adapt platform expands onto different playing fields, the demands of creating, maintaining, and innovating in the space promise to shift Nike toward being as much a technology, hardware, software, and service company as a footwear or sportswear one.

Ultimately, no matter what direction Nike takes, the relentless drive forward—spurred on by athletes who are always pushing to greater heights and limits—will remain at the heart of the company's endeavors; the relationship between athletic performance and athletic equipment is never static. Even when the goalposts shift mid-play—as happened with the new Air Zoom Viperfly, which was banned from competition by the World Athletics governing body—Nike continues to advance the limits of technology and design, and challenges the industry to do the same. Featuring a featherweight Atomknit upper, Zoom Air in the forefoot, and a split outsole built around an advanced carbon-fiber plate, the experimental design results from extensive athlete testing and proprietary technologies that have been continually improved upon for years, newly combined to extend the boundaries of athletic advancement.

As this and countless other examples and experiences from within Nike attest, there is no single recipe for how to successfully stay ahead of the curve, but Donaghu offers a counterintuitive theory: "I think that bringing naivete and lack of deep knowledge about things has been part of the secret sauce since the beginning, and I think it goes all the way back to Bill Bowerman. He didn't know anything about making shoes; he taught himself. He allowed himself to break more rules because he didn't know the rules."

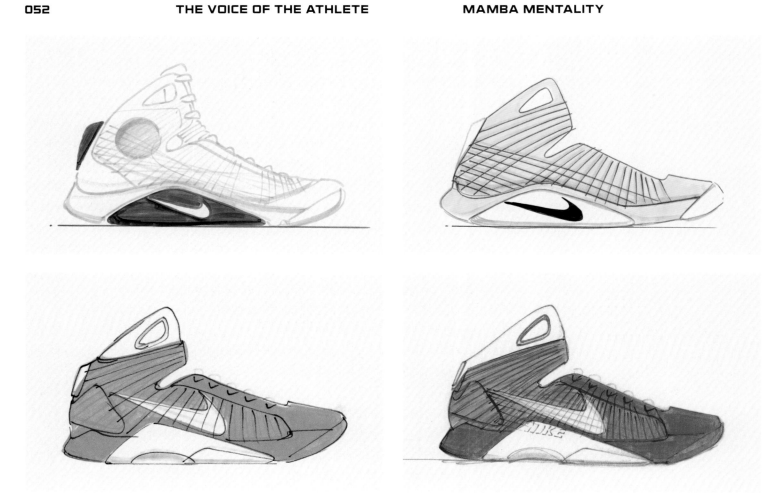

Hyperdunk sketches	Leo Chang	2008

Hyperdunk Lamar Odom House of Hoops	Black/Yellow/Purple/White	2008

Hyperdunk Pau Gasol House of Hoops	White/Yellow/Purple	2008

Hyperdunk Supreme Lithuania outsole	Green/Yellow/Red	2008

In the words of the vice president of the NSRL Matthew Nurse, "Data is useless until you turn it into knowledge." While the lab's researchers continually translate statistics into functional information employed by Nike designers, direct athlete insight continues to play an unassailable role in transforming statistical observations into performance innovations. The 2008 Hyperdunk provides a pinnacle example of this intersection. Designed by vice president and creative director of Innovation Eric Avar, the storied silhouette was the first Nike basketball shoe to feature Flywire technology and Lunarlon cushioning, which were developed on the back of NSRL data. The groundbreaking combination delivered unparalleled lightweight mobility and protection. It also sold Kobe Bryant on the design, which he wore while leading the USA team to a gold medal at the 2008 Summer Olympics in Beijing. Beyond precipitating the future of Nike basketball shoes, the Hyperdunk formed one of many links between Bryant and Avar, who went on to develop a more than decade-long relationship that redefined what an athlete–designer collaboration could deliver.

| Zoom Kobe I "Black Maize" | Black/White-Varsity Maize | 2006 |

| Zoom Kobe I "All-Star" | White/Red/Black/Gold | 2006 |

When the Zoom Kobe I debuted in 2006, it wed design cues from Nike's Huarache series with leading performance innovations, including heel and forefront Zoom Air units, a seamless internalized fit sleeve, and a carbon-fiber heel bucket. The shoe gained instant on-court credibility when Bryant wore it while recording a career-high eighty-one-point game on January 22, 2006—and its bold, technology-driven design foreshadowed the progressive thread that came to define Bryant's signature line, with each subsequent silhouette furthering the narrative. This boundary-pushing chronicle was the organic result of Bryant and Avar's shared intellectual curiosity and respective expertise. Rooted in an initial three-hour meeting that covered topics as disparate as philosophy, nature, and art, the pair's partnership maximized Bryant's uncanny ability to understand and articulate his sport's nuances, thereby questioning accepted notions of what a basketball shoe should look like and how it should perform. For his part, Avar and his team continually pushed, merged, and advanced Nike technologies to correspond to the player's evolving insights and performance requirements. Together, Bryant and Avar not only revolutionized the look of Nike Basketball; they forever changed hard-court footwear.

IN MEMORY OF
KOBE B. BRYANT

AUGUST 23, 1978 –
JANUARY 26, 2020

"THE PROCESS OF HELPING THE ATHLETE REALIZE THEIR POTENTIAL IS WHAT HELPS US REALIZE OUR OWN."

MARK PARKER

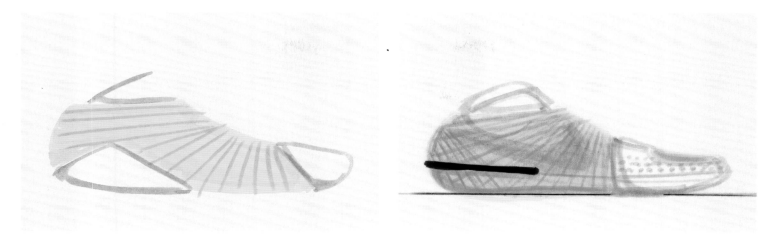

Zoom Kobe IV sketches	Eric Avar	2007

Zoom Kobe IV "Splatter"	Black/Black-White-Del Sol	2009

Zoom Kobe IV "Splatter" outsole		2009

Zoom Kobe V sketch	Eric Avar	2008

Zoom Kobe IX Elite sketch	Eric Avar	2012

Zoom Kobe V "USA"	White/Blue/Red	2010

Zoom Kobe V "USA" outsole		2010

| Zoom Kobe IX Elite "Devotion" from the Gumbo League Collection | Black/Metallic Gold-White | 2014 |

| Zoom Kobe IX Elite "Devotion" from the Gumbo League Collection outsole | 2014 |

Whereas Bryant's first three signature shoes hinted at a proclivity for toppling the status quo, the Zoom Kobe IV wholly reimagined the function and aesthetic of performance basketball shoes. An avid football fan, Bryant was inspired by his favorite players' boots and asked Avar to design a game-ready low-top. Avar first sought NSRL data proving Bryant's assertion that the bulky ankle padding provided by high-tops was superfluous. He then focused on adding stability while incorporating the enhanced range of motion and quick propulsion Bryant desired. The eventual design's revolutionary insight into natural motion fully manifested in the Zoom Kobe V, which dropped the shoe's collar even further—a profile that endured until the Zoom Kobe IX Elite arrived. Developed to support Bryant after an Achilles tendon injury, the ultra-high-top adapted Flyknit technology for basketball, providing a protective feel without limiting motion.

| Waffle Trainer | Blue/Yellow | 1976 |

| Waffle Trainer heel and outsole | 1976 |

While a basketball shoe digitally engineered down to a pixel stands performance worlds away from a running shoe constructed from a rubber sole glued to a nylon upper, it shares a foundational ethos that continues to define Nike innovation: always listen to the voice of the athlete. Beyond adorning the entryway of the NSRL, this mantra maps Nike's evolution. In the late 1950s Bowerman—then a veteran track coach—was dissatisfied with existing running spikes, which were composed of heavy leather and metal. With the guidance of a local cobbler, he began experimenting with plates and lasts.

After a bootmaker taught him how to fashion shoe patterns, he began crafting custom spikes by outlining runners' feet, measuring their width, noting anatomical minutiae, and integrating their performance and feedback. Churning out new designs on a weekly basis eventually led Bowerman to create the Moon Shoe. After debuting on elite athletes at the 1972 U.S. Track and Field Trials, it was adapted for everyday performance in 1974 as the Waffle Trainer, symbolizing Nike's foundational commitment to serve all athletes.

The ABC's of our most exotic training shoe.

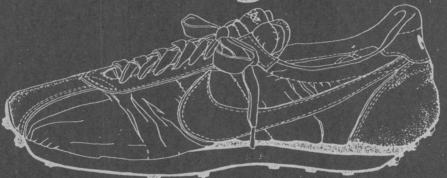

Aa

The Waffle. The design of the entire shoe begins here. The waffle is an original concept of Dr. William J. Bowerman, the famous track coach and head of the Nike research and development department. "Bill" Bowerman's penchant for waffles was to develop an entirely new concept in sole material.

The "waffle studs" provide cushion and traction. Cushion comes from the studs expanding into the space around them. A conventional ripple sole just isn't capable of this kind of cushion.

Greater surface area is achieved by running the waffle diagonal across the heel. The end result is low net weight, superb traction, and comfortable work outs. Bowerman's waffle bears U.S. Patent No. 3793750 and is also a great golf sole.

The midsole is nothing less than space age. It has bevels and flairs nearly everywhere. It's beveled at the heel and toe to reduce the effective lever.

The flairs and bevels help to prevent common running injuries by providing stability encouraging proper foot placement.

The compound of the midsole is a soft cushion crepe which provides shock absorbtion with limited weight. The midsole negates any transference of energy from the waffle material. Extra sole is placed under the most common stress points, the metatarsal heads, and elevated to the heel. This elevated heel, a constant in Nike/Bowerman design, reduces Achilles tendon stress.

Exclusively used Spenco innersole provides additional cushion to resist blistering and provide comfort.

Bb

Comfort. Besides using the finest innersole available, Nike's arch support used in the waffle trainers is one of the largest in production sportshoes.

The tongue is padded foam to protect the tendons running down the top of the foot and also guards against lace pressure.

The ankle collar and Achilles heel pad is super smooth which prevents rubbing and blistering.

The sock liner is smooth nylon which also reduces blow outs.

Cc

Durability. The powerful nylon upper is so sturdy and impervious to damage that it invites retreading with waffle material available from Nike. This retreading can extend the life of the shoe many times.

Lateral and Medial arch bandages and suede toe heel pieces are added for durability. The suede absorbs more glue to reduce separation and is double stitched.

The waffle trainer fits the widest range of shoe sizes of any trainer we've had on the market.

You can see the NIKE Waffle Trainer at your local dealer.

BLUE RIBBON SPORTS

HOT WAFFLES TO GO.

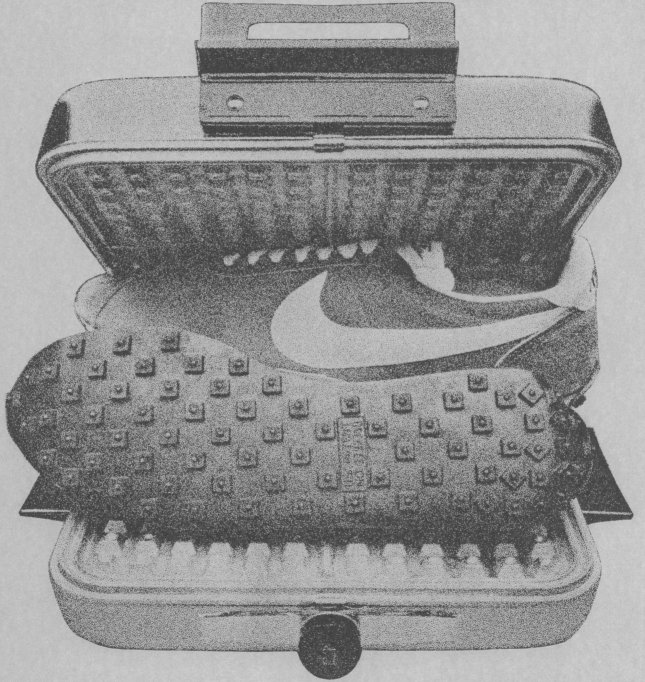

Come and get 'em. The best selling running shoes ever made are here. They're Nike Waffle Trainers. And they give you the kind of stability, cushioning and traction only a waffle sole can. So don't settle for substitutes. And don't wait. Because the original Nike Waffles are selling like hotcakes. Blue with yellow swoosh.

$00.00

(DEALER NAME)

| Blue Ribbon Sports Pre Montreal | Blue/White/Red | 1973 |

| Track spike made for Steve Prefontaine | Green/Yellow | 1973 |

| Triumph | Blue/Yellow | 1978 |

| Vainqueur | Lime/Black | 1978 |

| Track spike made for Mary Decker | White/Blue/Red | 1979 |

| Track spike made for Sebastian Coe | White/Black | 1980 |

| Zoom Ultra II | White/Red/Yellow | 1990 |

| Track spike made for Michael Johnson | Gold/Navy-Black | 1996 |

Zoom Super Fly and plate made for Maurice Greene	Red/White/Blue/Gold	2000

Zoom Superfly R3	Volt/Sequoia-Metallic Gold	2012

Zoom Matumbo 2	Volt/Sequoia-Metallic Gold	2012

Zoom Superfly R4	Volt/Sequoia-Metallic Gold	2012

Bowerman began tinkering with track spikes because he believed there was more to maximizing an athlete's speed than training techniques. His conviction that a lighter racing shoe with superior traction could make a runner measurably faster formed the core of Nike's track innovations for decades, as charted by the company's track spike genealogy. From Bowerman's early prototypes to the iconic 1996 gold track spikes designed by Tobie Hatfield and worn by Michael Johnson to claim 200- and 400-meter gold in Atlanta, the shoes' evolution plots Nike's increasing knowledge leading up to the seminal Zoom Super Fly II and subsequent custom spikes created in collaboration with sprinter Maurice Greene. Compiling the Zoom Super Fly II's revolutionary insights and technology, Greene's spikes introduced a plate so advanced that it became the template for all Nike spikes for the next sixteen years.

Zoom Superfly Elite made for Shelly-Ann Fraser-Pryce	Volt/Black-Pink Blast	2016

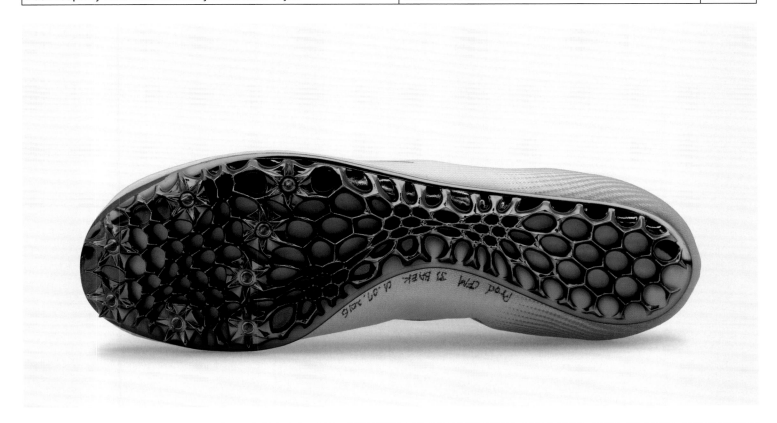

Zoom Superfly Elite plate	2016

Nike spikes made an international splash in the summer of 2012, with their Volt green hue spotlighting the world's fastest athletes as they competed in a number of sporting events. The technology on display, however, wasn't markedly new. The company's next significant innovation leap didn't debut until four years later in Rio, when computational design using generative algorithms and NSRL data enabled the creation of spikes precisely tuned to the needs of their respective athletes. The 2016 Zoom Superfly Elite serves as the foremost expression of this advancement. Its creation was led by Nike's Computational Design team, who combined the aforementioned technologies with rapid 3-D printing, facilitating an overnight prototype-to-trial process and producing customized plates that optimized stiffness and spike placement. The innovation's race-time results spoke for themselves: Nike athletes won 76 percent of that year's Olympic medals.

CUSHIONING THAT NEVER ENDS.

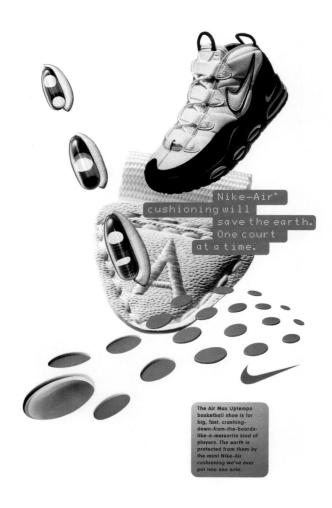

Nike-Air® cushioning will save the earth. One court at a time.

The Air Max Uptempo basketball shoe is for big, fast, crashing-down-from-the-boards-like-a-meteorite kind of players. The earth is protected from them by the most Nike-Air cushioning we've ever put into one sole.

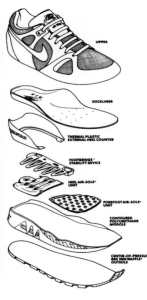

UPPER

SOCKLINER

THERMAL PLASTIC EXTERNAL HEEL COUNTER

FOOTBRIDGE™ STABILITY DEVICE

HEEL AIR-SOLE® UNIT

FOREFOOT AIR-SOLE® UNIT

CONTOURED POLYURETHANE MIDSOLE

CENTER-OF-PRESSURE™ BRS 1000 WAFFLE® OUTSOLE

It has been an unwritten rule that a running shoe can have stability or cushioning, but not both. The Air Stab, with its Footbridge™ stability device, breaks this rule, however, and allows excellent motion control without sacrificing cushioning and flexibility.

The Air Stab has

Better Cushioning:

- Polyurethane-encapsulated AIR-SOLE® units in the heel and forefoot significantly diminish impact shock and reduce the risk of injury.

- The Center-Of-Pressure™ BRS 1000 Waffle® outsole acts as a runner's first defense against impact shock, deflecting up into the midsole during ground contact.

Better Stability:

- Extensive research in the NIKE Sport Research Lab has shown that the Footbridge™ stability device provides motion control without sacrificing flexibility.

- The Air Stab is built on an anatomically correct last, giving the shoe a wide base of support and increased stability.

Air-cushioning advertisements and ephemera (above and opposite)	1987–2004

As diligently as Nike addresses the needs of its elite athletes, it works equally hard to deliver functional innovation for all athletes, upholding the Bowerman adage "If you have a body, you're an athlete." The company's evolution of cushioning technology, notably Nike Air, exhibits this ethos in action. Originally released in 1978 and visually exhibited for the first time on the 1987 Air Max 1, Air promises (as its original print advertisements confirm) "Cushioning That Never Ends." The technology's conversion across sports categories, such as in the Air Rio football boot, and its continual development—ranging from the 1995 arrival of Zoom Air to the debut of the Air Max 720 in

2019—sustain this promise. As explained by vice president of Cushioning Innovation Kathy Gomez, the company's ongoing expansion of Air is guided by two principles. The first is to highlight the technology's cushioning benefits, unencumbered by any other materials. The second is to push the limits of impact absorption with new geometries. The ensuing architecture must deliver an enjoyable underfoot sensation and a stable base. These considerations inevitably demonstrate a clear truth applicable to all Nike performance innovation: solving for functional needs results in intuitive and beautiful design.

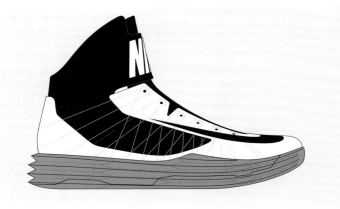

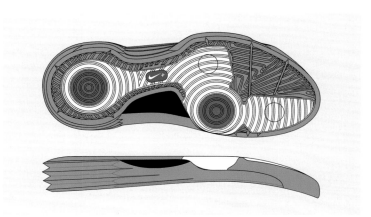

Lunar Hyperdunk sketches	Eric Avar	2012

Lunar Hyperdunk prototypes	c.2011

Hyperdunk+ Sport Pack "USA"	White/University Red-Obsidian	2012

The thread tying Air cushioning to the dawn of Lunarlon can be characterized as a dedication to transforming perception through performance. When ultralight Lunarlon first appeared—on the LunaRacer and Hyperdunk in the summer of 2008—it toppled terrestrial beliefs that copious cushioning required an ample upper. Conversely, taking inspiration from the weightless, springy movements of astronauts on the moon, the voluminous foam offered bouncy responsiveness that minimized impact and could be paired with an equally lightweight upper. The brainchild of Nike designers Kevin Hoffer and Eric Avar, Lunarlon required more than four years of development. Its instantaneous success, however, drove its rapid integration into performance footwear across numerous sport categories.

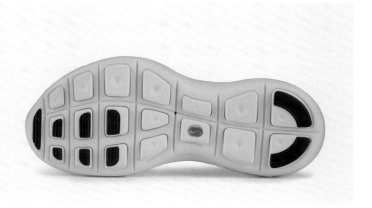

| LunarTrainer+ and outsole | White/Black-Volt-Metallic Silver | 2008 |

| LunarFly+3 and outsole | Pure Platinum/Blue-Black | 2012 |

| LunarMX+ and outsole | Dark Grey/Black-Volt | 2010 |

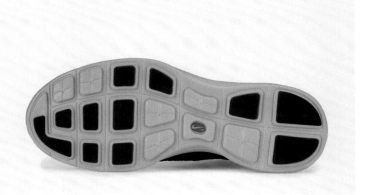

| Lunar Chukka Woven+ ND "Netherlands" and outsole | Black/Anthracite-Total Orange | 2010 |

React Hyperdunk 2017 Flyknit	Pale Grey/Metallic Silver-Sail	2017

Epic React Flyknit 2	Chile Red/Bright Crimson-Vast Grey-Black	2019

The advent of the React foam cushioning not only showcases how Nike's underfoot support has evolved since the Moon Shoe's day but also highlights the strides the company has made in translating NSRL insights into superior performance products. In the case of React, the dynamic operation began with in-house chemists and engineers testing more than four hundred chemical and processing combinations in search of a foam that was soft, responsive, and durable. They then trialed the winning composition on basketball players for more than two thousand hours before debuting it in the React Hyperdunk 2017 Flyknit. When subsequent athlete insight revealed that runners also wanted better cushioning and energy return wrapped up in a durable, lightweight shoe, Nike turned back to the proprietary foam. Employing NSRL data that pressure-mapped how runners move, in what direction, and with what force, they optimized cushioning and support to meet the sport's unique demands. They also used the information to inform superior midsole and outsole forms, and fed it into an algorithm that put the final touch on the 2018 Epic React Flyknit: it generated an original surface geometry that further amplified React's running performance—and hinted at a sport-specific future for the revolutionary technology.

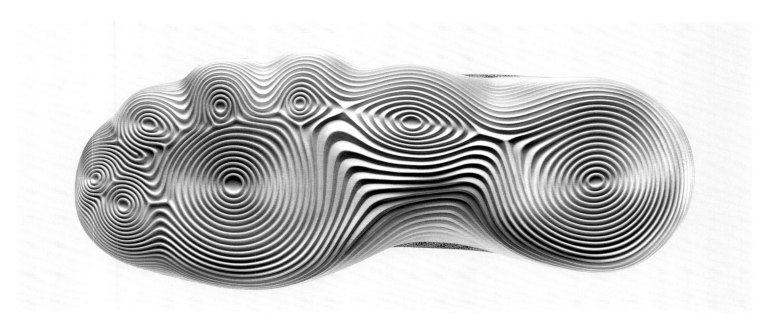

| React Hyperdunk 2017 Flyknit outsole | 2017 |

| Epic React Flyknit 2 outsole | 2019 |

| Odyssey React outsole | 2018 |

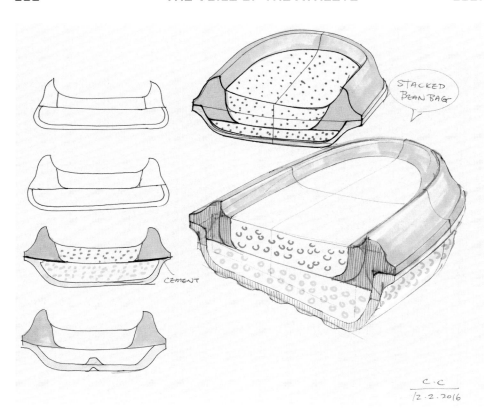

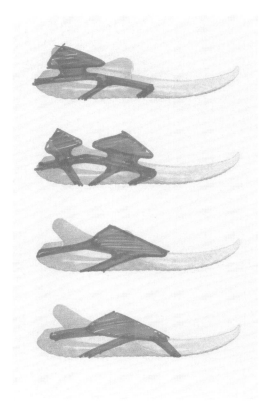

Joyride Air unit sketch	2016

Joyride prototype sketch	2017

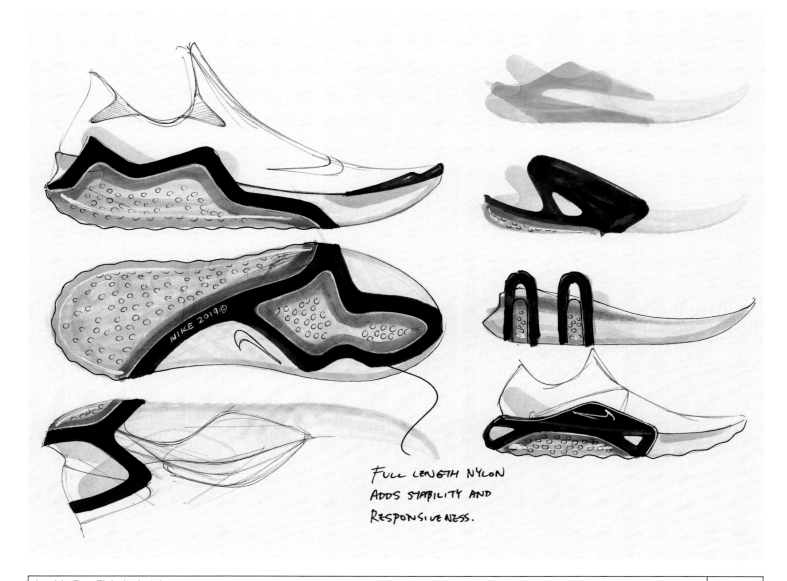

Joyride Run Flyknit sketch	2017

Joyride NSW Setter	Hyper Pink/Kumquat-Black-Racer Blue	2019

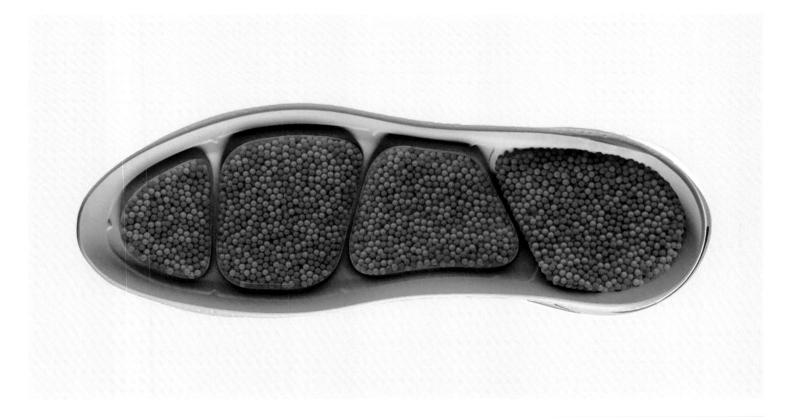

Joyride NSW Setter footbed showing TPE beads in zonally divided pods	2019

The 2019 introduction of the Joyride platform remixed the company's earlier cushioning breakthroughs into a novel system that tackles the multifaceted demands of modern life. Its first silhouette, the Joyride Run Flyknit, answered a request from athletes for a shoe that made running feel easy by placing thousands of tiny TPE beads directly underfoot. These colorful bubbles expand in all directions upon impact while remaining in their meticulously mapped zones, thanks to individual, transparent podlike enclosures. The resulting footbed dynamically responds to its wearer's foot strike, providing soft cushioning, smooth transitions, and a personalized feel. Within the year Nike had applied the technology to lifestyle silhouettes, including the Joyride NSW Setter, which debuted at Paris Fashion Week in 2019.

| Joyride CC3 Setter | White/Barely Volt/Total Crimson/Black | 2019 |

| Joyride CC3 Setter outsole | | 2019 |

"GOOD DESIGN IS FINDING THE RIGHT BALANCE BETWEEN SCIENCE & ART."

ERIC AVAR

"PEOPLE ASK ME WHY WE NEVER MADE A PRESTO 2.

I ALWAYS TELL THEM WE DID — IT'S CALLED THE NIKE FREE."

TOBIE HATFIELD

Free articulated shoe last	2003

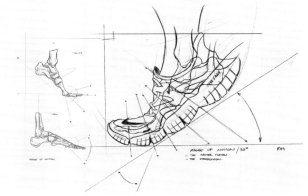

Free RN 5.0 anatomical sketch	2019

Free RN 5.0 anatomical sketch	2019

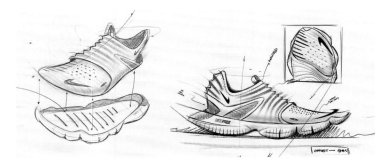

Free RN 3.0 sketches	2019

Free tooling evolution sketches	2019

Nike designers conceived of the idea that eventually birthed Free in 2001 after observing college runners cooling down without shoes in an attempt to strengthen their feet. An ensuing year of NSRL studies on the motion of bare feet proved the merit of this practice. It revealed that an uninhibited foot has a more natural strike and flexes more, which over time improves foot flexibility, balance, and strength. Working off these combined insights, Nike designers developed the 2004 Free 5.0 collection, which encouraged a natural stride via a longitudinally siped outsole. In 2014 new NSRL research revealed that as the foot loads, it expands and contracts on two planes: lengthwise and widthwise. This discovery prompted a recalibration of Free tooling, which led to a hexagonal siping pattern that better mimics how the body and foot react to force.

| Free 5.0 | Black/Blue/Silver | 2004 |

| Free 5.0 | Lime/Black/Blue | 2005 |

| Free 3.0 V3 | Orange/Purple/Red | 2011 |

| Free 3.0 | Black/Gold/White | 2007 |

| Free 4.0 | Blue/Green/White | 2005 |

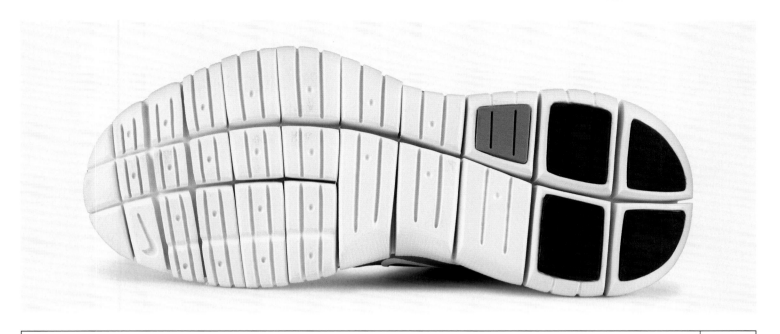

| Free 5.0 outsole | 2005 |

| Free 3.0 V3 outsole | 2011 |

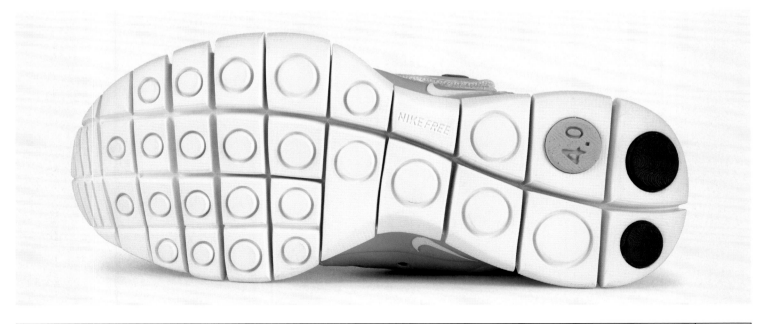

| Free 4.0 outsole | 2005 |

Free RN outsole | 2018

Free Train Force Flyknit outsole | 2016

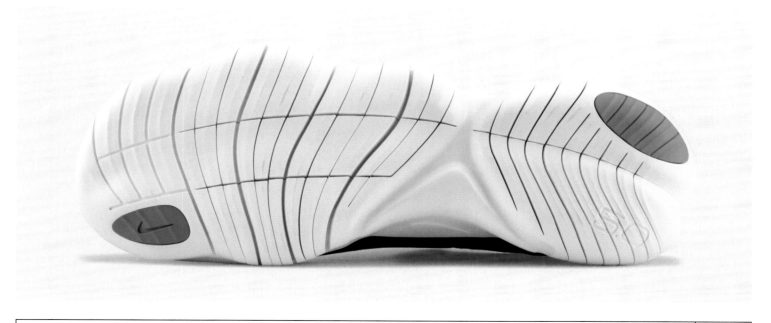

Free RN 5.0 outsole | 2019

| Free RN 5.0 | Indigo Force/Deep Royal-Blue Lagoon | 2019 |

| Free RN | Black/Total Crimson-Vast Grey-White | 2018 |

| Free Train Force Flyknit | Blue/White/Red | 2016 |

| Free RN 5.0 | Summit White/Black/Blue Hero/Volt Glow | 2019 |

| Free Trainer 7.0 | Grey/Red/White | 2007 |

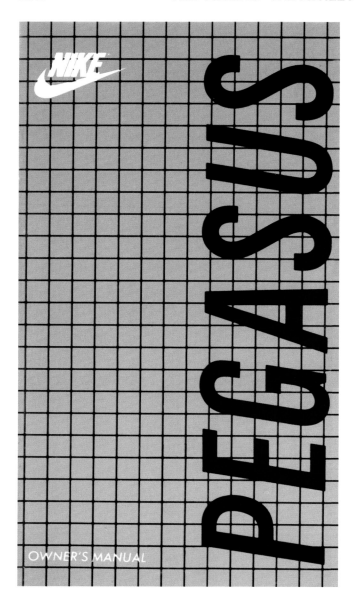

VARIABLE WIDTH LACING SYSTEM™

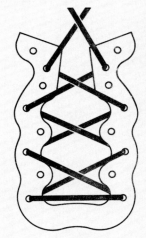

The Variable Width Lacing System™ found on the Pegasus offers greater control over the fit of the shoe through the use of staggered eyelets. Numerous variations can be utilized to create a custom fit:

Eyelet rows that are placed far apart are often used by runners with <u>narrow feet,</u> for a snug fit.

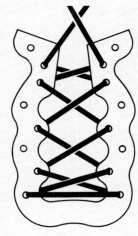

Eyelet rows that are placed closely together are recommended for runners with <u>wide feet.</u>

Pegasus Owner's Manual		1983

Pegasus	Grey/Red	1983

Pegasus Racer	White/Red/Lime	1991

As the Zoom Superfly Elite demonstrates, the company's most influential designs often make headlines due to their fantastic facades. The Pegasus—Nike's longest-running, best-selling product line—offers an inverse yet equally compelling storyline: it delivers premium performance to all athletes via slow, steady progress—akin to a runner completing a marathon. Since the Pegasus silhouette was conceived by Mark Parker in the early 1980s as a versatile, accessibly priced running shoe, it has been regularly upgraded with the era's latest technologies. The 2018 Air Zoom Pegasus 35 exemplified this

organic evolution by pairing the shoe's beloved cut-and-sew mesh upper with a full-length, articulated Zoom Air unit inspired by the curved carbon-fiber plate inside the pioneering Zoom Vaporfly 4% marathon shoe. Soon after, the Zoom Pegasus Turbo enhanced the design by incorporating super-resilient, energy-returning ZoomX foam. True to the stalwart shoe's step-by-step progression, in May 2020 the Air Zoom Pegasus 37 debuted the company's most recent innovations.

NEVER WILL SO MANY OWN SO MUCH FOR SO LITTLE.

It was one of those victories that, frankly, took us by surprise.

All we were after was an Air shoe with a slightly more down-to-earth price tag.

The more runners who experience Air, we reasoned, the fewer will settle for anything less. That was the theory.

Pegasus. That was the name.

Then our R&D department proceeded to run amuck. First, they incorporated the Nike Air-Wedge.™ That was fine. Because it gives the kind of long-lasting cushion you just can't find in any other shoe.

But then they started looking around for other innovations from some of our more specialized models.

Next thing we knew, the Pegasus was sporting the Waffle™ Center-of-Pressure™ outsole. For even more cushion. And greater stability. It also made the Pegasus great for running over any number of different surfaces. From grass to asphalt, to gravel and mud.

Then, they flared the heel for a touch more stability. Notched the suede at the first metatarsal for flexibility. And even went to a lighter EVA formulation in the midsole.

As a result, the Pegasus is not only a great training shoe, but at roughly 10 ounces in a size 9, it's more than light enough to race in.

We were stunned. And we told them—this is just too much

technology, too much versatility. The Pegasus is simply more shoe than we bargained for.

Then they reminded us. That's what a bargain is all about.

NIKE
Beaverton, Oregon

THIS NEW AIR-WEDGE IS OVER 10,000 MILES LONG.

It's hard to believe. But we just made something shorter without reducing its length.

Remember the NIKE-Air™ sole? Well, we just came out with a condensed version. The Air-Wedge.™

We did it the minute we learned from our survey that three out of four runners were heel strikers. With the Air-Wedge, we can now give those runners the protection of Air, but only where they need it most. Right under the heel.

True, the Air-Wedge is a lot shorter. But it reaches just as far— about 10,000 miles actually.

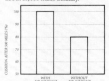

After 500 miles, shoes with the Air-Wedge lose none of their cushioning properties. Those with EVA foams, however, will suffer a 15% to 20% loss.

And probably even further. We don't know how much further because our lab technicians threw in the towel after watching the NIKE-Air sole successfully handle over 6,000,000 impacts.

That's the funny thing about Air. You'd think it would be fragile, susceptible to blow-outs, leaks, etc. When in reality it will outlast virtually every other part of the shoe, from the laces to the outsole.

That's not even the good news.

What's truly phenomenal about the Air-Wedge is that its cushion won't break down. It will absorb just as much shock on the first step as it will on the 5,999,999th.

Pretty remarkable. Especially considering the typical shoe with an EVA wedge will lose about 15 to 20 percent of its cushion after just 500 miles.

Such rapid compaction isn't just sad, it could be dangerous. Because, if you're a runner, you might as well hit your heel with a five pound hammer. That's how much shock is generated with every step.

Not so funny.

And, unless you like buying a new pair of shoes every 300 miles, not so cheap.

But the Air-Wedge does more than just keep its cushion. Accord-

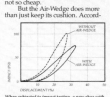

When subjected to impact testing, a new shoe with the Air-Wedge doesn't bottom out like a new shoe with EVA foam. Instead, it responds in a more linear fashion, delivering 12% better cushion. The steeper the slope on the curve, the harder the material becomes when it is compressed under your heel.

ing to tests carried out in our sport research lab in Exeter, New Hampshire, it gives better cushion the first day out of the box.

Whenever we stuck an Air-Wedge in a developmental shoe, shock absorption immediately jumped 12 percent. The reason being, the Air-Wedge simply doesn't bottom out, or get stiffer as it is compressed.

Okay, but how stable is it? Answer: surprisingly good. We also ran some direct comparison tests between two similar shoes, one with the Air-Wedge, the other with an EVA foam wedge. As far as controlling rearfoot motion, they both did the job equally well.

One last thing. Not all runners will run on the same amount of Air. We have scaled the pressure in the Air-Wedge according to shoe size, so that runners of all sizes will receive the appropriate amount of cushion.

Pegasus

Now where can you find this amazing device? In two new Nike models. The Pegasus. And the Odyssey.

We've made many claims about our NIKE-Air shoes. And with the introduction of the Air-Wedge, we're making even more.

But, then, we know it's going to let you down. A lot easier. And a lot longer.

NIKE
Beaverton, Oregon

"Never Will So Many Own So Much for So Little" and "This New Air-Wedge is Over 10,000 Miles Long" Pegasus advertisements   1983

| Pegasus | Grey/Blue | 1983 |

Air Zoom Pegasus 35	White/Volt-Gunsmoke-Atmosphere Grey	2018

Air Zoom Pegasus 35 outsole	2018

Air Zoom Pegasus 35	Elemental Rose/Barely Rose	2018

Air Zoom Pegasus 35	Blue Orbit/Blue Void/ Pure Platinum/Bright Citron	2018

| Zoom Pegasus Turbo 2 "Blue Ribbon Sports" | Orange Peel/White/Total Orange/Black | 2019 |

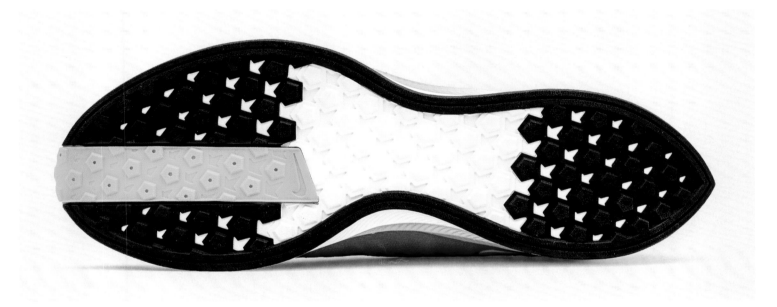

| Zoom Pegasus Turbo 2 "Blue Ribbon Sports" outsole | 2019 |

| Zoom Pegasus 35 Turbo | Gridiron/Black-Atmosphere Grey-Peat Moss | 2018 |

| Zoom Pegasus Turbo 2 | Black/Olive-Aura/White/Laser Crimson | 2020 |

| Pegasus Turbo NEXT% | Valerian Blue/Black-Lime Blast | 2020 |

| Pegasus Turbo NEXT% outsole | 2020 |

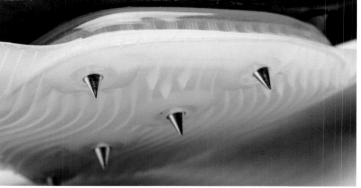

| Air Zoom Alphafly NEXT% Zoom Air pod | 2020 |
| Air Zoom Viperfly spike plate | 2020 |

| Air Zoom Alphafly NEXT% | Valerian Blue/Black-Lime Blast | 2020 |

| Air Zoom Viperfly | Valerian Blue/Black-Lime Blast | 2020 |

Showcasing the fruits of four years of performance innovation, a new suite of running shoes will debut in the summer of 2021. Springboarding off the Breaking2 design discoveries that resulted in the revolutionary Zoom Vaporfly 4%, the new footwear is expressly tailored to its race and runner. Middle-distance athletes will don the Air Zoom Victory, which places an articulated carbon-fiber plate between ZoomX foam and digitally engineered spikes. Nike marathoners will cover the distance in the Air Zoom Alphafly NEXT%. The latest iteration of the Vaporfly 4%, it incorporates a forefoot Zoom Air pod and redesigned carbon-fiber plate tuned to increase energy return.

The Air Zoom Tempo NEXT%, meanwhile, unites React and ZoomX foams to offer all athletes a superior training shoe. Developing these innovations also led Nike to conceive the Air Zoom Viperfly, an experimental, non-competitive design so groundbreaking that it challenges the tradition of sport. The Viperfly introduces an original split outsole, Zoom Air pods in the forefoot, and an advanced carbon-fiber plate that, extensive athlete testing revealed, offer a significant boost in energy return and traction. Finally, the performance footwear presents the next generation of Flyknit—Atomknit—which enhances heel lockdown and decreases materials waste.

Air Zoom Tempo NEXT% FE and outsole	Valerian Blue/Black-Lime Blast	2020

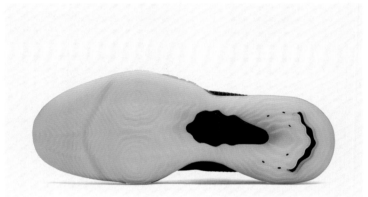

Air Zoom BB NXT and outsole	Valerian Blue/Black-Lime Blast	2020

Air Zoom Victory and plate	Valerian Blue/Black-Lime Blast	2020

Detail of the Air Zoom Victory Atomknit upper	2020

Detail of the Air Zoom BB NXT mesh upper	2020

2020 SUMMER GAMES IN 2021

"AS A DESIGNER, MY ARM IS AN EXTENSION OF AN ATHLETE'S DREAMS AND ASPIRATIONS."

JANETT NICHOL

| USA Women's Flyknit Airborne Top | 2020 |

| Germany Women's Dri-FIT AeroSwift Athletics Unitard | 2020 |

| USA Women's Dri-FIT AeroSwift Athletics Unitard | 2020 |

Novel race apparel for 2021 also marries the NSRL's most recent developments with those of the Nike Explore Team (NXT). Specifically, Nike track-and-field uniform pieces employ an entirely new Dri-FIT AeroSwift material that unites the trademark sweat-wicking technology with digitally engineered mesh. The U.S. women's 100-meter athletes, meanwhile, will wear a striking two-piece Flyknit uniform. Both the product of advancements in an apparel technology first introduced on the 2017 FE/NOM Flyknit Bra, the new designs are informed by full-motion capture of the body in race situations. Their strategic architecture addresses key areas of tension, slack, and sweat—and responds to thermal atlas maps that specify where breathability and mobility are most needed. The seamless garments, which are engineered pixel by pixel, provide highly structural support and cooling, completely eliminating the need for undergarments. The apparel also introduces an integrated lenticular veneer that transforms static shades into dynamic hues that mutate while the body is in motion, giving athletes a superhero-like appearance. Together the component parts combine to a signature Nike equation that expresses an enduring company conviction supported by nearly fifty years of evidence: athletes who look good and feel good perform better.

| HyperAdapt 1.0 | | Black / White-Blue Lagoon | 2016 |

| HyperAdapt 1.0 | Habanero Red/Black/Team Red/Habanero Red | 2018 |

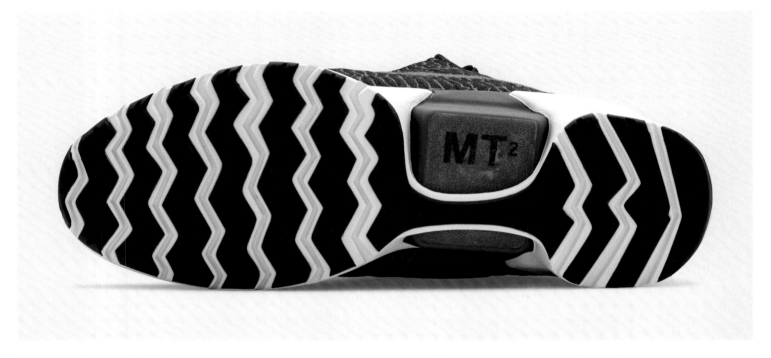

| HyperAdapt 1.0 outsole | | 2018 |

Beyond evolving performance products to serve ever stronger, more ambitious athletes, Nike is continually mining its data to imagine the future of sport. Its nascent self-lacing Adapt platform provides a peek at this disruptive road map. Aptly inspired by the futuristic Nike high-top worn by Michael J. Fox in *Back to the Future Part II* and guided by significant research into digital, electrical, and mechanical engineering, the smart technology debuted in the HyperAdapt 1.0. Designed by vice president of Creative Concepts Tinker Hatfield, with collaboration from a specialized team within the company's conceptual Space Kitchen, the directional shoe demonstrated that a product that instantaneously adapts to its wearer is no longer a futuristic theory; it's a tangible, attainable reality. Following its debut in 2016, the design became commercially available in 2017, and the technology has since been dialed in for basketball and lifestyle silhouettes, with more performance versions launched in 2020. Beyond representing Nike's firm innovation foothold, Adapt exemplifies the company's sustained sprint toward an increasingly customized, smarter, and faster future informed by athlete insights and progressive, science-informed products.

Adapt BB	Black/White-Pure Platinum	2019

Adapt BB outsole	2019

Jayson Tatum in the Adapt BB	2019

"THINK OF A PRODUCT THAT HAS THE INTELLIGENCE TO ADAPT TO YOUR BODY'S NEEDS IN THE MOMENT, AS YOU'RE DOING WHATEVER YOU'RE DOING. AS IF IT'S ATTACHED TO YOUR BRAIN."

MIKE YONKER

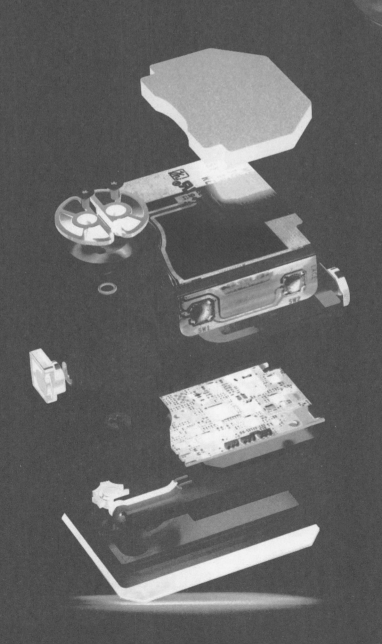

2 DESIGN THAT SPEAKS

Swoosh-only hat
Swoosh-only shorts
Swoosh-only Dri-FIT Long Sleeve Polo
Air Max 1
Air Walker Max
Air Max Light
Air Max 90
Air Max BW
Air Max 180
Air Max ST
Air Max 93
Air Max2
Air Max 95
Air Racer Max

Air Max 96
Air Max 97
Air Max 98 TL
Air Max Plus
Air Tuned Max
Air Max 2003
Air Max 360
Air Max 270
Air Max 720
Air Trainer SC High
Air Force 1 High
Air Force 1 High SC
Air Force 1 High Urban
Air Force 1

Air Force 1 High LE
Air Force 1 High L/M PRB
Air Force 1 × Busy P Low Supreme
Air Force 1 Premium by Mark Smith
Air Force 1 QK
Air Force 1 PRB
Air Force 1 × Undefeated
Air Force 1 × Bobbito High Premium
Air Force 1 Low Supreme
Air Force 1 Low PRM
Supreme Air Force 1 Mid
Lunar Force 1

Walk down any city street, and it will only be a matter of minutes—maybe even seconds—before you spot a Nike Swoosh. Over the course of a typical day, without realizing it, you may encounter the distinctive shape dozens, if not hundreds, of times. (In a completely unscientific study conducted by the author on a downtown street corner in California, 217 instances of the Swoosh were observed during a single lunch hour.) Over the course of its near fifty-year life span the logomark has become a ubiquitous addition to our visual landscape, so easily identified that for half of that time it has stood alone, without supporting typography, to represent the Nike brand.

The mark had relatively humble origins: it was created in 1971 by Portland State University graphic design student Carolyn Davidson as a freelance project for Phil Knight (who taught accounting classes at the school until 1969). The Swoosh first appeared in the same year on a pair of football boots called "The Nike," and in 1972 on the first line of Nike footwear produced by Blue Ribbon Sports, the company Knight and Bill Bowerman initially cofounded to distribute athletic shoes from Japan. However, it wasn't until 1978, as Blue Ribbon Sports ventured further into creating its own designs, that the company changed its name to Nike, Inc. It's impossible to imagine Davidson—even in her wildest dreams—had any notion that her work would one day be imbued with so much meaning for so many people around the world. But then again, if the Nike brand—ergo the Swoosh—stands for one thing, it's the idea that wild dreams can come true.

In the 2002 book *The Brand Gap*, author Marty Neumeier explains that the idea of a brand is little more than a collective amalgam of people's gut feelings about a product, service, or company. "When enough individuals arrive at the same gut feeling," he writes, "a company can be said to have a brand. In other words, a brand is not what you say it is. It's what they say it is." Companies that excel at marketing understand that everything they do—every product, every communication, every conceivable point of contact with a customer or potential customer, and even their corporate policies and practices—contributes to this perception. While this has long been the case at Nike, the success of its brand building has come through an ability to foster connection through emotive storytelling. Although the means, methods, and delivery change over time, the values at the core of Nike's brand expression remain the same—and the messages timeless. "We believe in the power of sport to make you better; that sport is one of those incredible forces that can help you to become the best version of yourself," says chief marketing officer Dirk-Jan van Hameren.

There are few examples that illustrate this decades-long approach better than "Just Do It"—the company's enduring and ubiquitous catchphrase that launched in 1988 with a series of thirty-second advertisements, one of which featured eighty-year-old Walt Stack traversing the Golden Gate Bridge on one of his daily 17-mile (27-kilometer) jogs. "People ask me how I keep my teeth from chattering in the wintertime," he says mid-stride, continuing with a perfectly timed pause, "I leave them in my locker." Those thirty seconds contain only scant views of Stack's Nikes, and no promises of boosted performance or feature call-outs. Instead, with equal parts humor and humanity, "Just Do It" offers a far more powerful call to action—the push to find that same drive within ourselves.

Teams at Nike have long understood that harnessing emotion in service of storytelling is a far more effective strategy for brand building than rattling off features and benefits. "Why do people get married—or do anything?" Phil Knight posited to the *Harvard Business Review* in 1992. "Because of emotional ties. That's what builds long-term relationships with the consumer, and that's what our campaigns are about. Our advertising tries to link consumers to the Nike brand through the emotions of sports and fitness. We show competition, determination, achievement, fun, and even the spiritual rewards of participating in those activities." While at the outset Nike considered itself production oriented, with success or failure predicated on the design and manufacture of innovative products, by the time of the aforementioned Knight interview, the company had undergone an incredibly consequential shift. "We've come around to saying that Nike is a marketing-oriented company," Knight said, "and the product is our most important marketing tool. What I mean is that marketing knits the whole organization together. The design elements and functional characteristics of the product itself are just part of the overall marketing process." The difference may seem subtle, or merely semantic, but this new perspective was crucial to the company's development into one of the most recognizable global brands. Even more remarkable, the shift can be largely attributed to the launch of one of the most consequential designs in Nike's history: Air Max.

It may seem difficult to comprehend in retrospect, but by the mid-1980s, Nike was in the midst of an identity crisis. The company's technical, performance-based output was being outpaced by more casual designs and aerobics-based footwear from the competition. Nike's attempts to branch out had missed the mark. There were layoffs, and the future was by no means certain. Tinker Hatfield—a champion pole-vaulter turned architect turned shoe designer—kept coming back to an idea that had occurred to him in Paris while looking at Renzo Piano and Richard Rogers's Centre Pompidou. Hatfield was struck not only by the juxtaposition of the alien Modernist structure with Paris's classic Beaux-Arts buildings (and the fact that whether you loved or hated it, you couldn't help but notice it) but by the architects' philosophical underpinning. If you could turn a building inside out, why not a pair of shoes? "That gave birth to Visible Air," the designer recounts. "You could see what made [the Air Max] different, what made it work better, and, therefore, made it more interesting and more overtly storytelling oriented."

The Air unit, Nike's premier cushioning technology, had been employed in the company's shoes since the Tailwind in 1979, but because it was buried underfoot, customers generally had little understanding of what it was or what it did. Working in close collaboration with Mark Parker—who led design and development at the time (and would later serve as CEO and chairman)—Hatfield sketched a shoe with a window in the midsole, exposing a cross section of the inflated unit within. The pair then drove every decision to emphasize the visual impact of the Air unit (which itself necessitated an entirely new manufacturing method to allow for a clear view of its insides). The shoe's original colorway featured a clean white upper while the midsole was framed in red, an approach which, according to Parker, was intended to draw the eye. "It's particularly compelling to see the technology in this case: design that speaks," says Parker.

When it came time to launch the Air Max, the organization knew that it would take more than a great design to overcome the headwinds the business was facing. "The Visible Air launch was a critical moment for a couple of reasons," Knight recounted. "Until then, we really didn't know if we could be a big company and still have people work closely together. Visible Air was a hugely complex product whose components were made in three different countries, and nobody knew if it would come together. Production, marketing, and sales were all fighting with each other. There was tension all the way around."

For the televised campaign, the company turned to now longtime agency partners Wieden+Kennedy, based in Portland, Oregon. Codirectors Paula Greif and Peter Kagan, who had helped define the look and feel of the burgeoning MTV network, were recruited to create a spot that would offer more vibe than narrative. The briskly paced sixty-second advertisement cut grainy Super 8 film of Nike stars Michael Jordan and John McEnroe with footage of amateur athletes, including Nike employees, competing in a variety of sporting events—punctuated repeatedly by a clip of the Air Max Air unit compressing under the weight of a runner's foot strike. Most notably, the Beatles' fuzz-drenched and overdriven recording of "Revolution" blared without interruption for the entirety of the commercial. As Knight explained, "We wanted to communicate not just a radical departure in shoes but a revolution in the way Americans felt about fitness, exercise, and wellness." By offering a more candid view of legends, such as McEnroe and Jordan, while simultaneously elevating the efforts of normal people pushing their limits, the film conveyed the universal humanity of sport. The repeated Air Max snippet served as a reminder that Nike was willing to go to extremes in pursuit of making every athlete better.

Unlike anything that had come before, the advertisement struck a chord. It may seem hard to believe now, but at the time original versions of classic songs by famous bands were rarely used in commercials—to say nothing of a smash hit by the most famous band of all time. Although Nike negotiated with Capitol Records and Yoko Ono—who was responsible for her late husband John Lennon's estate—to use the song, the remaining Beatles, through their publisher, Apple Records, objected to the usage and sued the company for US$15 million. "We got sued, and that made everything even more cool, because Yoko Ono got to fight with the rest of the Beatles," Hatfield reminisces. "The whole thing hit the market and was like a rocket ship. And Nike really hasn't stopped growing ever since."

Launched on March 26, 1987, the Air Max, of course, went on to become one of the most iconic and successful shoes in Nike's history, and Visible Air—in the many forms it now takes—remains the core technology at the heart of thousands of Nike designs. Although it was designed as a state-of-the-art performance running shoe, thanks in large part to successful marketing, the Air Max also found a huge audience outside sport. Steadily updated through the years with new technology and aesthetics, the Air Max has become a brand unto itself. Subsequent models—including Air Max 90, 95, 97, and 98—have become iconic in their own right. Much of the original line remains available (even customizable), and the company now celebrates March 26 as Air Max Day, providing an occasion to launch new models (2020 saw the release of the Air Max 2090, a futuristic riff on the Air Max 90) and engage with the sneaker community (in 2017 some particularly dedicated fans launched an Air VaporMax 117,500 feet [35,814 meters] into space).

The success of the Air Max as a "design that speaks," and its accompanying "Revolution" campaign, paved the way for Nike to dominate the cultural landscape through a two-pronged approach of daring, inextricably linked products and communications. It's impossible to consider Air Jordans without Mars Blackmon—director Spike Lee's Jordan-loving alter ego from the 1986 movie *She's Gotta Have It*. Bo Jackson, the first athlete in the modern era to play professional baseball and American football in the same year, became synonymous with "Bo Knows," the ultimate pitch for Nike's new cross-training shoes. And no matter your sport, the ongoing "Just Do It" campaign espoused the values going into every pair of Nikes.

It's unfair to call it a formula when so much effort has gone into keeping the messages fresh and potent, but Nike's playbook of hard-nosed determination, tongue-in-cheek irreverence, rock 'n' roll attitude, and limitless aspiration continues to propel the brand forward some thirty years later. "Each year there's a new generation of 'Just Do It' consumers with new expectations," says Greg Hoffman, former head of Global Brand Innovation. To best serve these customers, brand and marketing teams work diligently to stay at the forefront of trends in communication, interaction, retail, and sport. While the approach necessarily changes, at its core Nike's marketing rests on a powerful duality. "Of course it's about how we want people to feel about Nike," says Hoffman, "but more importantly, it's how we want people to feel about themselves."

"We tell stories, and through storytelling, we make people feel and help people do," elaborates van Hameren. "The breadth and the depth of our storytelling have become way more complex, and therefore the importance of being clear on what this brand stands for—the core of its values—is an even greater challenge creatively."

In today's diverse media landscape, where Nike's efforts extend far beyond national commercials to accommodate multiple platforms, scales, and geographies, creative officer, vice president of Brand Creative Gino Fisanotti is responsible for knitting together that cohesive narrative. Some of his teams' most notable recent work was the thirtieth anniversary "Just Do It" campaign that launched in 2018. "Many people remember one thing: thirty years of 'Just Do It,'" he says. "But if you really look at the entire campaign of that theme—of telling people, 'Hey, believe in your dreams. Go and do your best.'—you will probably see fifty, sixty, or seventy different executions. If you're in the U.S., you'll remember one, if you're in Germany, you will remember another, but the theme of what the brand stands for and how we're using sport as a unifier is the formula." Nike's aim is to maintain both global and local relevancy by identifying universal themes that take the brand and its customers somewhere new and then bringing those themes to life in different ways to engage different audiences.

The first film in the new series served as something of a teaser for what was to come. *Voice of Belief* features archival footage of a young Serena Williams practicing and receiving encouragement from her father, Richard Williams, interwoven with her first championship appearance in the U.S. Open, highlighting the star's now-legendary dream-come-true story. The next film, *Dream Crazy*, features narration from American football star Colin Kaepernick, who polarized NFL fans with his decision to take a knee during the U.S. national anthem prior to games as an effort to bring attention to police brutality and systemic racism. "Believe in something. Even if it means sacrificing everything," says Kaepernick. The film, and corresponding social media posts, created an instant furor—eliciting both praise and protest. While the ensuing controversy only served to bring more notoriety to the campaign, at the heart of the film was the powerful message Nike has championed for decades—sport has the power to transform people's lives and move the world forward.

Tellingly, not only did *Dream Crazy* feature top Nike athletes, such as Williams, LeBron James, and Eliud Kipchoge, but also ten-year-old wrestler Isaiah Bird, who was born without legs; wheelchair-bound basketball star and gold medalist Megan Blunk; and Alicia Woollcott, who was not only named homecoming queen as a high school senior but also played linebacker on the American football team. *Dream Crazy* was by no means the first Nike film to elevate the inspirational efforts of everyday athletes. Encouraging each of us to push our limits, to realize personal goals, and to define success by our own standards has long been a hallmark of the brand's ability to engage its customers. As the global pandemic surrounding COVID-19 unfolded in early 2020, the company's swift response brought this strategy to the fore with a campaign dubbed "Play Inside," which featured a rousing call to action: "If you ever dreamed of playing for millions around the world, now is your chance." Within hours of launching, the social media-driven campaign had been amplified by Nike's stable of top athletes (including Williams, Jordan, James, Cristiano Ronaldo, Sue Bird, and Elena Delle Donne), while the company made access to its Nike Training Club app free for anyone to use. By bridging the gap between social responsibility and personal ambition, and top athletes and relative unknowns, Nike's communications highlight the brand's unique ability to shape a purposeful global conversation and community connected through sport.

Nike's ability to maintain relevancy at a global scale isn't simply by virtue of its size and reach. In 2017 the company announced a reorganization of its marketing around twelve international cities: Barcelona, Beijing, Berlin, London, Los Angeles, Mexico City, Milan, New York, Paris, Seoul, Shanghai, and Tokyo. By building programs and communications around specific localities, Nike is able to keep its finger on the pulse of a much broader range of cultural trends than would be possible sitting behind a desk in Beaverton, Oregon—with the ultimate goal of better anticipating the needs and wants of a far more diverse group of customers. Van Hameren posits, "If the brand is a person in the context of a city, we ask, who would be an interesting person in that city to be right now? What things do you want them to be aware of? Are we a great buddy to play basketball—or explore the coolest new gym trends—with? Are we going to tell you about something new that's going on in music? Is there a marathon coming up? If we can transpose ourselves into the person we want to be for a specific subset of customers, we get to the insights and creative expressions that will have our brand, as a person, be more relevant for that group."

One of the sharpest examples to bring this strategy to life is the 2018 spot *Nothing Beats a Londoner*, a highly energetic and humorous romp through the city's sporting life. Highlighting the diversity, resilience, and competitiveness of the megalopolis's residents, and leaning into neighborhood-specific tropes and subcultures, the short film won acclaim for its attitude and authenticity. While that may come off as seamless over the course of the film's three-minute run time, it's actually the result of hundreds of hours of carefully orchestrated research into the habits, activities, and desires of the city's inhabitants and the careful casting of 258 real young athletes from London neighborhoods, such as Brixton, Dalston, and Peckham.

Newer entries in the "Just Do It" campaign also bring the company's globally local stance to the fore. *Juntas Imparables* (*Unstoppable Together*) highlights the challenges overcome by Mexico's top female athletes—playfully starting with the capital city's legendary traffic jams. *Just Do It: Tokyo*, narrated by tennis phenom Naomi Osaka, questions established values and highlights the diversity of a more youthful Japan. *Helden* (*Heroes*) features a range of German athletes working toward a more equitable future through sport—set to a German-language recording of David Bowie's uplifting anthem of the same name (recorded in Berlin some forty years earlier). Zeina Nassar, a female boxer who helped to overturn an international regulation prohibiting women from competing in a hijab, is featured in the short film, among others, and plays a leading role in another subsequent spot focused on her inspirational story.

Another key theme to resurface under the banner of "Just Do It" is the positive influence of sports on girls. As the company's 1995 campaign "If You Let Me Play" made clear, women who participate in athletics when young are less likely to get breast cancer, more likely to leave abusive relationships, and suffer less depression. In the lead-up to the 2019 Women's World Cup, Nike launched a series of films aimed at shining the

spotlight on diverse female athletes, such as Nassar, who have transformed the playing field and brought inspiration to all. In *Dream with Us*,
a diverse cross section of young female athletes metaphorically takes the
field with Alex Morgan, Megan Rapinoe, Mallory Pugh, and the rest of the
U.S. Women's National Team as actress Viola Davis asks, "Do you want
to be the generation that ends gender inequality?" The next film, *Dream
Further*, follows ten-year-old Makena Cook as she gets pulled into a
variety of footballing roles on and off the field, and finishes with the statement, "Don't change your dream. Change the world." With the ultimate
success of the U.S. Women's National Team, the events proved to be a
moment of inspiration for all athletes, regardless of gender, and validated
Nike's desire to treat it as it would any other football tournament, rather
than specifically one for women.

Nike's fantastic growth, coupled with an ingrained desire to cultivate the
unexpected, has led it to continually explore new ways to connect with
and expand its fan base. By the mid-1990s, sustained interest in classic
designs led to the first "retroed" footwear—retooled models of the Air
Force 1, Air Jordan I, Air Jordan III, and Dunk (among others) destined for
the street instead of the playing field. Although the Air Max may have
transformed Nike from within more than any other shoe, the Air Force 1
worked in the opposite direction. Originally designed by Bruce Kilgore in
1982 as the first basketball shoe to incorporate Nike's Air unit technology,
the rugged, utilitarian design was an instant success both on and off the
court. In the urban cores of cities up and down America's East Coast, the
Air Force 1 helped to define emerging hip-hop fashion, and its collectabil-
ity among sneaker connoisseurs almost single-handedly ignited the
craze for "retroed" shoe designs. As a testament to the design's enduring
legacy, more versions of the Air Force 1 have been produced than any
other Nike shoe—while limited-release, special-edition versions created
in conjunction with other brands, artists, designers, musicians, retailers,
and fashion labels rank among the most coveted and collectable
shoes in the company's history.

The popularity of the Air Force 1 coupled with the rise of street fashion
taught Nike that there were significant opportunities to build the brand
beyond the playing field. If the best brands aim to be as relatable as
people, they also understand that the most interesting people are multi-
dimensional. Sneakers didn't have to be relegated to the locker room but
could be equally at home in art galleries, high-end boutiques, and runway
shows. Exhibitions, such as 2004's *White Dunk: Evolution of an Icon* in
Tokyo—where twenty-five Japanese artists were invited by Mark Parker
to interpret the Nike Dunk however they saw fit, with the entries displayed
in a larger-than-life pop-up shoe box adjacent to the Prada store in the
city's ever-fashionable Aoyama neighborhood—were hugely influential
in defining a new approach for broader cultural engagement.

The Nature of Motion, a temporary exhibition coinciding with Milan Design
Week in 2016, offered visitors a view of expressive and unexpected collaborations with ten of the design world's most progressive practitioners,

including Lindsey Adelman, Martino Gamper, Max Lamb, Bertjan Pot, Shane Schneck, and Clara von Zweigbergk. The exhibition, which also featured an array of playful and experimental underfoot studies by Nike's in-house team (ranging from a modular outsole constructed of Velcro hair rollers to a design inspired by the tactile sensation of stone reflexology paths), won critical and popular acclaim by demonstrating the depth of Nike's innovative material and technological design capabilities in a completely unexpected, noncommercial format.

The following year *Objects of Desire*, a New York City-based multimedia exhibition curated by *Out of Order* magazine's Dorian Grinspan, focused on Nike's legacy of creative collaboration. Newly commissioned works and past campaigns were framed (and reframed) under the banners of resilience, determination, and strength. *I, David*, a film directed by Niclas Gillis, with sets designed by artist James Casebere, featured David Hallberg, a principal dancer for both the Bolshoi Ballet and American Ballet Theatre. In the work, Hallberg's dance through shallow water evokes the tension, release, and triumph of his comeback from a debilitating injury. An ACG poncho designed by Errolson Hugh, the creative force behind Berlin-based streetwear label Acronym, accentuates his movements and—in a role somewhere between set piece and second skin—belies its technical roots to become a channel for artistic expression. Operating like this at the intersection of culture, creativity, artistry, and sport allows for Nike to explore new avenues of connection with new audiences, and lets the company set an agenda rather than follow one.

"In the past, the thought was, any time you communicated, you communicated with the majority of your consumer base," says Hoffman. "Now you have the opportunity to communicate directly to individuals. As we grow and get bigger and bigger, we have to double down on getting more specific to the individual that you're talking to without making it feel like it's a big brand that's doing the talking." To do so, Nike has long stood at the forefront of the digital landscape, from racking up the first viral YouTube spot to hit a million views (which went viral because of a debate surrounding whether it actually showed Brazilian footballer Ronaldinho repeatedly striking a goalpost's crossbar with freakish precision) to building a personalized infrastructure for running workouts and health tracking (Nike+ and the FuelBand). While today's variegated digital ecosystem is on the one hand exceedingly complex for brands to navigate, on the other hand it offers—as Hoffman notes—unprecedented access directly to the customers they most want to reach. With a digital footprint that spans multiple platforms, scales, and geographies, Nike today boasts a massive online presence to serve every imaginable customer.

At the forefront of these efforts is the company's SNKRS app, a hub for Nike's most ardent and active fans. SNKRS is first and foremost a place where Nike+ members can stay up to date on and access the company's rarest and most desirable new designs. However, over its short life span, the app has added a host of innovative features aimed at delivering unique experiences that bridge the divide between virtual and physical space as well as build community. In 2017 Nike launched SNKRS Stash, a digital service offering fans the ability to unlock exclusive products by finding "hidden" drop sites through the augmented reality functionality of their smartphones. When Nike partnered with celebrity chef David Chang on the SB Dunk High Pro "Momofuku," pairs could only be purchased by using the SNKRS Cam to take a picture of a John McEnroe poster hanging in Chang's flagship East Village restaurant in New York City. Elsewhere within the app are a multitude of short-form, screen-based avenues for relatable storytelling around new designs or "drops," sneaker collecting, and street fashion.

Using insights based on data generated from SNKRS, Nike has been able to develop fresh approaches to product creation, storytelling, and community building. The Air Force 1 "De Lo Mio" is a prime example. Digging into SNKRS data for New York City in 2018, Nike's digital team found that the highest concentration of app users was based in a handful of predominantly Dominican neighborhoods. New York City native César Pérez, an artist and fashion world up-and-comer, was tapped to help create a shoe fine-tuned to connect with Nike's Dominican fans. A lenticular Swoosh that changes color from blue to red, showing the whole spectrum in different lights, was selected to signify the inherent diversity of people from the Dominican Republic. Other features, such as the domino-themed lace clips and heel tabs embossed with *República Dominicana*, offer a more literal nod to the culture. To promote the design, six New York-based photographers of Dominican heritage were selected to share their unique perspective, lending even greater authenticity and artistry to the project. Needless to say, the shoes were an instant hit and sold out almost immediately (a restock a few weeks later again sold out in less than five minutes). The success of the program has the SNKRS team looking at further opportunities to be equally specific in other geographies, while the Air Max 95 "De Lo Mio" launched to similar acclaim in the spring of 2020.

Amalgamated localized data is also driving a new approach for the company's latest brick-and-mortar storefronts—an evolution of the company's NikeTown retail outlets that first opened in the 1990s. New stores in Melrose and Long Beach, California, as well as Tokyo's Shibuya neighborhood, called Nike Live, offer a more curated experience based on highly targeted, regional buying patterns, app usage, and engagement of regional Nike+ members. The Melrose store is heavier on running gear, bright, bold colors, and the Cortez (a classic 1970s model), while Long Beach offers an expanded selection of womenswear. The Shibuya location makes heavier use of digital connectivity with specialized vending machines accessed through Nike+, quick pickups for online orders, and live customer-service support through a chat app called Line. While this backbone of regionalized data has enabled the company to create more specific boutiques in some locations, Nike's largest flagship stores—such as those in Shanghai and New York City—use the same digital capabilities to also offer a more personalized shopping experience. New York's House of Innovation features an entire floor dedicated to the Nike Speed Shop, which offers a curated selection based on local trends, backed by a Sneaker Bar featuring the latest styles along with expert consultations for Nike+ members. With the company's plans to extend its direct-to-consumer business, customers can continue to expect an increasing emphasis on creating data-enriched experiences that weave together the convenience of shopping online with the tactility of traditional retail.

Wherever Nike decides to go in the future, it is certain not to rest on its laurels. Founded on the idea of athletic drive and the pursuit of ever greater achievement, the company's inherent brand is progression. With product and marketing as two sides of the same coin, that means never-before-seen products necessitate never-before-seen marketing—whether it's the message or the delivery mechanism. "If people are expecting what's new and better from Nike, it's because there's a culture here—within ourselves—where we just believe that [the work] can always be better," says Fisanotti. The creative director ascribes Nike's enduring appeal to its ability to continually conjure "cultural relevance." To him and the marketing teams at Nike, that means being anchored to your DNA and values while always staying ahead of the game.

That same potent mix of timelessness and progressivism is why the original "Revolution," "Just Do It," and "If You Let Me Play" campaigns feel as relevant today as they did upon release. And it's why a Knight quote from 1992 still succinctly encapsulates the company's approach to brand building. "You have to be creative," he said, "but what really matters in the long run is that the message means something. That's why you have to start with a good product. You can't create an emotional tie to a bad product, because it's not honest. It doesn't have any meaning, and people will find that out eventually. You have to convey what the company is really all about, what it is that Nike is really trying to do."

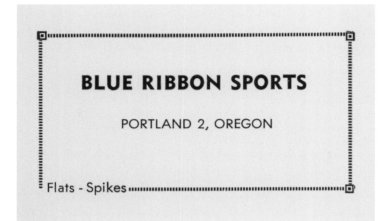

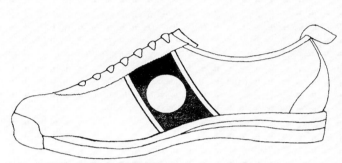

The "Nike hole" was one of many rejects.

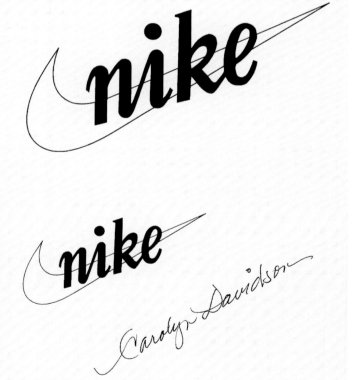

Early Swoosh branding development	1970s

In early 1972, as Phil Knight plotted to evolve Blue Ribbon Sports into the company that would become Nike, he identified the need for a memorable logomark to adorn the nascent company's footwear. Then-graphic design student Carolyn Davidson was tasked with imagining a simple, fluid emblem that communicated motion— just like the company's potential names, which ranged from animal-related labels, such as Falcon, to the eventual winner, Nike, inspired by the Greek goddess of victory.

Original Swoosh design by Carolyn Davidson (top) and original Nike shoebox (bottom) | c.1971

Nike patented Davidson's winged design on June 18, 1971, and one year later it adorned the vamp of the company's first running shoe, the Cortez. Since then, the logo has officially appeared in myriad sizes and colors, and been unofficially employed by copycats, such as the

Kinney Company, which attempted to appropriate the symbol in the late 1970s by turning it upside down. First colloquially and later formally, the checklike mark was branded the Swoosh, synonymous with the sound (and look) of speed.

Original Blue Ribbon Sports logo		1966

Blue Ribbon Sports logo		1967

Original Nike logo	Carolyn Davidson	1971

Blue Ribbon Sports logo		1972

Nike "Baby Teeth" wordmark	Geoff Hollister	1976

Nike Futura Swoosh logo	Allen Powers	1976

Swoosh Pinwheel logo		1976

Futura wordmark		1976

Just Do It logo	Ron Dumas	c.1989

Swoosh logo in PMS 172 (Nike Orange)		1995

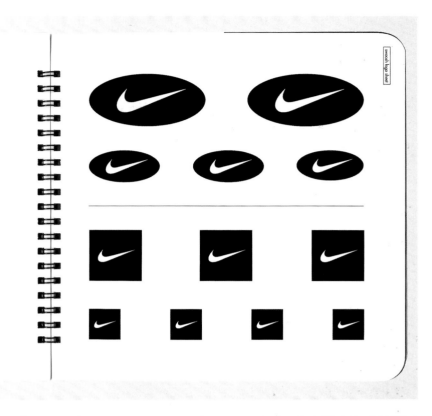

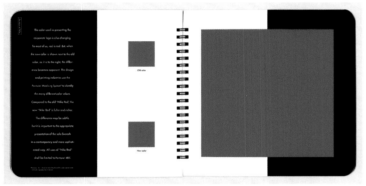

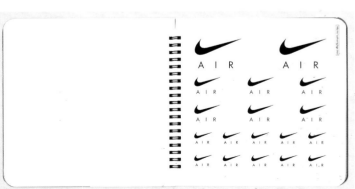

Swoosh Brand Manual | Ron Dumas | 1995

"I Dream" and "Evaporating the Sweat" advertisements, featuring Andre Agassi | 1996–97

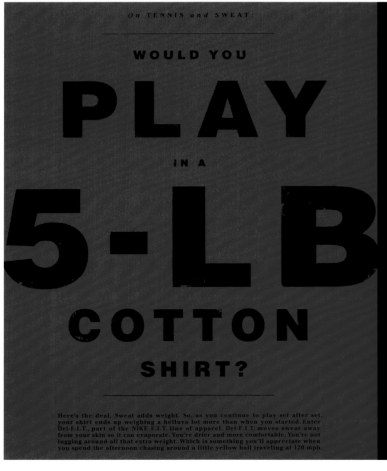

"Dry Shirts Don't Get Thrown Into the Stands" advertisement, featuring Andre Agassi | 1997

| Swoosh-only hat, autographed by Andre Agassi | c.1996 |

| Swoosh-only shorts, autographed by Andre Agassi | c.1996 |

| Swoosh-only Dri-FIT Long Sleeve Polo, autographed and worn by Andre Agassi at the 1996 U.S. Open | 1996 |

In the early 1990s the Swoosh's cultural weight reached critical mass, so Nike began using it as a stand-alone design, free of the wordmark that had spelled out its origins since 1972. The text-free logo made its first appearance on apparel during the 1992 Wimbledon tournament, with tennis star Andre Agassi sporting a Swoosh-only hat. Furthering this evolution, in 1995 the company introduced a comprehensive visual brand manual created by longtime Nike designer Ron Dumas. The rules clarified approved uses of the logo on its own and accompanied by branded typography. They also standardized Nike Orange, the company's official color, tweaking it from Pantone Matching System (PMS) Warm Red to PMS 172, which remains its formal designation. By 1996, Nike had developed a full collection of Swoosh-only products.

"Just Do It" graphic for Nike apparel | 1989

If someone says you run or throw like a girl, ask them to be a little more specific.

Just do it.

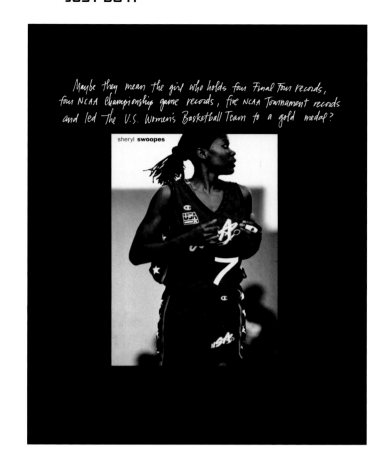

Maybe they mean the girl who holds four Final Four records, four NCAA Championship game records, five NCAA Tournament records and led the U.S. Women's Basketball Team to a gold medal?

sheryl **swoopes**

gail **devers**

Or the girl who conquered Graves' disease and went on to become the first woman in 45 years to win a gold medal in the 100 meters and 100-meter hurdles in world competition?

picabo **street**

Or could they mean the girl who is the only American to win a World Cup Downhill title and was twice named U.S. Female Alpine Skier of the Year?

"Throw Like a Girl" women's brochure, featuring Briana Scurry, Sheryl Swoopes, Gail Devers, and Picabo Street | c.1997

"Just Do It." The urgent linguistic foil to the Swoosh's speedy aesthetic, Nike's now-famous catchphrase entered the company's lexicon in 1988, articulating its promotion of sport as a powerful agent of personal and collective progress. Early "Just Do It" print advertisements underscored this transformative potential. The imperative declaration punctuated poignant storytelling that directly connected everyday athletes to Nike superstars, postulating self-discipline as the key to overcoming obstacles and achieving unlikely dreams. Nike has subsequently employed "Just Do It" to continually connect with and empower consumers—and ultimately shape timely conversations that extend beyond sport, as demonstrated by its thirtieth anniversary "Just Do It" campaign, titled "Dream Crazy."

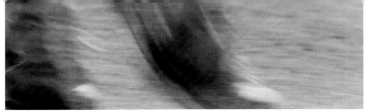

Walt Stack.
80 years old.

Just do it.

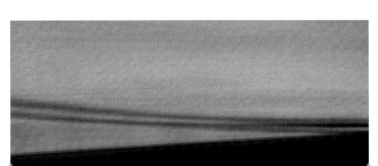

The first film in the "Just Do It" campaign series, featuring Walt Stack (above and opposite)	1988

Perhaps no Nike advertisement embodies the timeless nature and universal appeal of "Just Do It" better than the commercial that introduced the mantra. Released in 1988, it highlights Walt Stack, an eighty-year-old runner laboring across the Golden Gate Bridge on what is revealed to be his daily 17-mile (27-kilometer) jog.

In his simple shorts and Nike running shoes, Stack personifies the steadfast athlete fueled by tenacity rather than talent. Nike's celebration of this act of will in place of a straightforward product push forged a powerful emotional connection with consumers that set an enduring benchmark for future brand expressions.

An early film in the "Just Do It" campaign series, featuring Priscilla Welch (above and opposite) | 1988

Priscilla Welch.
Winner, New York Marathon
at age 42.

Just do it.

Air Max 1	White/Light Neutral Grey/Red	1987

Air Walker Max	White/Royal Blue	1988

At the same time Nike was hitting its stride with galvanizing marketing campaigns, it was discovering the innate narrative possibilities of its products, defined by chairman Mark Parker as "design that speaks." The Air Max 1, which debuted in 1987, epitomizes this elemental approach to storytelling and marked the first time consumers could see the Air in a Nike shoe. Designed by vice president of Creative Concepts Tinker Hatfield in collaboration with Parker, the shoe's Visible Air overtly spun an intriguing tale by placing its differentiating characteristic on display through a midsole window. This deliberately arresting approach has since become a defining trait of Nike design.

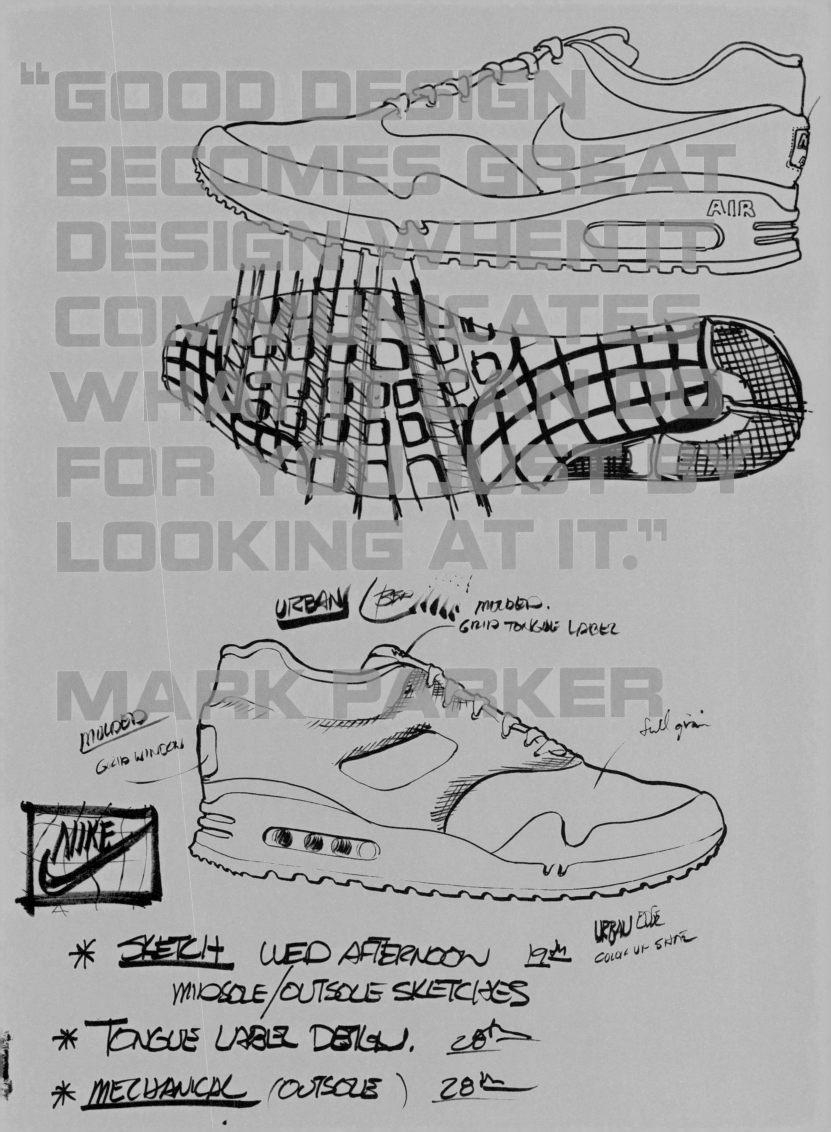

AIR

URBAN LBR   MOLDED.
                 GRIP TONGUE LABEL

MOLDED   full grain
GRIP WINDOW

NIKE

URBAN EDGE
COLOUR UP SHAPE

* SKETCH   WED AFTERNOON   19th
     MIDSOLE/OUTSOLE SKETCHES

* TONGUE LABEL DESIGN.   20th

* MECHANICAL (OUTSOLE)   28th

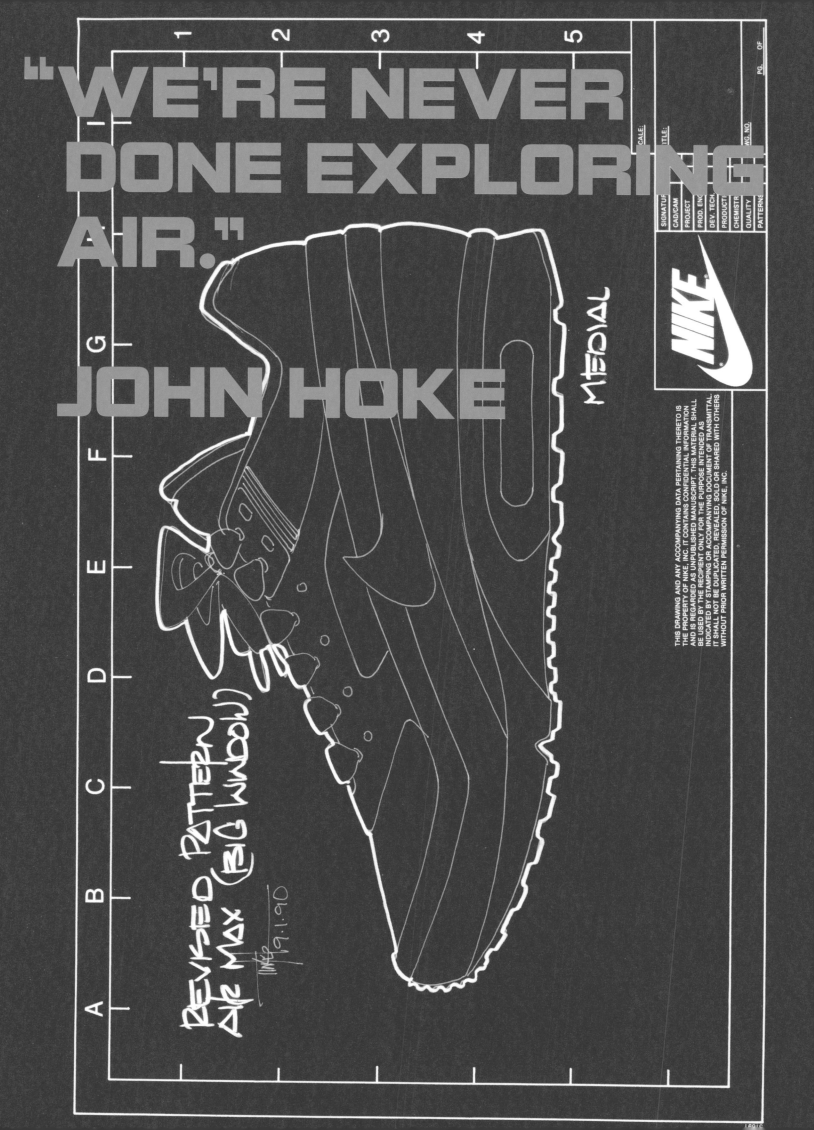

| Air Max Light | White/Black/Red | 1989 |

| Air Max 90 | White/Black/Grey/Infrared | 1990 |

| Air Max BW "Persian Violet" | Black/Persian Violet/White | 1991 |

| Air Max 180 | White/Ultramarine-Solar Red-Black | 1991 |

| Air Max ST | White/Black-Solar Red | 1992 |

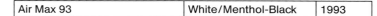

| Air Max 93 | White/Menthol-Black | 1993 |

| Air Max2 | Wolf Grey/White-Turquoise | 1994 |

| Air Max 95 | Black/Neon Yellow-White | 1995 |

| Air Racer Max | White/Purple/Orange | 1995 |

| Air Max 96 | Blue/Purple/Silver | 1996 |

| Air Max 97 | Metallic Silver/Varsity Red-White-Black | 1997 |

| Air Max 98 TL | Midnight Navy/Green Chili-White-Hyper Blue | 1998 |

| Air Max Plus | Grey/Red/Navy/Black | 1998 |

| Air Tuned Max | Dark Charcoal/Celery-Saturn Red | 1999 |

| Air Max 2003 | Silver/Light Blue | 2003 |

| Air Max 360 | Metallic Silver/White-Flint Grey-Varsity Red | 2006 |

| Air Max 270 | Black/Black-Total Orange | 2018 |

| Air Max 720 | Dark Smoke Grey/Black-Laser Fuchsia | 2019 |

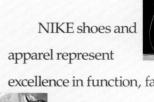

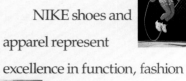

NIKE shoes and apparel represent excellence in function, fashion and technology. Special care is devoted to providing the utmost in comfort and performance, no matter what your sport or activity.

Top: Mini Airborne, Stretch Short, Cross Trainer Low. *Left:* Kiara, Outbreak High
Right: The Strand Top, The Strand Short, Women's SC, Gear Logo Tank, Signature Short. CC-X

NIKE-AIR IS NOT A SHOE.

Air Revolution

A PRINCIPLE THAT WORKS.

At the Nike Sports Research Lab, one thing is more important than a love of sports.

A passion for science.

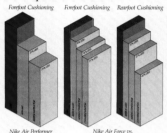

Forefoot Cushioning   Forefoot Cushioning   Rearfoot Cushioning

Nike Air Performer and Air Protector vs. Avia 460 and Reebok Instructor.   Nike Air Force vs. Reebok 6600, adidas Conductor, and Converse Weapon.

That's why, to make sure our research is valid and objective, our scientists and engineers regularly present their findings to institutions such as The American College of Sports Medicine.

We conduct basic and applied research projects, to find new methods of improving cushioning, flexibility, stability, and support.

Our findings helped us develop Nike-Air to begin with. And the Sports Research Lab continually puts Nike-Air to the test.

Using accepted standard testing methods, we measured the impact on different shoes when the foot strikes the ground. The lower the force transmitted through the shoe, the better the cushioning. Here's what we found:

Aerobics: Forefoot cushioning is crucial because the forefoot strikes the ground first in nearly all maneuvers. Better forefoot cushioning reduces the shock that can cause injury to the foot and lower leg.

We tested our Air Protector and Air Performer against the Reebok Instructor Low and the Avia 460. The Nike shoes provided 29% more cushioning than Reebok, and 21% more than Avia.

Basketball: A player lands from a jump with the force of up to ten times his weight. Better forefoot and rearfoot cushioning can reduce shock and the chance of injury.

We tested the Nike Air Force against the adidas Conductor, Converse Weapon, and Reebok 6600.

The Air Force was shown to have the best forefoot cushioning (16% better than adidas, 21% better than Converse, and 8% better than Reebok) and the best rearfoot cushioning (21% better than adidas, 40% better than Converse, and 12% better than Reebok).

Running: We conducted impact studies with the Air Max and nine competitors' shoes. Compared to shoes with conventional midsole materials, the Air Max provided an average of 13% better rearfoot cushioning, and 15% better forefoot cushioning.

Nike-Air never ends: These tests were conducted with new shoes. Yet further tests prove that Nike-Air retains its cushioning properties indefinitely,

These are the results of impact testing conducted to measure the change of cushioning that occurs during a typical run or workout. A better cushioning score means that less shock is transmitted to the foot and leg. Two midsole cushioning systems of the same thickness were tested: a Nike Airsole ■ and molded EVA ▪.

while other systems begin to lose their cushioning with the very first step. So the superiority of Nike-Air increases with use.

For instance, after 534 miles, the Air Max retained 98% of its cushioning properties. After 410 miles, an EVA-cushioned shoe retained just 67% of its cushioning. After just 40 miles, shoes using Tiger-Gel™ had already lost 8% of their cushioning.

It's a matter of how different cushioning systems work.

In conventional systems, like EVA, the midsole has small cells containing bubbles of air. When the foot strikes the ground, the air is squeezed out and the cell walls break down or compact.

But in an Airsole, the gas can't escape. The Airsole remains undamaged, mile after mile.

The research that supports these findings assures us that we can provide the best cushioning possible in an athletic shoe.

But in a tough, confusing, retail marketplace, it provides you with an equally important measure of comfort. The facts.

JUST DO IT. Pull on a pair of Nike Air Max™ running shoes. Feel the unrivaled cushioning of the Nike Air-Sole! Feel the resilience of the flex grooves. Feel the support of the thermoplastic support straps. Don't feel the impact of the road.

Women's and Men's Air Max

Low Martin, world-ranked marathoner. Mark Coogan, world-ranked steeplechaser.

The Air Max® shoe is the technical response to multi-milers' need for **greater impact protection throughout the stride—** anatomically correct cushioning, support and flexibility from heelstrike to toe-off.

NIKE-AIR® cushioning is the dominant athletic shoe technology of this generation. Key to its unending command of impact protection and performance comfort is a unique versatility. This allows NIKE to continually cross the boundaries of convention with authentic applications of NIKE-AIR® cushioning. **For Fall '95, the proof is found in a new series of Air Max® shoes with maximum-volume, visible Air-Sole® units in the forefoot.** Compared to previous forefoot Air-Sole® units, the new Air Max forefoot units provide at least 3-5 times as much NIKE-AIR® cushioning volume.

air max

Air Max advertisements and ephemera (above and opposite)   1987–95

The March 26, 1987, launch of the Air Max 1 personifies how Nike design and marketing exponentially combine to express compelling stories. By focusing the Air Max 1's advertising narrative on its Visible Air unit rather than its singular silhouette, the introductory campaign laid the foundation for an unfolding Air Max chronicle instead of a solitary chapter. Its print advertisement copy supported the framework by clarifying Nike Air as a technology with endless application possibilities. Nike has delivered on this promise time and again with an archive of Air Max styles that have endlessly evolved the Air Max legend and, as of 2013, earned it its own annual holiday: Air Max Day, celebrated globally on March 26.

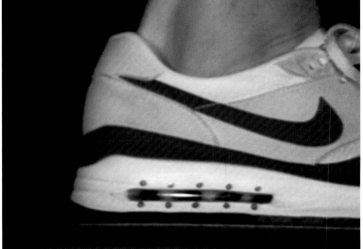

| *Revolution* film for the Air Max 1 (above and opposite) | 1987 |

Nike's *Revolution* film formed the centerpiece of the debut Air Max 1 campaign. Set to the Beatles' anthem of the same name, the grainy Super 8 black-and-white film featured amateur athletes as well as icons, such as Michael Jordan and John McEnroe, participating in the fitness revolution sweeping America. By pairing a representative cross section of individuals with a famous soundtrack, Nike introduced a democratized vision of sport directly associated with the Visible Air technology spliced between physical feats.

THE BEST ON EARTH.
Air Jordan from Nike.

THE BEST ON MARS.
Ditto.

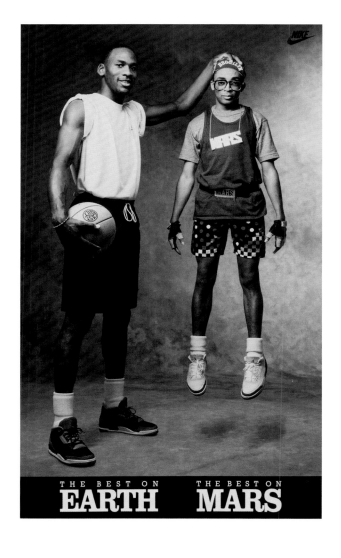

THE BEST ON
EARTH

THE BEST ON
MARS

| Early Air Jordan advertisements | 1984 |

| "Spike and Mike" Air Jordan advertisements, featuring Michael Jordan and Spike Lee (above and opposite) | 1988 |

As Nike honed its potent recipe of narrative products and evocative communications, it subsequently broadened its cultural influence, inextricably embedding itself in the era's social context. Starting in 1988, this savvy expression came in the form of a collaboration with movie director Spike Lee, who appeared in a series of Air Jordan television advertisements as Mars Blackmon, the Air Jordan-obsessed character from Lee's 1986 hit movie *She's Gotta Have It*. Together Blackmon and Michael Jordan formed an iconic duo, coined "Spike and Mike," that gave the signature sneakers (and Nike) elevated street credibility and reach.

1-800-305-2420

| "1-800" print campaign, featuring the Air Penny II | 1996 |

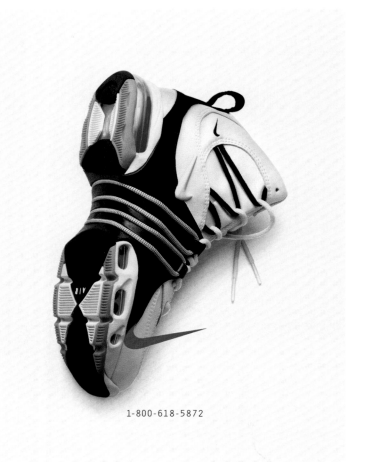

1-800-618-5872

| "1-800" print campaign, featuring the Air Max Mundo | 1996 |

1-800-650-6941

| "1-800" print campaign, featuring the Air Alarm | 1996 |

1-800-931-2354

| "1-800" print campaign, featuring the Air Zoom Flight 5 | 1996 |

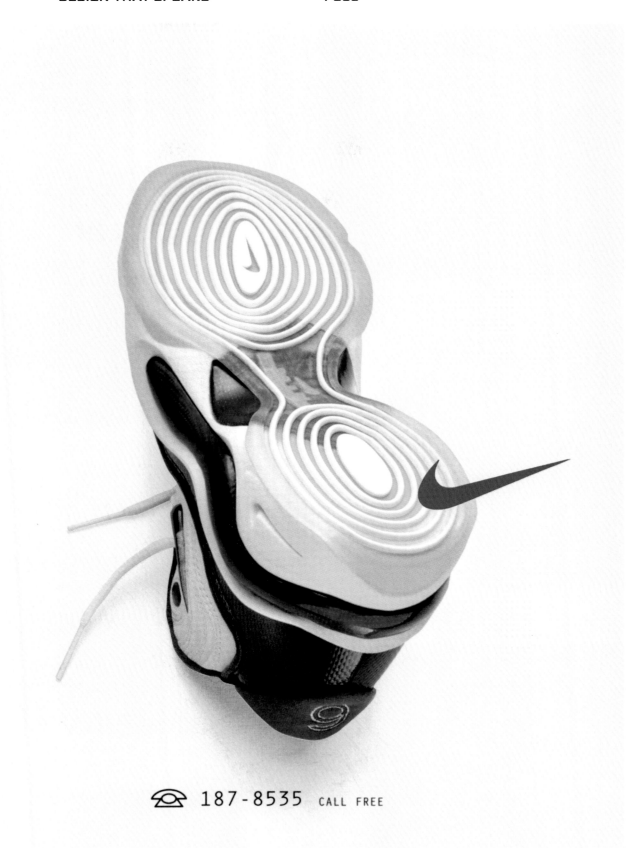

187-8535 CALL FREE

| "1-800" print campaign, featuring the Air Zoom Flight 96 | 1996 |

As the Swoosh logo and Nike's increasingly iconic footwear designs began to speak for themselves, the company said less. Specifically, in a series of print advertisements often referred to as the "1-800" ads, Nike introduced bold sneakers on white backgrounds, accompanied only by a Swoosh and a phone number. Consumers calling the number could hear prerecorded messages from various Nike icons, designers, and athletes, such as tennis player Jim Courier. Beyond showcasing the shoes, the advertisements hinted at the philosophical undercurrent that continues to inform both Nike product creation and brand expression: an unapologetic irreverence for convention, even its own.

Air Trainer SC High	White/Grey/Orange	1990

Monday–Wednesday–Friday film series (opposite) and "Bo Knows" advertising campaign (above), featuring Bo Jackson	1988–89

No audit of Nike's advertising archive would be complete without the inclusion of the 1989 "Bo Knows" campaign, a sequel to the 1988 *Monday–Wednesday–Friday* film series, which introduced the idea of cross-training into the Nike domain. Both of these influential campaigns featured Bo Jackson—the first modern athlete to play professional baseball and American football in the same year—wearing a version of the Air Trainer, the company's premier cross-training shoe, while excelling at various athletic activities. In the inaugural "Bo Knows" commercial, a variety of Nike athletes—ranging from Michael Jordan to Joan Benoit Samuelson—attest to Jackson's expertise with the catchphrase "Bo knows," positioning the athlete as an authority on all things sport, including shoes. In a coup of pitch-perfect timing, the advertisement debuted just after Jackson's lead-off home run in the 1989 Major League Baseball All-Star Game.

Just do it.

"Together" campaign, with banner (above) and film (opposite) featuring LeBron James | 2014

While Nike's early brand expressions frequently placed its products in secondary spots, the company's later campaigns have increasingly relegated them to the background, focusing instead on the power of sport to connect communities, influence culture, and fuel dreams. The 2014 "Together" campaign—released ahead of basketball star LeBron James's return to Cleveland, Ohio, his hometown—exemplifies the potential of this practice.

Its film focuses exclusively on the pride and anticipation that preceded the star's arrival, amplifying these emotions with a stirring speech by James, images of the city's diverse populace, and a call for Clevelanders to band together in pursuit of a shared goal: an NBA championship. A ten-story, 25,000-square-foot (2,320-square-meter) banner welcoming James back to Cleveland, unveiled in tandem with the film, reiterated this unifying message.

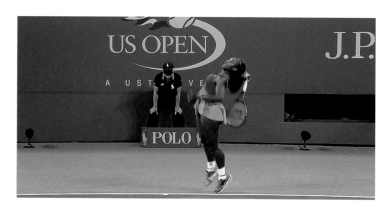

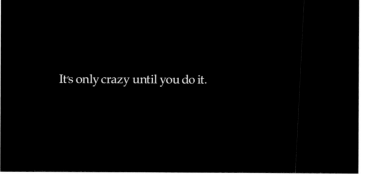

It's only crazy until you do it.

Voice of Belief film, featuring Serena Williams (above and opposite) | 2018

Thirty years after the first "Just Do It" advertisement, Nike presented *Voice of Belief*, a film starring Serena Williams. Hailing Williams's rise from aspiring tennis prodigy to the greatest athlete of all time, it merged archival and match footage with a voiceover by Williams's father and first coach, Richard Williams, articulating the young athlete's dream of winning a Grand Slam. Concluding with the text "It's only crazy until you do it. Just Do It," the film tangibly connected Nike's tagline to the realization of crazy dreams—and introduced the greater "Dream Crazy" campaign, which celebrated the enduring yet always evolving "Just Do It" message.

Girls from Compton don't play tennis. They own it. ✔ Just do it.

You don't have to change who you are to change your world.

Just do it.

It's only a crazy dream until you do it.

Believe in something, even if it means sacrificing everything.

Just do it.

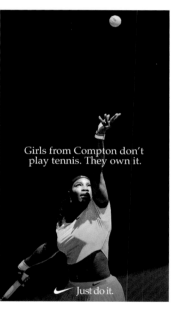

Girls from Compton don't play tennis. They own it.

Just do it.

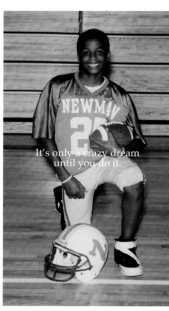

It's only a crazy dream until you do it.

Don't wait until you've won a ring to play like it.

Just do it.

It's only a crazy dream until you do it.

If you need a reason to dream crazy, here's eleven.

Just do it.

| "Dream Crazy" billboard | Union Square, San Francisco, California | 2018 |

| "Dream Crazy" print campaign (above and opposite) | 2018 |

The second film in the "Dream Crazy" series emphasized the campaign's egalitarian message and clarified its greater expression. Narrated by former National Football League quarterback Colin Kaepernick, it highlighted the unlikely stories of athletes who reject excuses and defy odds in pursuit of their crazy dreams. Commemorating household names, such as LeBron James, Serena Williams, Shaquem Griffin, and Eliud Kipchoge, as well as extraordinary young athletes—such as basketball phenom and wheelchair athlete Megan Blunk; homecoming queen and high school linebacker Alicia Woollcott; and Isaiah Bird, a ten-year-old wrestler born without legs—the film and its accompanying campaign posters introduced "Just Do It" to a new generation of athletes.

Dream Crazy film, narrated by Colin Kaepernick (above and opposite) | 2018

Created in collaboration with longtime creative agency Wieden+ Kennedy, the multimedia "Dream Crazy" campaign explicitly demonstrated the power of sport to move the world. Implicitly it also paid homage to the hard work and no-excuses ethos that have helped Nike realize its own crazy dream: to become the world's largest sneaker and sportswear brand. Moreover, the campaign's idealistic narrative and Nike's use of Colin Kaepernick as a spokesperson revealed how the company's "Just Do It" ideology influences its increasingly vocal support for a level playing field for all.

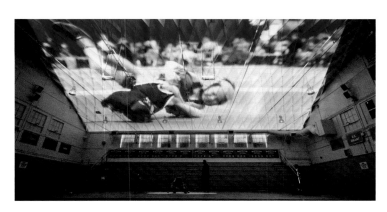

LEBRON OPENS HIS 'I PROMISE' SCHOOL

IF YOU EVER DREAMED OF PLAYING FOR MILLIONS AROUND THE WORLD,

NOW IS YOUR CHANCE.

PLAY INSIDE, PLAY' FOR THE *WORLD*

Dear Athletes,

Why do we love sporting comebacks so much? It's not as simple as a moment of boastful pride or a shallow victory.

It's because in that moment, we saw and felt the impossible made possible. It is because of the inspiring nature of what we humans are capable of when we don't give up.

We've all been underestimated and counted out at some point. We've all felt overpowered by someone or something that at that moment felt much stronger than us. It could have been a tougher opponent, a nasty hill or a ruptured Achilles.

But whatever it was, in those moments we felt like it was all over, and so did everyone else.

But we didn't give up, we didn't quit and because of that, things started to change, and then, to faith's surprise, we were on top again.

YOU CAN'T STOP SPORT. / US

That's why sports will always remind us we can make it back. No matter how deep down we fall. Again and again and again, sports will prove to us that we can make it back from anything.

Back from injury, back from loss, back from 3-1, 6-1 or 3-28, back from everyone thinking we were history.

And that's why comebacks have a way of leaving a mark on us all, we hold onto them and bring them out when we need it most. And that is right now.

And even if right now there isn't a trophy or championship to win, there is something much bigger to comeback from and to.

Now more than ever, we need to see ourselves in sporting comebacks and remember that there is nothing we are not capable of.

"You Can't Stop Us" digital advertising campaign, athlete letter | 2020

In 2020—following the arrival of the COVID-19 pandemic—Nike again evidenced its activist position with the "Play Inside, Play for the World" campaign. Reacting in real time to stay-at-home orders, the social media-driven initiative urged athletes to do their part by playing inside. In tandem, the company engaged consumers via virtual competitions, such as the Living Room Cup.

Nike soon followed the humanitarian missive with the digital "You Can't Stop Us" campaign, which glorified the resilience that underpins comeback victories. Grounded in a film titled *Never Too Far Down* that was narrated by LeBron James, the campaign drew a straight line between a champion's steadfast resolve and the perseverance needed to surmount the moment's unprecedented challenges.

| *Nothing Beats a Londoner* film (above and opposite) | 2018 |

While the success of Nike's international campaigns highlights its capacity to strike an influential common chord, its ability to cultivate hyperlocal conversations is an emerging talent, fueled by the rise of digital media and a commitment to meeting athletes where they are. "Nothing Beats a Londoner," a 2018 Instagram-led campaign that extolled the resilient mind-set of the city's inhabitants through the lens of sport, provides a blue-chip example of this capacity. The accompanying film features 258 local youths, plus cameos by their athletic heroes. From the true stories that inspired the film's script to its locations and soundtrack, it authentically reflected its audience's reality.

| "If You Let Me Play" advertisement | 1995 |

In 1984, Nike celebrated the introduction of the women's marathon to the Olympic Games with an advertisement that praised those who had lobbied international sporting authorities to reject the archaic belief that women were physically incapable of running the distance. Joan Benoit Samuelson further obliterated this myth when she won the inaugural race. Having trained for the event alongside Mark Parker and other Nike teammates, she became an enduring icon of the company's advocacy for gender equity. In the summer of 1995, Nike continued its crusade with *If You Let Me Play*, a statistics-based film that lauded the long-term benefits of providing girls with access to sport.

"In 1979 Joan Benoit was 23 Years Old and Winning" advertisement, featuring Joan Benoit Samuelson	1995

"There is No Finish Line" fortieth-anniversary poster, featuring Joan Benoit Samuelson	2019

Air Force 1 High	White/Silver	1983

Air Force 1 High outsole		1983

When the Air Force 1 introduced Air technology to basketball in 1982, its utilitarian aesthetic instantly captivated sport and street culture, with its status only rising over time. Currently Nike's most iterated design of all time, the sneaker has enabled the company to converse with entirely new audiences through limited-edition releases and special-edition collaborations that have reimagined the iconic canvas in homage to people, places, teams, and moments. Whether aligning with like-minded brands, artists, or fashion designers—or tapping its own in-house design team—Nike has employed the Air Force 1 to precipitate new creative and cultural exchanges.

"CONCEIVED FOR BASKETBALL BUT ADOPTED BY THE STREETS, THE AF1'S CONFIDENT SWAGGER TRANSCENDS TIME."

FRASER COOKE

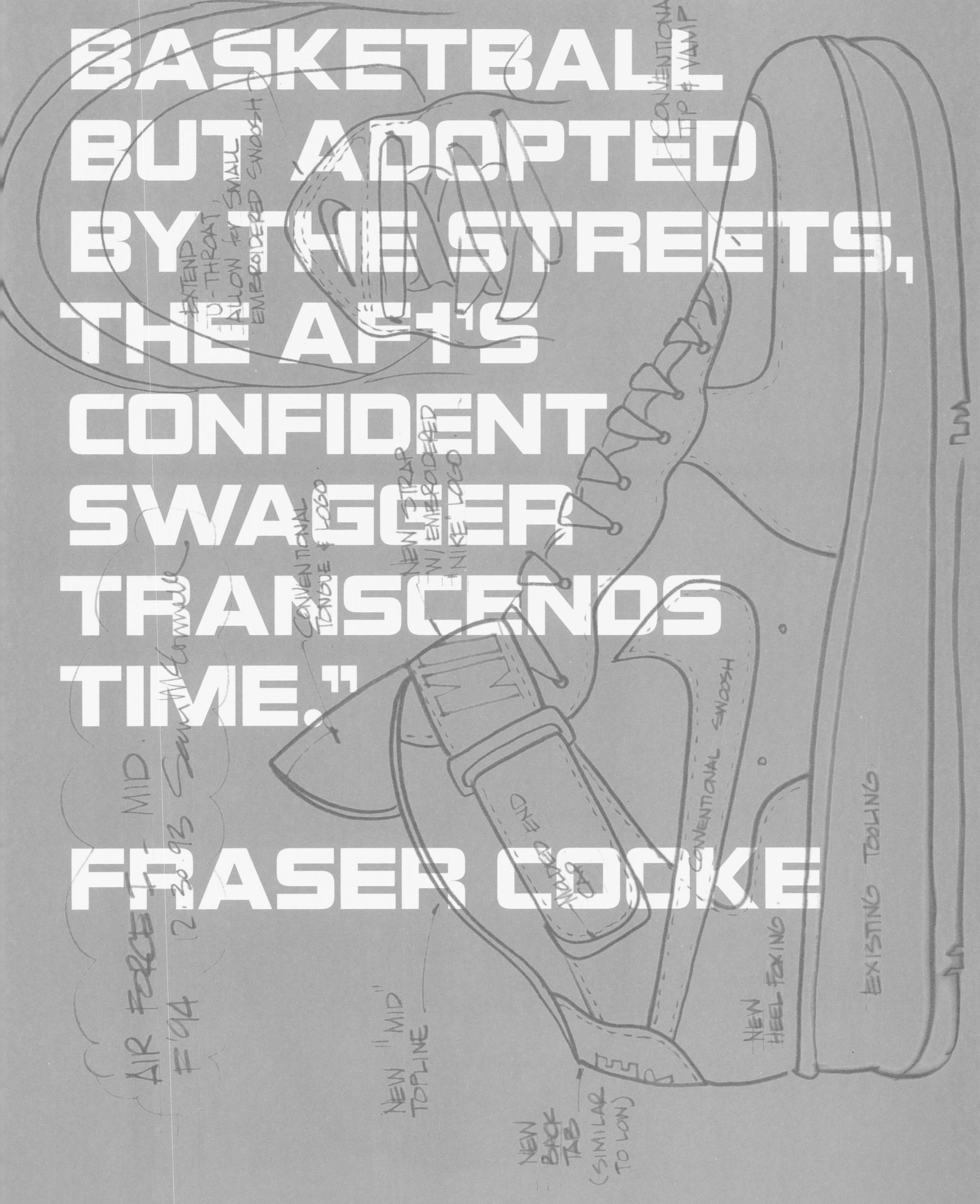

AIR FORCE 1 LO

Sizes	6-15
Upper	White/Silver

Full-Grain Leather Upper: Durable and supportive for long wear.

Perforated Full-Grain Leather Toe Piece: For increased breathability.

Variable Width Lacing System™: Allows the upper width to be adjusted by staggering the eyelets while also providing a snug, comfortable fit.

Spenco® Rearfoot Padding: Provides heel security, blister protection and cushioning for the Achilles tendon.

Sockliner *PermaFoam™:* Molds to the pressure pattern of the foot for a uniquely personalized fit.

Midsole *NIKE-Air™ Unit:* Provi[des] cushioning than conve[ntional]. Reduces impact on mu[scles]. Helps reduce leg fatigu[e].

Outsole *Concentric Circle Outsole:* [trac]tion and minimal resis[tance to] movements.

Profile The Air Force 1 Lo is th[e...] with the NIKE-Air mids[ole sys]tem which in the past [...] NIKE technical running [...] Air midsole provides u[...] ioning than conventio[nal...]

Continued on back

4/83

AIR FORCE 1 HI   4190

Sizes	6-17
Upper	White/Silver

Full-Grain Leather Upper: Durable and supportive for long wear.

Perforated Full-Grain Leather Toe Piece: For increased breathability.

Variable Width Lacing System™: Allows the upper width to be adjusted by staggering the eyelets while also providing a snug, comfortable fit.

Proprioceptus Belt: To decrease the chance of ankle injury.

Hinged Eyelet Design: Allows ankle mobility without sacrificing stability.

Spenco® Rearfoot Padding: Provides heel security, blister protection and cushioning for the Achilles tendon.

Dipped Achilles Pad: Prevents Achilles tendon irritation during normal foot flexion.

Sockliner *PermaFoam™:* Molds to the pressure pattern of the foot for a uniquely personalized fit.

Midsole *NIKE-Air™ Unit:* Provides up to 30% more cushioning than conventional midsoles. Reduces impact on muscles and joints. Helps reduce leg fatigue.

Outsole *Concentric Circle Outsole:* For optimum traction and minimal resistance to pivoting movements.

Continued on back

NIKE

4/83

| Air Force 1 High SC | White/Blue | 1995 |

| Air Force 1 High Urban | White/Brown | 1993 |

NIKE ®

AIR FORCE 1

OWNER'S MANUAL

The Advantages of "Air":
   Studies show that the larger the player, the more cushioning is needed since the increase in force generated against the bottom of the foot during play exceeds the increase in the sole area that is absorbing the impact. Scientists have shown that the Air-Sole® provides up to 30% more cushioning than conventional basketball shoes.

   In addition to providing superior cushioning, the flow of gas throughout the Air-Sole® unit during foot contact creates a conforming foot bed, providing stability for side-to-side maneuvers.

   Moreover, studies show the Air Force I to be 20% more resilient than conventional basketball shoes. A "resilient" material is one which returns energy that is put into it. The resiliency of the Air-Sole,® with its return of energy to the player, reduces fatigue and makes possible those important fourth quarter rallies. And, unlike conventional midsoles, the Air-Sole® will not lose its cushioning, resiliency or stabilizing capability with use. The Air-Sole® contained in the Air

Force I is with you every step of the way.
   Strap yourself in and take to the sky. The Air Force I...it's earned its wings.

FEATURES
Concentric Circle Outsole:
   The concentric circle outsole pattern is designed for two purposes: To provide optimal traction during side-to-side and front-to-back maneuvers, and to provide minimal resistance to pivoting movements that apply large and potentially injurious pressures to the ankle, knee and hip joint.

   In tests done in the NIKE Sports Research Laboratory, the Air Force I was compared with conventional European shell outsole patterns. Results show that while having similar resistance to side-to-side and front-to-back movements, the NIKE concentric circle outsole demonstrated a lower maximum torque, or lower resistance to twisting movements. This study indicates that while performing as well, the concentric circle design may be safer than conventional outsole patterns.

Concentric Circle Outsole:

Traction Characteristics ■ *Air Basketball Concentric Outsole*
■ *Conventional Outsole*
■ *Conventional Outsole*

Resistance to Translation

| 1.00 | 1.10 | 1.20 | 1.30 |

Static Coefficient of Friction

Resistance to Rotation

| 70 | 80 | 90 | 100 | 110 | 120 | N•m |

Maximum Torque – 180 Degree Turn

Syntex® Rearfoot Padding: Provides heel security, blister protection and cushioning for the Achilles tendon.

PermaFoam Sockliner: Molds to the pressure pattern of the foot for a unique, personalized fit.

Dipped Achilles Pad: Prevents Achilles tendon irritation during normal foot flexion.

Proprioceptus Belt: Exerts slight pressure to the base of the tibia and fibula (the two bones between the knee and ankle). This pressure allows the body's sensory receptors to monitor ankle joint positioning and thus decrease the chance of ankle injuries.

Hinged Eyelet: Allows ankle mobility without sacrificing stability.

Variable Width Lacing System:™ Allows you to vary the upper width by staggering the eyelets while also providing a snug, comfortable fit.

Full Grain Leather Upper.

Nylon Mesh Arch Side Panels: Help to keep in-shoe temperatures to a cool minimum.

AIR

| Air Force 1 Owner's Manual | 1982 |

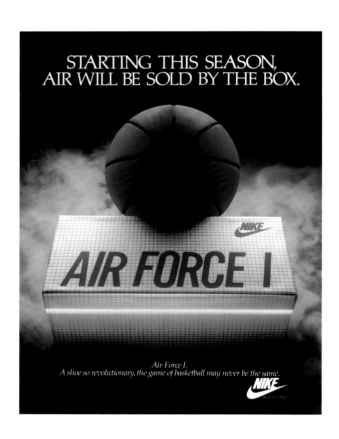

Air Force 1 advertisements and ephemera | 1983

Extracts from the Air Force 1 thirtieth-anniversary "1thology" poster   2012

| Air Force 1 "Linen" | Beige/White/Pink | 2000 |

| Air Force 1 "Atmos" | Medium Grey/Twilight Blue | 2001 |

| Air Force 1 "Black Album" | Black/White/Black | 2003 |

| Air Force 1 High LE "Sheed" | White/Varsity Red | 2003 |

| Air Force 1 High L/M PRB "Tokyo Stash" | Light Grey/Magnet | 2003 |

| Air Force 1 "Vibe" | White/Blue-Black | 2003 |

| Air Force 1 × Busy P Low Supreme | Black/Varsity Blue | 2004 |

| Air Force 1 Premium by Mark Smith | Cashmere/Cashmere-British Tan-White | 2004 |

Air Force 1 QK "Mister Cartoon"	White/Classic Green-Varsity Red	2005

Air Force 1 PRB "Ueno Sakura"	Light Bone/Light Bone-Watermelon-White	2005

Air Force 1 × Undefeated "Shemagh"	Varsity Purple/Varsity Purple-Harbor Blue-Light Charcoal	2006

Air Force 1 × Bobbito High Premium "Beef 'N Broccoli"	Army Olive/Baroque Brown-Soft Grey	2007

Air Force 1 Low Supreme "Krink"	Metallic Silver/Metallic Silver-Gum Light	2008

Air Force 1 Low PRM "BHM"	Midnight Fog/Black	2012

Supreme Air Force 1 Mid "Red"	Varsity Red/White-White	2014

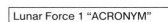

Lunar Force 1 "ACRONYM"	White/White-White	2017

From top left, artworks by: Atsushi Kamijo, Eiji Nakayama, Eisaku Kito, Hajime Sorayama, Haruo Suekichi, Hideaki Hirata, Hitoshi Yoneda, Jun Goshima, Junichi Taniguchi, Katsuya Terada, Keiichi Sato, Kenji Ando, Kow Yokoyama, Masakazu Katsura, Naoki Sato, Shinichi Yamashita, Shuji Yonezawa, Takayuki Takeya, Yoshikazu Yasuhiko, Yasuhito Udagawa, Yasushi Nirasawa, Yukio Fujioka, Yuji Oniki, and Yukihiro Suzuki.

| *White Dunk: Evolution of an Icon* exhibition | Toyko, Japan | 2004 |

In 2004 Nike's perpetual quest to connect with new audiences manifested as the *White Dunk: Evolution of an Icon* exhibition, which opened in Tokyo before traveling to Paris and Los Angeles. The gallery-like pop-up exhibition featured artworks by twenty-five Japanese artists—from animators, illustrators, and toymakers to craftspeople, sculptors, and graphic designers—who were invited by Nike chairman Mark Parker to take an all-white Dunk and "Let it inspire [them]. No limits." The success of Nike's first foray into an exhibition format set the tone for increasingly experimental future brand expressions.

| *The Nature of Motion* exhibition for Milan Design Week | Milan, Italy | 2016 |

"Experiments in Natural Motion" experimental shoe designs for *The Nature of Motion* exhibition	2016

The Nature of Motion, a temporary exhibition for Milan Design Week 2016, evinced Nike's growing legacy of unconfined cultural engagement. Devoid of commercial product, the multiroom show juxtaposed experimental footwear creations by Nike designers with conceptual objects created in collaboration with ten progressive contemporary designers. Employing everything from Velcro hair rollers to cork to recycled Flyknit yarn, the radically diverse displays shared a singular characteristic: the investigation of natural motion, which also aligned the designs with Nike's ongoing mission to expand human potential.

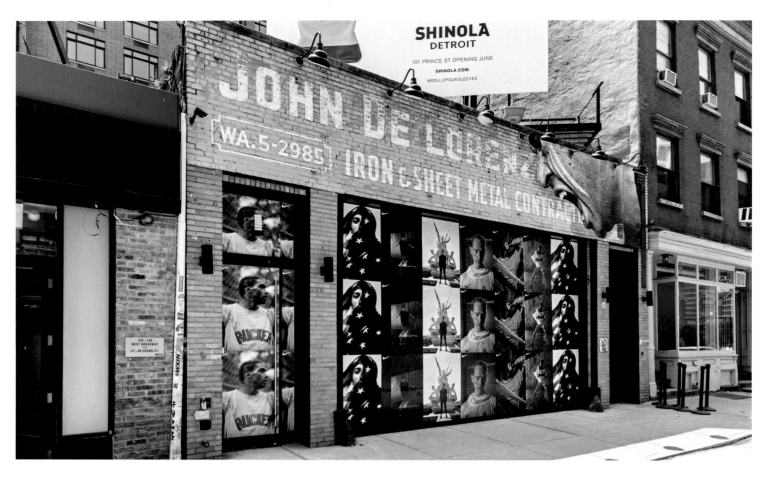

| *Objects of Desire* exhibition | New York City, New York | 2017 |

The 2017 multimedia exhibition *Objects of Desire* in New York City similarly presented an immersive intersection of sport and culture. Curated by Dorian Grinspan, editor-in-chief of *Out of Order* magazine, *Objects of Desire* featured both archival works of Nike athletes wearing Nike innovations and newly commissioned works, including the film *I, David*. Directed by emerging filmmaker Niclas Gillis, the expressive work stars David Hallberg, a principal dancer for the American Ballet Theatre, wearing a NikeLab ACG Poncho.

I, David film, featuring David Hallberg, at the *Objects of Desire* exhibition | New York City, New York | 2017

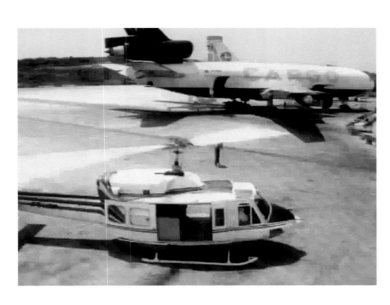

Airport film, featuring Brazil's National Football Team (above and opposite)	1998

No matter their platform, the success of Nike's brand expressions hinges upon its ability to authentically engage its respective communities. The *Airport* film, featuring Brazil's National Football Team, illustrates this simple truth. Created in anticipation of the 1998 World Cup, it featured the team's top players performing mesmerizing tricks in a paradoxically banal airport. This stark juxtaposition hinted at the game's transition from a traditional European style of play to the spontaneous, creative approach favoured by the Brazilian squad and was underscored by the rise of small-sided (five-a-side) football. In short, it ensured that everyone aspired to become a Brazilian footballer.

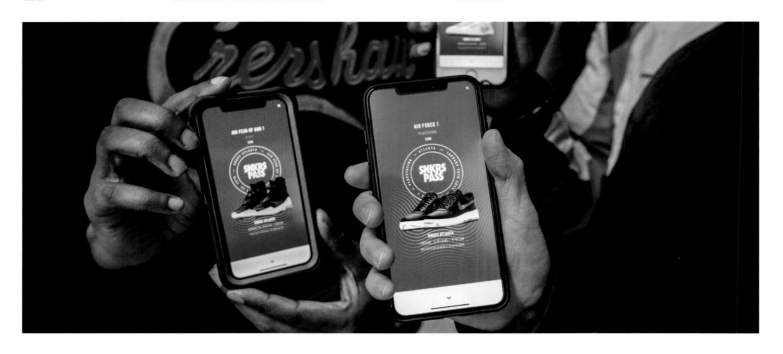

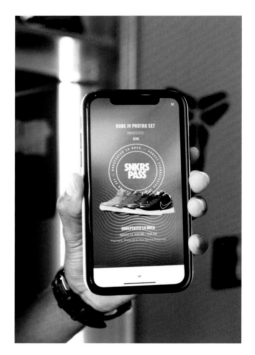

SNKRS drops	Various locations	2019

Since its 2015 launch, the SNKRS app has operated as a litmus test for Nike's most advanced digital initiatives. Branded as the ultimate sneaker destination, it alerts users to the company's newest, rarest footwear. In addition to providing online "passes" to purchase these covetable styles, the app invites users to acquire them via innovative experiences, such as SNKRS Stash, which employs augmented reality to unlock access to exclusive products "hidden" at local drop sites. At the same time, the app delivers user data to Nike, allowing for the company to better anticipate and meet user needs and desires.

Air Force 1 "De Lo Mio" campaign imagery   2018

Air Force 1 "De Lo Mio"	White/University Red-Sport Blue	2018

The 2018 Air Force 1 "De Lo Mio" is a prime example of how SNRKS's circular discourse can augment Nike's ability to deliver elevated experiences and products. When the app's data revealed that its highest concentration of New York City users was in predominantly Dominican neighborhoods, Nike commissioned designer César Pérez—a New York City native of Dominican descent—to create a shoe that paid homage to the Dominican community. Nike then invited six New York-based photographers of Dominican heritage to snap the sneaker on members of the Dominican community. The shoe sold out almost immediately upon initial drop and restock.

| Nike NYC, House of Innovation 000 | New York City, New York | 2018 |

| Nike Shanghai, House of Innovation 001 | Shanghai, China | 2018 |

Nike's use of localized data is increasingly more evident around the globe, as the company tailors its physical stores to their respective communities. In Shanghai, New York, and Paris, flagship stores have evolved from standardized NikeTowns to uniquely designed Houses of Innovation—each showcasing locally relevant designs, decor, and offerings that seamlessly integrate the company's digital platforms.

Nike Live stores in Los Angeles and Tokyo also rely upon Nike app usage, regional buying patterns, and NikePlus member engagement to inform dynamic, highly customized environments. Based upon the company's declared focus on direct-to-consumer business, these spaces are just a mere preview of progressively curated retail expressions.

"NIKE HOUSE OF INNOVATION IS ABOUT REINFORCING A SPACE TO CELEBRATE AND TELL STORIES."

ANDY THAEMERT

3 DREAM WITH US

Air Jordan III
Dunk High
SB Dunk Low Pro
SB Dunk High
Zvezdochka
Kobe IX Elite Premium Low HTM
HTM2 Run Boot Low TZ
Lunar Flyknit HTM
Sock Dart HTM
Air Force 1 HTM
Air Woven Boot HTM
Air Moc Mid HTM
Air Footscape Woven HTM
Zoom Macropus LC Priority HTM
Air VaporMax Moc 2 × ACRONYM
Air Presto Mid Utility × ACRONYM
Air Monarch IV × Martine Rose
Air Monarch
Nike × MMW Free TR 3 SP

R.T. Air Force 1 Mid
R.T. Air Force 1 Low
R.T. Air Force 1 Boot SP
R.T. Dunk Lux High
R.T. × Victorious Minotaurs Collection
The Ten
NikeCourt Flare 2.0 PE × Virgil Abloh
Blazer Studio Mid × Virgil Abloh
NikeCourt Day Dress × Virgil Abloh
Shox Glamour SW × Serena Williams
Studded Leather Jacket × Serena Williams
Denim Skirt × Serena Williams
Studded Dress × Serena Williams
French Open Catsuit × Serena Williams
Nike × sacai LDWaffle
Nike × sacai Blazer Mid
Gyakusou Transform Jacket
Gyakusou Helix Shorts
Gyakusou Short Sleeve Packable Jacket

Gyakusou DF Utility Speed Tights
React Element 87 × Undercover
NIKECraft
React LW WR Mid iSPA
iSPA Air Max 720
iSPA Joyride Envelope
Air VaporMax Flyknit 3
Air VaporMax Flyknit Gaiters iSPA
iSPA Zoom Road Warrior
iSPA OverReact Flyknit
iSPA Drifter
iSPA Flow 2020
iSPA Short
iSPA Inflate Vest
iSPA Inflate JKT

In fall 1987, Nike cofounder Phil Knight and Tinker Hatfield—an architect turned shoe designer with only a couple years of experience under his belt—were sitting at a conference room table across from Michael Jordan's parents, waiting for the basketball star to appear. In the month prior, some of Jordan's key contacts within the company had left, and purportedly Jordan was also thinking about moving on. Following their departures, the task of designing Jordan's next signature shoe fell on Hatfield—who had turned heads with his groundbreaking design for the Air Max. After three frenzied and sleepless weeks of design and development, a first prototype was finally sitting on the table, shrouded under a black cloth. It wasn't lost on Knight or Hatfield that Jordan's high-profile endorsement deal may well be on the table too.

When Jordan arrived, the designer recounted what he had seen and heard on a recent visit to Chicago. Hatfield had accompanied the ballplayer to a tailor, who was making him suits, and learned of his penchant for Italian leather shoes. He saw firsthand that Jordan had an eye for style and was savvy enough to comment on the detail of a lapel or the rise of a hem. Hatfield played back how Jordan wanted a sneaker that would be lighter and less restrictive to complement his dexterity and aerial acrobatics on the court. The star's interest was piqued, and once the cloth came off the prototype on the table, Jordan grasped the shoe immediately, smiling.

The Air Jordan III was a departure from anything that had come before. Like an architect designing a house, Hatfield had listened intently to the needs and wants of his client and connected the dots between offhand observations to deliver a design that would go beyond all expectations. The shoe's upper combined a suedelike nubuck embossed in a distinctive elephant skin pattern with a soft leather called floater that is tumbled after the tanning process to bring out the natural grain. Jordan wanted to wear a new pair every game, and these wouldn't require breaking in. Borrowing from the Air Max, a window in the midsole exposed the company's premier cushioning technology in the heel. The Nike Swoosh was relegated to a distinctive plastic tab at the back, while a new logo—a silhouette of Jordan hanging in midair—was emblazoned on the front and center of the tongue. Rising to just below the ankle, the shoe met Jordan's demand for something lighter and more flexible. With a single design, Hatfield had fused performance and fashion in a way that had never been done before. Jordan was sold. Knight was relieved.

The success of the Air Jordan III was instrumental in establishing the company's approach to athlete collaboration. For Nike's designers, creating a rapport with athletes of the highest caliber, garnering their feedback, and translating those insights into new designs has resulted in a continually improving product cycle—where innovations beget innovations and the evolution of style knows no boundary. One of the more instructive lessons of the Jordan III, perhaps due to Hatfield's architectural training, was that true collaboration with athletes also included recognizing who they are as three-dimensional human beings beyond sport. Intuiting and synthesizing those unique strands into the final product helped to push the company's designs in new and unexpected directions (Andre Agassi's denim tennis shorts come to mind). With street style and hip-hop ascending to the mainstream, the Air Jordan III wasn't just a success on the court; it was a defining moment for the company as a brand with broad cultural cachet, and it helped give rise to sneaker culture as we know it today.

If Hatfield and Jordan's partnership became the paragon for athlete collaboration in popular sport, the emergence of Nike SB (Skateboarding) established a novel approach for harnessing subculture to create a new level of energy around limited-edition, specialized collaborations. After a handful of unsuccessful attempts to crack the skateboarding market, in the early 2000s, Sandy Bodecker—a former product wear-tester whose visionary creativity fueled Nike's entrée into football and action sports, and who would later go on to lead the Breaking2 effort—was tapped to lead the charge. Bodecker understood that for a company of Nike's scale, authenticity and subtlety would be the keys to connecting with the sport's naturally rebellious following. "Action sports athletes have always been about creativity, self-expression, challenging norms, and trying and doing things that have never been done before," Bodecker later explained. "They were the antithesis of what Nike was as a traditional sports brand. But clearly at the time we started Nike SB, the world was changing, and for Nike to stay current and youthful, and to broaden our appeal, it made sense to try to establish a real connection with this new and growing group of nontraditional athletes. From the very beginning, skaters had adopted sneakers as part of their uniform, so we kept things really basic and respectful—and tried not to be something we weren't."

"The nature of skateboarding is to adapt to whatever's in front of you, whether it's a ramp or an obstacle, it's not a structured thing like other sports—there are no rules," says Kevin Imamura, Nike SB Footwear R&D, and a near twenty-year veteran of the SB business. "Because of that mind-set, skateboarders use whatever's at their disposal—whether it's a casual surf shoe or an old basketball shoe. Nike had decades of incredible shoes that had already been used by skateboarders but weren't intended for skateboarding. We realized we could make some slight tweaks and they would be incredible skate shoes."

The Dunk first hit the market in 1985 as the company began partnering with some of the biggest NCAA basketball programs (with the novel two-tone design giving team colors a boost). Following its release, the style was quickly embraced by the then-underground skater community, so in 2002 it was selected to serve as the cornerstone of the nascent SB business. But it wasn't the addition of extra padding to the tongue or a Zoom Air unit to the sockliner, or even changing the composition of the outsole to offer more grip that made the shoes a runaway success. A novel launch strategy included partnering with four skaters, each of whom worked with Nike to devise his own version of the shoe. The Dunk's utilitarian design offered an ideal customizable, chameleonic canvas—and Danny Supasirirat, Gino Iannucci, Richard Mulder, and Reese Forbes all came up with wildly differing approaches to suit their personal styles.

Unlike other sports, performance and fashion have always been insep-
arably intermingled in skate culture. The vibe and appearance of a deck are
as critical as the hardware itself, while the broader scene encompasses
graphics, fashion, music, and lifestyle. By the time the SB Dunk Low Pro
Supreme "Black Cement" and "White Cement" appeared a year later to
instant acclaim (with a design that riffed on the iconic material palette and
colors of the Air Jordan III), Nike SB had not only established a firm footing
in the skate world but had propelled sneaker culture to a whole new eche-
lon by sparking demand for limited quantities sold through specialized
retailers in specific locales. Dunk collaborations with other skaters, artists
(such as Futura, Pushead, and Geoff McFetridge), complementary brands,
and even musicians (including U.N.K.L.E., De La Soul, and the Melvins)
followed, establishing a vibrant cultural feedback loop within the company.

While the Nike SB Dunks were essentially an exercise in product veneer-
ing, another contemporaneous collaboration would prove to be extremely
impactful on the company's design and innovation programs. Australian
industrial designer Marc Newson catapulted to fame in the 1990s on the
basis of his work for Italian brands, such as Alessi, Magis, and Cappellini,
which merged technical prowess with space-age millennial optimism.
From the outset of the partnership, it was clear that Newson didn't just
want to make another pair of shoes. Together with chairman Mark Parker,
who had a personal interest in exploring modularity within footwear
design and was a key collaborator throughout the project, the pair
wanted to demonstrate that shoe construction could be rethought from
the ground up. Released in 2004, the Zvezdochka (aptly named after the
Russian dog launched into space aboard *Sputnik 10* in 1961) did just
that. The design's four discrete components—a perforated, cagelike outer
shell; interlocking outsole; wetsuitlike inner sleeve; and Zoom Air unit
insole—could be assembled and worn in different combinations to suit a
range of applications and environments. By virtue of its modular construction, Zvezdochka also eliminated the adhesives needed in traditional
footwear—one of the stickiest barriers, literally and scientifically, to recycling shoes. While the unique aesthetic may have been divisive, there's
no question that the design pushed the team to think differently about the
materiality, construction, and even philosophy behind shoe production.
The Considered line from 2005, for example—shoes developed specifically around material sourcing for ecological circularity—resulted directly
out of the work for Zvezdochka, although the look and feel couldn't have
been more different. Ultimately the shoe sold in relatively small quantities,
but to this day, company veterans point to it as a pivotal benchmark and
turning point for design, because nothing was out of bounds and every
step of the shoemaking process could be questioned, if necessary.

Over the last two decades, as the lines between the worlds of high fashion,
streetwear, and sportswear have broken down, Nike has secured a unique
position as a brand with permission to play—and push boundaries—in
virtually any arena. One of the key components of this trajectory has been
collaboration. Working with athletes has been at the heart of the company
since Bill Bowerman's days of cobbling shoes under the grandstand at the

University of Oregon, and this intense form of partnership remains at the core of Nike's approach to design. The Air Jordan III, however, paved the way for stylistic and narrative elements drawn from athletic personality to play as important a role as performance innovations. The SB Dunks demonstrated that footwear could serve as a canvas for Nike to engage meaningfully with culture in order to build authentic connections with new audiences. The Zvezdochka revealed the value of external provocateurs to instigate new thinking and serve as change agents within the organization. Naturally, all of these strategies are layered upon the intricate web of collaboration that already exists within the company. New shoes don't simply leap from a designer's desk to the street. Countless professionals, from material scientists to marketing managers, all contribute their expertise to bring a successful product to life. Knowledge sharing, co-creation, and teamwork are essential building blocks in the Nike universe—and it's this foundation that underpins the success of the company's work with outside collaborators.

It's unlikely that Bowerman ever imagined his shoes would make it to Paris Fashion Week, but with high-profile designers, such as Chitose Abe, Virgil Abloh, Kim Jones, Martine Rose, Jun Takahashi, Riccardo Tisci, and Matthew Williams, counted among Nike's roster of collaborators, today the brand is as likely to turn up on the catwalk as on the track. One of the key actors in bringing these relationships to fruition is senior director of Influencer Marketing Special Projects Fraser Cooke. Based in Tokyo, far beyond the boundaries of Beaverton's berm, Cooke likens his role to an A&R man in the record industry—keeping a finger on the pulse, scouting for new talent, and forging relationships that may or may not lead to fruitful endeavors down the line. Coming out of London's streetwear scene, Cooke joined Nike in the early 2000s as the company was ramping up its efforts to connect with audiences outside traditional sport. "I have to hand it to Mark Parker and his team, they did foresee that there was something worth spending time looking at," Cooke reflects. "There was always a culture of collaboration at Nike, but I think they realized there's this other way of working with people to bring unusual, challenging, and interesting ideas forward that otherwise wouldn't exist." Although these designer collaborations only represent a small fraction of Nike's business, over the last two decades, as they have taken on greater and greater prominence, they have helped expand both the boundaries of sport, and the notion of what the Nike brand encompasses.

To make these collaborations work, teams dedicated to footwear and apparel are charged with representing Nike's side of the design partnership. A top-flight roster of talent—many of them graduates of the world's most prestigious fashion and design programs, such as London's Central Saint Martins or Design Academy Eindhoven—has been recruited to bring their unique talent to bear on the company from within. Nathan Jobe, senior footwear creative design director, likens the team to a disruptive force for co-creation (whether hosting external designers or working across teams within the company to distribute and fertilize new design concepts). Given the high-profile nature of the partnerships, both Jobe and his counterpart in apparel, Jarrett Reynolds, are quick to point to the demanding pace and nature of the role. "It's hectic and crazy, and that's why I love it," says Reynolds. "No two days are the same, and no two collaborators are the same." Even with dozens of projects in the pipeline at different stages of development, and more being lined up, Reynolds and his team meticulously prepare for meetings weeks in advance— polling colleagues in other departments to determine if there are specific needs to be addressed, curating color and material samples, generating construction ideas, and producing prototypes to share with collaborators. "It's a balance of stepping on toes, pushing, and finding the magic in the middle," says Reynolds. "I have to stand up for Nike in the meeting, but then when we walk away, I have to stand up for the designer so their vision doesn't get diluted."

For Nike's teams, a truly meaningful collaboration results in something neither party could achieve on its own. The company's legacy of innovation, technical expertise, extensive design resources, and deep archives offers external designers the chance to engage with a veritable feast of opportunities. The collaborators in turn not only bring their cachet but also a unique creative spirit completed by skill sets that typically sit outside sportswear. According to Reynolds, the worst way to start a collaboration is by collaborating. Or as Jobe explains, "The whole team is involved, and we'll sit in a room all day long. We show them what we're into and ask what they're into. We'll share ideas around form, culture, music— everything to kind of influence it. It may seem abstract, but it takes the pressure off them coming in and feeling like they have to solve a problem for Nike." In the best cases, entirely fresh results emerge from the confluence. Limited in quantity, hyped in anticipation of release, sold out instantly, and reverberating throughout the digital content landscape, Nike's collaborations have become a key brand differentiator.

Such was the case with "The Ten," the 2017 reappraisal of ten iconic models from Nike (and Nike-owned brands Jordan and Converse), done in partnership with Off-White creative director Virgil Abloh. Relying on a cut-and-paste mentality, the collection aimed to subvert the gravitas of the iconic originals through acts of removal, remixing, and recontextualization. "The important thing about 'The Ten' for me is that it's Nike recognizing its icons from the past, but showing them for the design integrity of the future," Abloh wrote in a 132-page treatise on the project titled *Textbook*. He describes it as "a postmodern idea about design, culture, innovation, and athletic performance all intertwined into one." Although the shoes were originally designed for sport, "The Ten" recognizes that they now occupy a far bigger space in culture writ large. The first five models (dubbed "Revealing") were conceptualized in a single marathon session guided by Jobe's team. Layers and elements of each shoe were stripped away to create something recognizable yet unexpected, while a system of tags and labels playing off Nike's internal shoe samples were devised to highlight the origins of each design. With the other five models (under the banner "Ghosting"), translucency was prioritized through material substitutions to call attention to elements and forms that may have gone undetected in the original. Although the initial concepts were developed quickly, the intentionally imperfect, interventional details—such as exposed, unreinforced heel counters; overprinted text blocks; and deliberate yellowing—proved difficult to replicate in factories accustomed to standardization and rooting out imperfections. Ultimately Nike's willingness to challenge its own processes in partnership with Abloh helped make the collection the viral sensation it became.

From furniture to fashion, Abloh's larger-than-life persona rests on an intrinsic ability to transform the all-you-can-eat buffet of our infinitely scrolling culture into accessible amuse-bouches perfectly timed to the public's appetite. Nonetheless, harking back to his teenage aspirations, Abloh made it clear throughout *Textbook* that these are techniques and tools available to all—and for those who missed out on "The Ten," creating your own icon takes little more than setting a blade, stencil, or zip tie to an old pair of shoes. A series of "Off Campus" workshops hosted by Nike and Abloh in New York and London further extended Abloh's notion of the collection, representing a figurative baton pass to the next generation of aspiring designers.

In 2018 Nike paired two of its biggest stars, Abloh and Serena Williams, to create new models of the NikeCourt Flare, Blazer, and Air Max 97 for Williams's French Open appearance. One year later the duo reunited with Nike's design teams to put together an entire look—including a dramatic ruffled cape, crop top, and skirt adorned with a distinctive black-and-white print. Emblazoned with the words *Mother, Champion, Queen, Goddess* in French, the outfit was just the latest in a long line of provocative fashion statements by the reigning star of center court. "Serena's an example of a world-class athlete who's got really strong opinions about what works for her," says Parker, who developed a close working relationship with Williams during his time at the helm of the company. "She's not shy, and she doesn't have as much of a filter between how she thinks and what she expresses—which I like." Serena's candid approach may make her a demanding collaborator, but Parker maintains that her high standards and sharp fashion sense help push Nike to be better. "She has a very particular view of what works for her aesthetically and how she wants to feel when she gets out on the court," says Parker. "But also she knows what she needs in terms of support and protection to perform at the highest level." To that point, two of Williams's most celebrated and controversial on-court looks, the black catsuit worn at the 2018 French Open and the denim miniskirt and knee-high boots worn at the 2004 U.S. Open, were designed with functionality beyond aesthetics—the former aimed to help mitigate postpartum blood clots and the latter to help her recover from a knee injury. Nonetheless both the boots and catsuit were banned for not hewing closely enough to the established guidelines of decorum. For Nike, the controversy only fuels conversation. In a pitch-perfect response to the catsuit ban, the company ran an advertisement stating, "You can take the superhero out of her costume, but you can never take away her superpowers."

For almost two decades, Williams's unapologetic vision of transposing couture to the tennis court has helped Nike broadly carve out a hybrid territory between sports and fashion, opening the door to further partnerships and possibilities. So when Naomi Osaka, the Japanese tennis phenom, became a Nike athlete, it was natural that she was partnered with Chitose Abe, the progressive womenswear designer behind the Japanese label sacai and some of Nike's most successfully elegant and irreverent collaborations. Osaka's ensemble built off the language Nike and Abe had developed since her first collection in 2015, transforming traditional sportswear silhouettes into something altogether new through layering, cutting, and splicing. "I've always been inspired by classics," Abe says. "Working with traditional silhouettes and ideas that often come from utility or performance-based sportswear, I'm interested in creating new hybrids that combine different fabrics and shapes to create an unexpected yet wearable result." That Abe spent eight years as a pattern cutter for Rei Kawakubo and Junya Watanabe at Comme des Garçons before starting her own line is evident in the playful and unexpected constructions that have become a hallmark of her work with Nike. Fresh takes on a tech fleece, with a subtle band of knit mesh lace tucked into the inside of the garment, and the Nike Windrunner, reshaped to burst in an explosion of pleats, elevated Nike's prosaic classics into a new feminine dimension. For sacai, these interventions are not merely ornamental but accentuate and exaggerate the movement of the wearer—a fashion statement descended from sport.

Sacai's 2019 Spring / Summer show during Paris Fashion Week saw the debut of the Nike × sacai LDWaffle and Blazer Mid—shoes that immediately took the sneaker world by storm and became two of the most sought-after models of the year. "We were in a meeting looking at putting one bottom on top of another," says Jobe, "and then had the idea that it would be a lot cooler to smash the two shoes together and have them live at the same time." In a process not dissimilar to other sacai collaborations, the designs fuse multiple archival products into something wholly original. Abe talks about her work as a fusion of the polar notions of stability and betrayal—of the familiar and unique. In the case of the LDWaffle and Blazer Mid, stability comes from the recognizable retro color schemes, while betrayal comes to life through doubled elements, such as the Swooshes, laces, and tongues, and the oddly interposed midsole inserts. New women's models of the Air Force 1—Shadow and Shadow SE—serve as a good example of how Nike's cutting-edge collaborations inform its "in-line" category work. Building off the vocabulary established by sacai, the shoes feature doubled elements and boast a playful, less reverential take on the original Air Force 1.

While design teams working with sacai continue to help Nike build a bridge toward the world of fashion from sport, the company's longstanding collaboration with Jun Takahashi has worked inversely, working from fashion toward sport. Takahashi founded his high-end streetwear label Undercover in the early 1990s and had long been on Nike's radar, but it wasn't until he began running seriously—and couldn't find any gear that suited him—that the impetus to work together took hold. Gyakusou, meaning "running in reverse," was so named after Takahashi's punk rock-inspired running club (while most runners follow a clockwise path around Tokyo's Yoyogi Park, Takahashi's crew staked new territory by literally going the other way). Launched in 2010, and offering seasonal updates biannually, Gyakusou has become a core component of Nike's running business by continually bringing a new perspective on both stylistic and performative elements. "Jun offers up a real runner's insight," says Reynolds. "How lucky are we to be able to work with one of the best designers in the world who can also run a marathon? It's a weird, perfect storm."

The success of the Gyakusou program rests in the nebulous space between Nike design and Takahashi, where the company's ability to harness advanced technologies and materials in concert with a progressive designer's vision fuels a new kind of innovation. From the outset of his partnership with Nike, one of the critical changes Takahashi wanted to make was to adopt a more sensitive color palette—substituting the bold, bright, contrasting colors normally associated with sports for neutral tones that blend with both the urban and natural landscape. Based on Takahashi's own experience, Gyakusou also prioritizes practical problem-solving for urban runners. Most of the garments feature specially constructed pockets, often concealed, to hold items such as keys, a credit card or money, and a phone, so they don't come in contact and create distraction. Elements such as heat-mapping data, realized through stitching that allows for more breathability where the body needs it, have been incorporated into garments for both their functionality and aesthetics.

One of the most distinctive ideas to emerge from the ongoing collaboration was 2016's Utility Speed Tights, a design that fuses runners' staple shorts and tights into a single garment. Takahashi felt strongly that he wanted to wear tights to run because of the compression and insulation they offer, but he also felt awkward just standing around in line at the café on his way home. Layering shorts over tights would solve the issue of modesty but result in more waistbands, more weight, and more chaffing if they didn't nest together well. Working with Reynolds in his Tokyo studio, the pair spontaneously started playing with the idea of combining the best elements of both. "We imagined what would happen if you left a pair of shorts on a pair of tights for a million years—they would become one thing," says Reynolds. For him, it was one of the highlights of his career. "There was no intention going into that meeting that we were going to create this new thing. You don't get many opportunities to create an entirely new silhouette." The design has become a hallmark of Gyakusou and has subsequently been adapted and adopted in various forms across a range of Nike's regular running apparel, demonstrating how ideas from collaborations help fuel the broader business.

While Gyakusou operates on seasonal deadlines, Nike's ongoing collaboration with the artist Tom Sachs has been marked by a more long-form and open-ended approach to problem-solving—emerging from

Sachs's innate curiosity and contrarian nature and filtered through Nike's product-creation expertise. When Sachs contributed a work to a charity event sponsored by Nike in 2009, the artist didn't miss his opportunity to bend the ear of Parker. Over the course of dinner, Sachs relayed just how terrible he thought Nike's products (specifically his own pair of ACG boots) had become. After patiently weathering the litany of complaints, Parker called Sachs's bluff and invited him to Beaverton to see how Nike works. "One of the best parts of my job is getting to be a student for the rest of my life," recounts Sachs. "So the gift that Nike gave me was the opportunity to go crazy and research all this." After digging into the Nike archives and meeting with developers and designers in the Innovation Kitchen, he quickly learned that making shoes is nowhere near as simple as it may seem.

In the art world, Sachs is known for his intensive DIY process, meticulously reconstructing vernacular objects, well-known consumer items, and historical and cultural icons—from teahouses to space vehicles—out of everyday materials. Working with Nike on products that were to be manu-factured at scale pushed the artist outside of his (atypical) comfort zone. At the same time, Sachs leaned on Nike to explore materials that had never been used in products before—automotive air bags, mainsails for boats, and even NASA's space suits. Three years into their partnership, the first fruits of their collaboration debuted as a part of Sachs's 2012 exhibi-tion at New York City's Park Avenue Armory, *Space Program: Mars*. Based on the idea of manned space travel, the NIKECraft Collection included the Mars Yard Shoe, Trench, Marsfly Jacket, and Lightweight Tote, with each design offering functionality beyond its primary use (such as a zipper pull that doubles as a storage container or a paracord that can be used as a tourniquet). The products were worn by Sachs and his team as they manned their imaginary mission during the show's run and were offered to guests through the exhibition's adjunct retail display.

As an indication of Sachs's dedication to the Nike partnership (and his pull-no-punches attitude), in 2015 he and his studio team became the company's first city-based wear-testers. Most wear-testing happens away from public scrutiny in such places as rural Colorado, but the consensus at Nike was that something different might emerge based on feedback solicited from people in a metropolitan environment. Sachs took the role—one he still maintains today—with aplomb. "Some of our collabora-tors will be like, 'Yeah, that looks good,'" notes Reynolds. "Tom says, 'Cool. I'll let you know in a month.' He's going to test it and wear it and make it not work. He'll take it until it fails, and from that failure, we make it better. It's real. He's our athlete. He tests stuff harder than anybody tests stuff."

As an indication of Sachs's dedication to wear-testing, after five years of trialing the Mars Yard Shoe in his studio, the artist revisited the design in 2017 to improve its perceived failings. The Mars Yard 2.0 was stronger, more breathable, and featured a new outsole more appropriate for urban use (in adherence with the Mars theme, the original was based on a shoe for desert conditions). The original Vectran upper (a highly tensile fiber similar to Kevlar that's used by NASA) was replaced to make a cooler-wearing shoe. In a unique touch, an antimicrobial cork insole was offered for those who wanted to go sockless.

Sachs's relationship with Nike also enables him to produce things on a scale that is impossible within a bespoke artistic practice. Sometimes, as was the case with the NIKECraft Poncho, the two worlds collide. In development for more than four years, the Poncho began with an idea Reynolds had for a slimline pack that could rapidly deploy into rain gear. He had figured out the mechanics of how to get the poncho out of the pack but had not solved for easily getting it back in so it could be used again. When he shared his progress with Sachs, the artist was intrigued and began toying with the concept in his studio. "When I saw his first prototype, I viewed it as a magic trick," says Sachs. "Later, when I stumbled across the parachute release mechanism of a dragster and saw how it folded back, I saw how the problems that we were having with the complexity of the release mechanism were solved in other parts of industry."

"I was at my in-laws' house on Christmas Eve at like 9:00 at night when I got a FaceTime call from Tom," says Reynolds. "He had figured out this new way to do it. That totally made my Christmas that year." For Reynolds, who shares a patent for the mechanism with Sachs, it was an outstanding example of how collaborators can help push ideas forward when Nike can only go so far.

For Sachs, his work with Nike isn't an adjunct to his artistic practice; the two endeavors have become fully integrated. Not unlike how Isamu Noguchi viewed his commercial lighting and furniture designs to be fundamentally the same as fine arts, Sachs's collaborations with Nike sit comfortably within a broader portfolio. "The ideas in this collection—transparency of materials and of construction—are very well reflected, and I'm really honored by this body of work," he says. "They have the same value and integrity of the sculptures I make in the studio." Back at Nike, the influence of having a prominent artist such as Sachs working alongside apparel and footwear designers has welcomed a degree of idiosyncrasy—be it in different materials, construction techniques, or frame of reference—to recast the company's approach to performance-based problem-solving.

The cumulative success of Nike's collaborations has enabled the internal teams working on them to grow creatively while establishing a thrust for innovation within the company's sportswear division. Although innovation at Nike has typically focused on solving problems for traditional athletes, Jobe sees things differently. "Our athlete is someone with a busy lifestyle who lives in a big city. They start their day at 8:00 in the morning and maybe don't get home until 3:00 a.m., because they went out to a club. They might not live in close proximity to where they work or go to school or whatever they do, so they're traveling long distances on foot, by bike, bus, or train. They're in their shoes the whole time—exposed to the elements. That's just the reality. It's where we go and take chances with innovation." Exploring this line of thinking, and working in close collaboration with colleagues across the business, led the team to develop the React Element language, as well as the Air Max 270 and 720 Air units, all of which have become staple platforms for the company. With their approach validated by developments such as these, and blockbuster hits including Abloh's "The Ten" and sacai's LDWaffle, the team was ready to try something different: a collaboration with themselves.

Hybridizing their internal work process with the ethos driving products for the urban athlete, the team developed a guiding philosophy of "improvise, scavenge, protect, adapt." Condensed into acronym form, iSPA soon became the label for their output. With free rein to explore their ideas, the iSPA team serves as a kind of forward assault for sportswear—pushing the boundaries of design with provocative, never-before-seen aesthetics and concepts that are purposefully ahead of their time. These ideas are informed both by what's happening across campus and on the other side of the world. In the past the team traveled numerous times as a group, seeking out inspiration from unlikely places (and learning as much from esoteric fashion designers as from experts in nonintuitive areas, such as wood joinery and moss gardening). Back in Beaverton, the "scavenge" part of their ethos comes to life as the group liberally borrows ideas, materials, and technologies from elsewhere in the company and transmutes them into something wholly original. Even the iSPA logo reflects this strategy—the *I* is from Air Max, the *S* is from Shox, the *P* is from Presto, and the *A* is from VaporMax—all while managing to look like something that comes from the future.

Guided by narrative themes, such as "State of Emergency," where everything is designed to be quickly adorned, lightweight, and adaptable in response to both natural and man-made disasters, and "Synth Colony," a farther-out take on communal living and sharing, the group has been able to push Nike's aesthetic envelope while building on its legacy of innovation. Although the designs may seem outlandish to the uninitiated, all of the features (such as closure systems, additional traction, and cages) have been developed with the performance needs of urban athletes in mind. One of the more succinct and clever examples of the iSPA ethos (hitting all four pillars of improvise, scavenge, protect, and adapt) is the Air VaporMax Flyknit Gaiter iSPA, a kind of shroud or spat designed to swiftly transform the Air VaporMax Flyknit into an all-conditions water-resistant gaiter boot. In addition to their responsibility for the ever-expanding roster of projects with outside designers, iSPA is already working three seasons ahead. "People will ask me what my favorite collaboration is," says Jobe, "and literally it's working with my own team. We all add incremental value through our expertise, and we've taken pride in how we've created a fluid process of sharing insights and ways to articulate this concept."

At Nike, everything is rooted in one form of collaboration or another. The company began as a collaboration between a former runner and his coach. Collaborations with athletes serve as the foundation for Nike's approach to product creation. Collaborations across functions and disciplines reinforce the knowledge-sharing that sparks creativity. Collaborations with external design partners have helped push the company in exciting, and sometimes unexpected, directions to find new audiences and address new problems. As company leaders look to the future and see the landscape of sport being indelibly altered by forces both large and small, collaboration—ranging from partnerships with individuals to those with communities, institutions, and organizations—will increasingly move beyond mere products to encompass broader initiatives and experiences centered on the company's values and mission.

In February 2020 Nike convened the first of a series of conversations, dubbed Future Sport* Exchange, that aim to offer a window into this more open-ended approach to engagement. Hosted by the *Gentlewoman* editor Penny Martin, a roundtable forum of forty-three creative talents, including Yoon Ahn, Errolson Hugh, Simon Jacquemus, Max Lamb, Cynthia Lu, Martine Rose, and Matthew Williams, probed at what the future of sustainability might look like for fashion, design, and sport. With no predetermined outcomes in mind, and everything from product to business models up for discussion, the conversations simply strive to get at the core of what collaboration is truly about: promoting diversity of thought.

"I think what makes a good collaboration is the ability to really bring different points of view to the table and to listen with empathy, and listen more deeply to what someone says—to what's behind the word," says Parker. "The ability to be open to a new point of view, something that might challenge your current view of whatever, gives you a different perspective. I love these eclectic or eccentric combinations of people who wouldn't normally work together but come together—and you can see the wheels turning. You go, 'Wow, I never thought of that.' If you have that kind of openness, with those diverse points of view coming in with really talented people that can actually execute ideas and conversations into something that is compelling to other people, that's a pretty good formula." For Nike, it's a formula that has stood the test of time and will only continue to expand.

Air Jordan III	White/Fire Red-Cement Grey-Black	1988

While the Air Jordan III was Michael Jordan's third signature shoe, its creation process marked a first in Nike history: it established athlete collaboration as an instrumental driver of innovation. This evolution can be directly linked to the shoe's designer, Tinker Hatfield. When Hatfield was tapped to design the Air Jordan III in fall 1987, he united candid insights from Jordan with his own detailed observations of the athlete's inimitable performance and style. The shoe's mid-top height answered Jordan's request for lighter, more flexible footwear, while its distinct appearance aligned with his elevated aesthetic. The Air Jordan III was also the first Jordan shoe to feature the Jumpman logo, a visible Air unit, elephant-print leather, and super-soft prewashed leather, which nullified the need for break-in time.

Air Jordan I catalog cover | 1985

| Dunk High | White/Red | 1985 |

| SB Dunk Pro Low "Ishod Wair" advertisement | 2015 |

| SB Dunk Pro advertisement | 2011 |

Nike's first successful forays into skateboarding were serendipitous, with the discriminating sport culture organically embracing the 1985 Air Jordan I and Dunk due to their superior performance, durability, and style. The 2002 launch of the Nike Skateboarding (SB) brand flipped the script. Instead of expecting the sport to adopt existing Nike innovations, Nike SB—under the leadership of Nike veteran Sandy Bodecker—enlisted top skaters to inform skateboard-specific silhouettes, starting with the SB Dunk. Responding to athlete insights, Nike designers incorporated a Zoom Air unit into the shoe's heel, bolstered its tongue padding, and enhanced its outsole grip. To give the launch collection additional street credibility, Bodecker recruited recently signed skaters Reese Forbes, Gino Iannucci, Richard Mulder, and Danny Supasirirat to collaborate on custom designs.

SB Dunk Low Pro "Mulder"	White/Orion Blue-White	2002

SB Dunk Low Pro "Supa"	Safety Orange/Hyper Blue-White	2002

SB Dunk Low Pro "Blue Lobster"	Nightshade/Dark Slate	2009

SB Dunk High "De La Soul"	White/Firefly	2015

SB Dunk Low Pro "Pigeon"	Medium Grey/White-Dark Grey	2005

| Zvezdochka | Black/Light Graphite | 2004 |

| Zvezdochka outsole | | 2004 |

| Zvezdochka | Royal/Light Graphite | 2004 |

| Zvezdochka | Kiwi/Light Graphite | 2004 |

"MARC CAME IN AND WE HAD A VERY FREE-FORM, ORGANIC CONVERSATION THAT WENT ALL OVER."

MARK PARKER

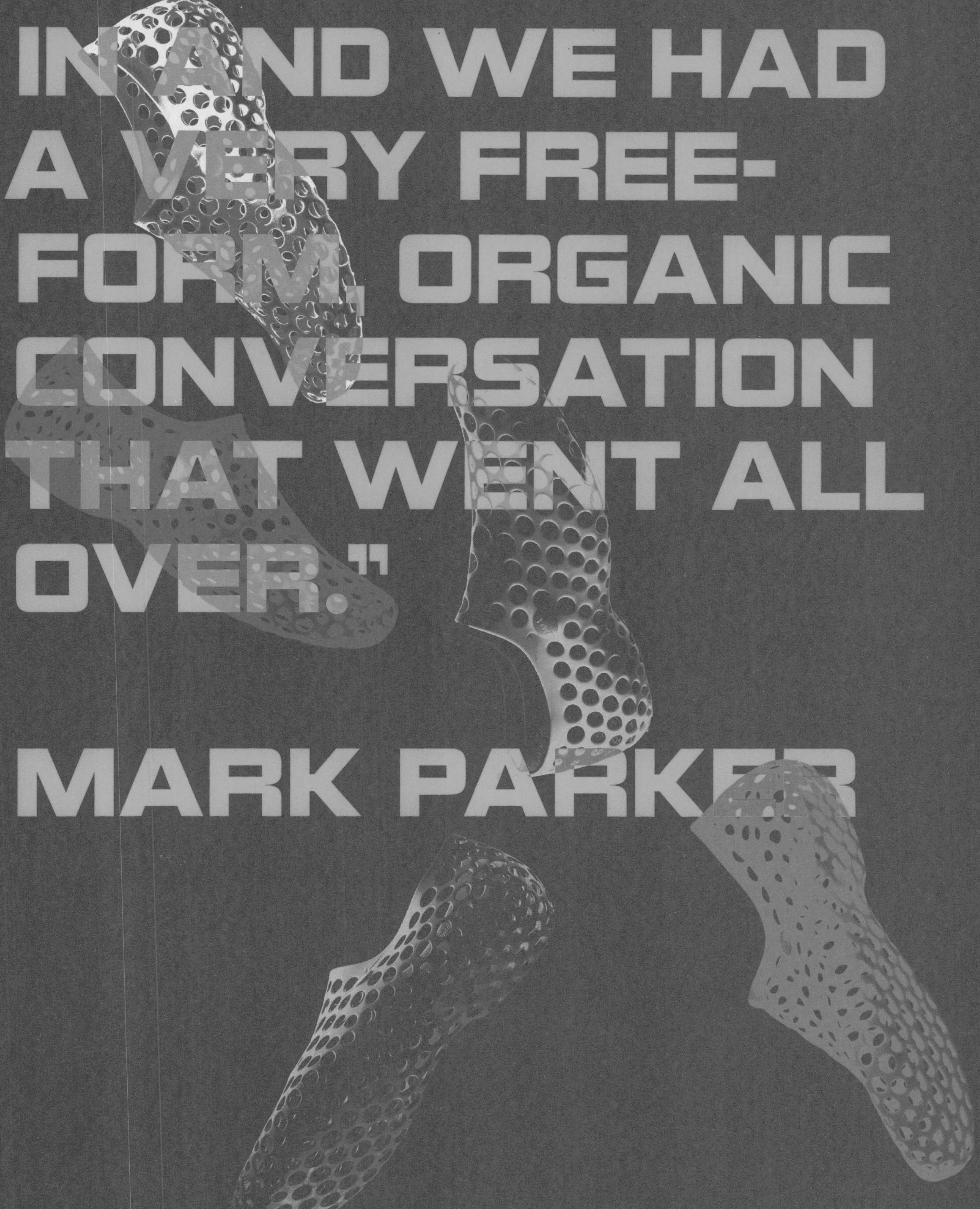

"EXPLORATION
IS BEST DONE
TOGETHER."
MARK PARKER

| Zvezdochka interlocking shoe components | 2004 |

If the Air Jordan III and SB Dunk proved the commercial merits of collaboration, the Zvezdochka—created with Australian industrial designer Marc Newson in 2004—revealed the potential of external partnerships to capsize conventional thinking. Named after a Soviet space dog launched into orbit aboard *Sputnik 10*, the Zvezdochka was imagined as a multipurpose shoe for cosmonauts. Comprised of four interlocking, interchangeable parts—an outer cage, outsole, inner sleeve, and insole—the modular design eliminated adhesives and marked one of Nike's first explorations of closed-loop creation. While the design's retail success was modest, its experimental ethos prompted an immediate and enduring internal shift at Nike—one that fostered radical new ways of approaching innovation and collaboration.

HTM logo	2012

Kobe IX Elite Premium Low HTM "Milan"	Black/Reflect Silver-Multi-Color	2014

In 2002 Nike's cross-pollination practices generated a stand-alone collaborative line: Nike HTM, an ongoing design alliance between Hiroshi Fujiwara, founder of Japanese fashion label, fragment design; vice president of Creative Concepts Tinker Hatfield; and Nike chairman Mark Parker. Initiated by Parker as a way to materialize a spontaneous intellectual exchange, HTM collapsed the designers' varying styles and approaches into a free-form partnership that updated classic Nike silhouettes, starting with the Air Force 1; introduced new Nike design concepts, such as the Sock Dart; and showcased innovative Nike technologies, including Flyknit. Beyond garnering a fervent global fan base that anxiously awaited its impromptu drops, HTM continually fed an experimental internal culture that greatly influenced future Nike designs by validating the promise of purposeful rule breaking.

HTM2 Run Boot Low TZ "Black"	Black/White	2010

Lunar Flyknit HTM	White/Black-Volt	2012

Sock Dart HTM	Pink/Black-Blue	2004

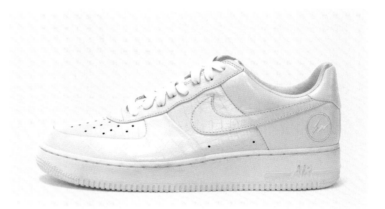

Air Force 1 HTM "Fragment"	White/White/White	2008

Air Woven Boot HTM	Khaki/Quasar Purple-Rainbow	2002

Air Moc Mid HTM	Black/Light Stone	2002

Air Footscape Woven HTM	Varsity Royal/Varsity Royal-Neutral Grey	2005

Zoom Macropus LC Priority HTM	Black/Black-Net-Team Red	2006

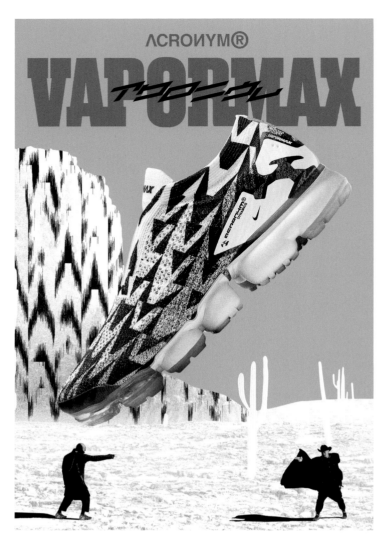

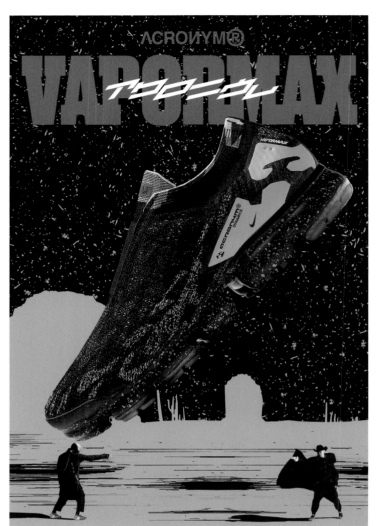

Air VaporMax Moc 2 × ACRONYM (top) and Air Presto Mid Utility × ACRONYM (bottom) advertisements | 2018

Nike's collaboration with Acronym cofounder Errolson Hugh began in 2015, with Hugh applying his utility-focused, high-impact design philosophy to the Lunar Force 1 by incorporating an easy-entry zipper into the shoe's statement upper, which he also accented with bold color blocking. He employed this same ethos in the Air Presto Mid Utility × ACRONYM, first released in 2016, and the 2017 NikeLab AF1 Downtown × ACRONYM. Meanwhile, collaboration on the 2018 Air VaporMax Moc 2 × ACRONYM, moved the ongoing design exchange into new territory. The shoe's functionality was already so advanced that Hugh and his team focused exclusively on pushing the silhouette's aesthetics to their functional edge, resulting in an aptly futuristic camouflage-like upper pattern iterated from the brand's wordmark.

| Air VaporMax Moc 2 × ACRONYM | Light Bone/Volt-Light Bone | 2018 |

| Air Presto Mid Utility × ACRONYM | White/Black-Dynamic Yellow | 2018 |

| Air Monarch IV × Martine Rose | Medium Soft Pink/Black | 2018 |

| Air Monarch IV × Martine Rose | Black/Black-Black | 2018 |

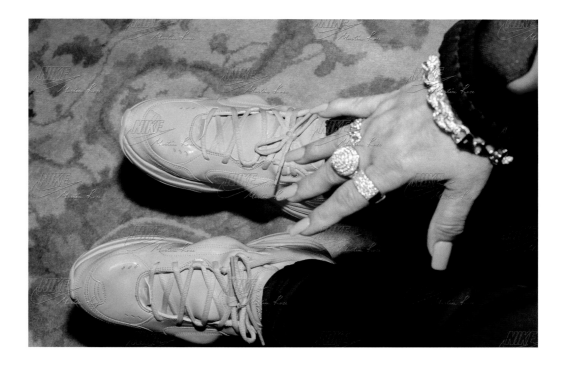

| Nike × Martine Rose Collection campaign imagery | 2018 |

Air Monarch	White / White-Navy	2002

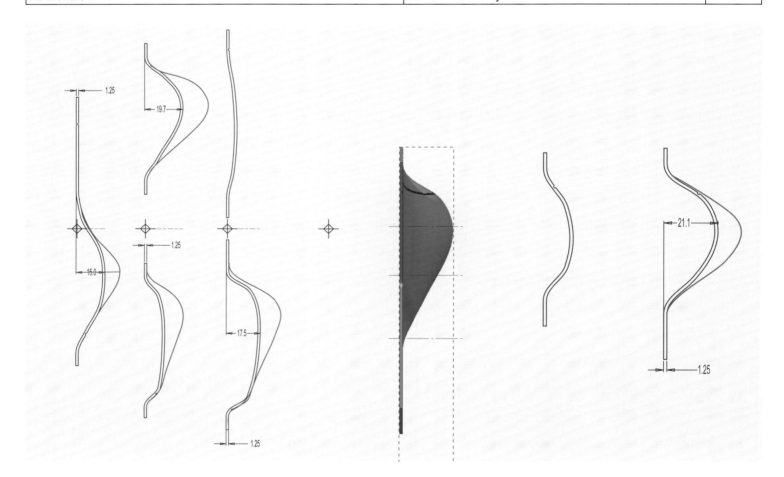

Air Monarch IV × Martine Rose design exploration	2017

Extending its track record of collaborating with external partners to expand the language of iconic designs, Nike enlisted Martine Rose to reimagine the Air Monarch in 2017. Originally released in 2002, the design was widely considered an average, very American shoe until the British designer radically distorted its proportions, transforming it from the ordinary to the extraordinary. For the Air Monarch IV × Martine Rose, this meant fitting a U.S. size 18 upper on a size 9 outsole. Evolving the design from prototype to commercial production pushed both Nike and Rose, precipitating new shapes and ideas that—unsurprisingly for both parties—flout expectations.

Nike × Martine Rose design prototypes | 2017

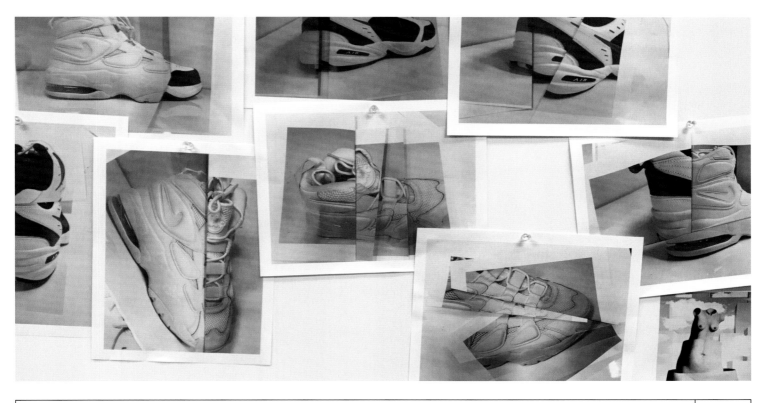

Nike × Martine Rose inspiration board | 2017

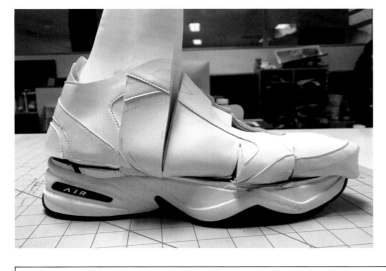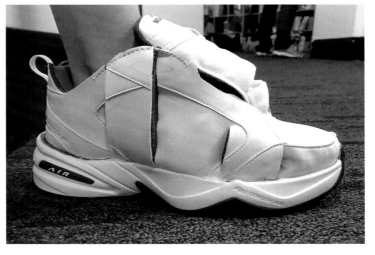

Air Monarch IV × Martine Rose prototypes | 2017

Nike × MMW Series 003 Collection campaign imagery   2019

| Nike × MMW Free TR 3 SP | Black/Black-Black | 2019 |

| Nike × MMW Free TR 3 SP | Black/Black-University Red | 2019 |

The juncture of Nike and Matthew M. Williams (MMW) united Nike's innovation legacy and heritage designs with Williams's ultramodern style to hypothesize the future of training apparel. Expressly formulated for high-intensity outdoor interval workouts, Nike × MMW apparel balanced cutting-edge design tools, such as data-driven patterns and knits, with the designer's acute attention to individual expression. Footwear, ranging from the Nike × MMW Free TR 3 SP to the Nike × MMW Joyride, similarly anticipated multifunctional requirements.

| R.T. Air Force 1 Mid | Vachetta Tan/Black | 2014 |

| R.T. Air Force 1 Low | Vachetta Tan / Black | 2014 |

| R.T. Air Force 1 Boot SP | Vachetta Tan/Black | 2014 |

| R.T. Dunk Lux High | White/Black | 2016 |

| R.T. Dunk Lux High | Black/White | 2016 |

| R.T. Air Force 1 High Victorious Minotaurs Collection | Sunblush/Bordeaux-Team Orange | 2018 |

| R.T. Air Force 1 High Victorious Minotaurs Collection | Gym Red / Opti Yellow-Black | 2018 |

R.T. Air Force 1 Collection campaign imagery | 2014

| R.T. × Victorious Minotaurs Collection Logo T-shirt | 2018 |

| R.T. × Victorious Minotaurs Collection Basketball Shorts | 2016 |

| R.T. × Victorious Minotaurs Collection Basketball Pants | 2018 |

| R.T. × Victorious Minotaurs Collection Mesh Jersey Dress | 2018 |

R.T. × Victorious Minotaurs Collection Varsity Jacket	2017

R.T. × Victorious Minotaurs Collection Tank Top	2016

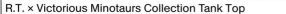

R.T. × Victorious Minotaurs Collection T-shirt	2016

According to senior creative design director for Apparel Special Projects Jarrett Reynolds, Nike's multiyear collaboration with Riccardo Tisci epitomized teamwork. "We can help bring Riccardo into the world of sport performance, which is our expertise. On the other hand, Riccardo's vision pushed our design to a place we wouldn't have arrived at on our own." In practice, the partnership married Tisci's high-fashion irreverence with Nike's innovative materials and sports code, resulting in invariably dramatic footwear and apparel with a cultlike following.

| The Ten: Blazer Mid × Virgil Abloh | White/Black-Muslin | 2017 |

| The Ten: Chuck Taylor All-Star Vulcanized Hi × Virgil Abloh | White/Cone-Ice Blue | 2017 |

Most design collaborations showcase the layering of their partners' respective aesthetics. Nike's 2018 collaboration with Virgil Abloh—founder of the fashion label Off-White—conversely stripped ten archetype Nike designs down to their essential foundations before reconstructing them around two main themes: "Revealing," which removed external facades to form new designs based on the shoes' essential features, and "Ghosting," which employed translucent materials to showcase the designs' defining characteristics. The purpose of the exercise, Abloh declared, was to both expose the physical elements of "The Ten" as well as pull the philosophical thread that he believes binds athletes and designers: what propels them to be the best comes from within.

| The Ten: Air Max 90 × Virgil Abloh | Sail/White/Muslin | 2017 |

| The Ten: Zoom Fly × Virgil Abloh | White/White-Muslin | 2017 |

| The Ten: Air Presto × Virgil Abloh | Black/Black-Muslin | 2017 |

| The Ten: Air Force 1 Low × Virgil Abloh | White/White-Sail | 2017 |

| The Ten: Hyperdunk Flyknit × Virgil Abloh | White/White-White | 2017 |

| The Ten: Air Max 97 × Virgil Abloh | White/Cone-Ice Blue | 2017 |

| The Ten: Air VaporMax Flyknit × Virgil Abloh | Black/White-Clear | 2017 |

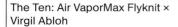

| The Ten: Air Jordan 1 × Virgil Abloh "OG Chicago" | White/Black-Varsity Red-Black | 2017 |

The Ten: Nike × Virgil Abloh Collection campaign image   2017

"THE WAY WE WORK WITH VIRGIL . . . IT'S LIKE A LUNATIC INVENTED THE PROCESS. STARTS HERE, GOES THERE, SWITCHES BACK, GOES LIKE THIS, AND THEN WE'RE LIKE, 'FREEZE!'"

JARRETT REYNOLDS

MOTHER
CHAMPION
QUEEN

"LOGO"

GODDESS

NikeCourt Flare 2.0 PE × Virgil Abloh for Serena Williams Queen Collection	Grey/Black/Silver	2018

Blazer Studio Mid × Virgil Abloh for Serena Williams Queen Collection	Wolf Grey / Cool Grey-Pure Platinum-Volt	2018

U.S. Open NikeCourt Day Dress × Virgil Abloh for Serena Williams Queen Collection	2018

Virgil Abloh's subsequent collaboration with Serena Williams for the 2018 U.S. Open further illustrated the complementary qualities of athletes and designers by linking Abloh's magpie eye with Williams's feminine, powerful style. Titled the Queen Collection, the signature performance footwear and apparel celebrated Serena as both a champion athlete and a woman. The pair united again in 2019 with the Virgil Abloh for Serena Williams Cape-Jacket and Skirt, which were emblazoned with the words *Mother, Champion, Queen, Goddess* in French. Launched to coincide with the 2019 French Open, the outfit aimed to inspire a new generation of athletes everywhere.

| Shox Glamour SW × Serena Williams | Black/Silver | 2004 |

| Shox Glamour SW and compression sleeves × Serena Williams | Black/Silver | 2004 |

| Serena Williams at the 2004 U.S. Open | New York City, New York | 2004 |

Serena Williams's collection with Virgil Abloh is just one manifestation in a nearly twenty-year partnership with Nike, a collaboration underpinned by a close working relationship with Mark Parker. The company's chairman praises Williams's unapologetic nature and astute understanding of personal performance needs and style preferences for pushing Nike to higher design planes. On-court expressions of this synergy range from Williams's controversial 2004 U.S. Open look—a denim jacket and miniskirt, studded black tank top, and knee-high black boots—to her 2018 French Open catsuit, which were both hastily banned from the competition due to their unconventional appearances. Instead of kowtowing to these reprimands, Williams and Nike continue to defy the status quo and celebrate the champion's bold nature, as evidenced in January 2020, when they again collaborated to form a team of emerging New York City-based designers tasked with creating a range of footwear and apparel inspired by the athlete.

Studded Leather Jacket × Serena Williams	2004

Denim Skirt × Serena Williams	2004

Studded Dress × Serena Williams	2004

French Open Catsuit × Serena Williams	2018

| Serena Williams at the 2018 French Open | Paris, France | 2018 |

| Nike × sacai LDWaffle | | Green Gusto/Black-Varsity Maize-Safety Orange | 2019 |

| Nike × sacai LDWaffle | Pine Green/Clay Orange-Del Sol-Sail | 2019 |

| Nike × sacai LDWaffle | Black/Anthracite-White-Gunsmoke | 2019 |

| Nike × sacai Blazer Mid | Varsity Maize/Midnight Navy-White-Varsity Red | 2019 |

| Nike × sacai Blazer Mid | Black / University Blue / Sail / White | 2019 |

If each of Nike's external collaborations illuminates a different aspect of the company's design ethos, its alliance with fashion brand sacai underscores its penchant for creation through studied subversion. Just as Nike has routinely upended design and technology standards in the name of innovation, sacai founder Chitose Abe is renowned for her unique ability to splice, slice, and layer archetypal silhouettes into arresting hybrid fashions—say, a Windrunner jacket transformed by an eruption of back pleats or two Nike icons mashed together to form the Nike × sacai LDWaffle. Since joining forces in 2015, Nike and Abe have continually blurred the line separating fashion and sport, even venturing into performance apparel via a subtly insurgent on-court look designed for tennis phenom Naomi Osaka.

81J SAFETY

Nike × sacai Collection campaign imagery | 2019

| Gyakusou Transform Jacket | 2019 |

| Gyakusou Helix Shorts | 2019 | Gyakusou Helix Shorts | 2019 |

Taking cues from its name, which means "running in reverse" in Japanese, the Gyakusou Collection initially took an inverse approach to conception. The biannual running collection, launched in 2010 in collaboration with Jun Takahashi—the founder of Undercover, a high-end streetwear brand—based its early designs on Takahashi's stylistic insights, namely a desire for neutral tones, coupled with Nike innovations. As Takahashi's passion for running grew, so did the collection's attention to utility. From concealed pockets designed for essentials to body-map data integrated into zones of breathability, each season advances the modern uniform of running, leading to progressively more revolutionary designs, such as the Gyakusou DF Utility Speed Tights, which combined shorts and tights into a single garment.

Gyakusou Collections campaign imagery   2010–16

Gyakusou Collections campaign imagery   2010–16

Gyakusou Short Sleeve Packable Jacket	2018

Gyakusou DF Utility Speed Tights	2016

React Element 87 × Undercover outsole prototypes | c.2017

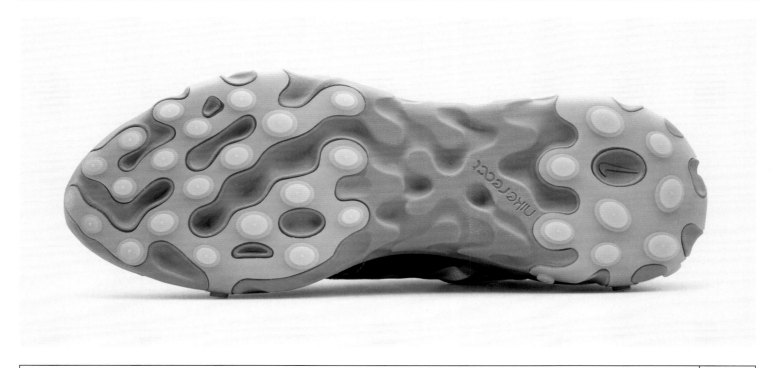

React Element 87 × Undercover outsole | 2018

Since its inception, Gyakusou footwear has overlaid Nike's cutting-edge innovations with Jun Takahashi's autograph aesthetic. In 2018 the designer and Nike flip-flopped the exchange; instead of bringing fashion to sport, it brought sport to fashion, introducing the React Element 87 × Undercover at Paris Fashion Week on the Undercover runway. The extraordinary shoe combined inspiration from heritage Nike running shoes, particularly the Internationalist, with advanced React cushioning. The sculptural foam unconventionally offset the familiar silhouette, which further declared its original identity via reflective and transparent details, signature Undercover branding, and four vibrant colorways.

| React Element 87 × Undercover | Light Beige Chalk/Signal Blue-University Red-Black-Classic Stone | 2018 |

| React Element 87 × Undercover | Green Mist/Linen-Summit White-Deep Burgundy-Black | 2018 |

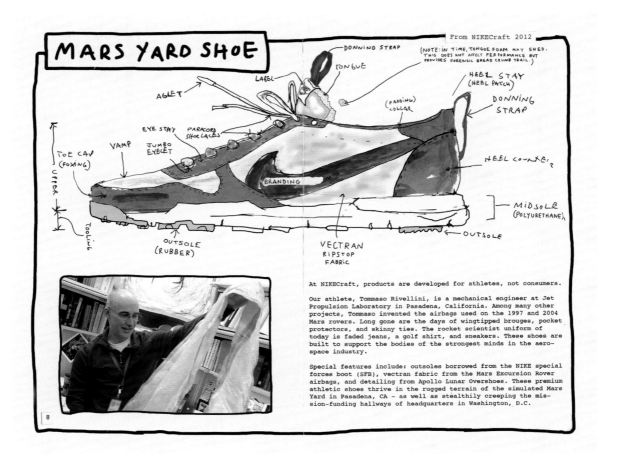

NIKECraft Mars Yard Shoe specifications sheet | 2012

| NIKECraft Mars Yard Shoe | Natural/Sport Red-Maple | 2012 |

NIKECraft Lightweight Tote | 2012

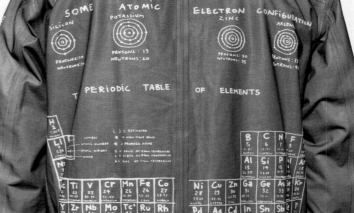

Detail of the NIKECraft Marsfly Jacket | 2012

Detail of the NIKECraft Trench | 2012

| *Space Program: Mars* exhibition | Park Avenue Armory, New York City, New York | 2012 |

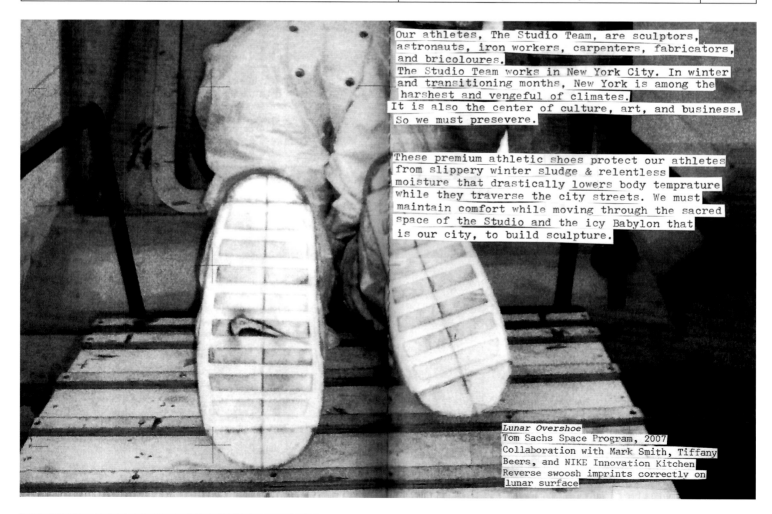

Our athletes, The Studio Team, are sculptors, astronauts, iron workers, carpenters, fabricators, and bricoloures.
The Studio Team works in New York City. In winter and transitioning months, New York is among the harshest and vengeful of climates.
It is also the center of culture, art, and business. So we must presevere.

These premium athletic shoes protect our athletes from slippery winter sludge & relentless moisture that drastically lowers body temprature while they traverse the city streets. We must maintain comfort while moving through the sacred space of the Studio and the icy Babylon that is our city, to build sculpture.

Lunar Overshoe
Tom Sachs Space Program, 2007
Collaboration with Mark Smith, Tiffany Beers, and NIKE Innovation Kitchen
Reverse swoosh imprints correctly on lunar surface

| Lunar Overshoe: A Letter to Sandy Bodecker, from Tom Sachs | 2007 |

Do you own your things or do your things own you?

We all die alone and we die without our sneakers.

Spend time caring for and repairing your old
things. Build a personal history with your
possessions. When they don't serve you anymore
pass them on with generosity and without delay.

Just because you posses something doesn't mean you
have to keep it. There is freedom in having less.
More can be a burden. It takes time to manage your
possessions. How do you want to spend your time?
Time is the only thing you have in limited supply
and the thing you control most.

21

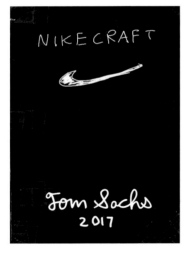

Pages from the *NIKECraft: Mars Yard 2.0* zine | 2017

As innovations such as React and Free reveal, serendipitous encounters often provide transcendent discoveries. The same can be said for opportune collaborations—just take the partnership between artist Tom Sachs and senior creative design directors Nathan Jobe and Jarrett Reynolds. Initiated by an auspicious 2009 encounter between Nike chairman Mark Parker and Sachs, which quickly snowballed into wear-testing and design exchanges, the idiosyncratic intersection combines the artist's unique DIY engineering processes with Nike's data-driven innovation and scalable manufacturing methods. In 2012 this collaboration spawned NIKECraft, a capsule collection inspired by Sachs's research into space travel and a shared obsession with durable product performance. The introductory NIKECraft Collection anticipated the needs of manned space missions by integrating hardy materials—such as space suits, automotive air bags, and mainsails for boats—into the artisanal-looking Mars Yard Shoe, Trench, Marsfly Jacket, and Lightweight Tote. A heightened focus on multifunctionality manifested in zipper pulls that doubled as storage containers, paracords that served as tourniquets, and myriad details merging visual interest with purpose.

"FAILURE IS ALWAYS AN OPTION"

In NIKECRAFT 2012 we attempted to channel the vision of John Ruskin, who in 1849 wrote of the changing times and the loss of handmade quality in the age of mechanical production. The Mars Yard Shoe was an expensive attempt at building a durable yet light weight athletic shoe that would last and even support the act of being repaired instead of replaced. We failed. The flexible Vectran fabric used in the upper part of the shoe is unbelievably strong in tension, abrasion resistance, and heat resistance. It passed every possible test we threw at it, but no one could guess what we could only learn by using it in real life.

Vectran, though very strong, failed quickly under folding fatigue, just like a paper clip which breaks when folded twice. That's why you'll see it tear in the corners. This was compounded by using only a single layer of vectran (to save weight and increase breatheability) without a liner material against the user's sock.

Every material has its strengths and weaknesses.

Some of the red tongue donning straps tore out. They were not sewn through the tongue ███████████ as specified by me in the studio in NYC. We have repaired many of these straps by hand in the NYC studio. On 2.0 each strap is secured through the tongue with an X box stitch. It might seem like overkill, but the X provides visual confirmation that this detail won't fail because of me.

We provide an optional cork sock liner because many users rock the shoe sockless and research shows that cork has natural antimicrobial properties. Try it and see if you like it. Yes this shoe comes with 2 pairs of sockliners. Use one and save another for later, to extend the life of the shoe.

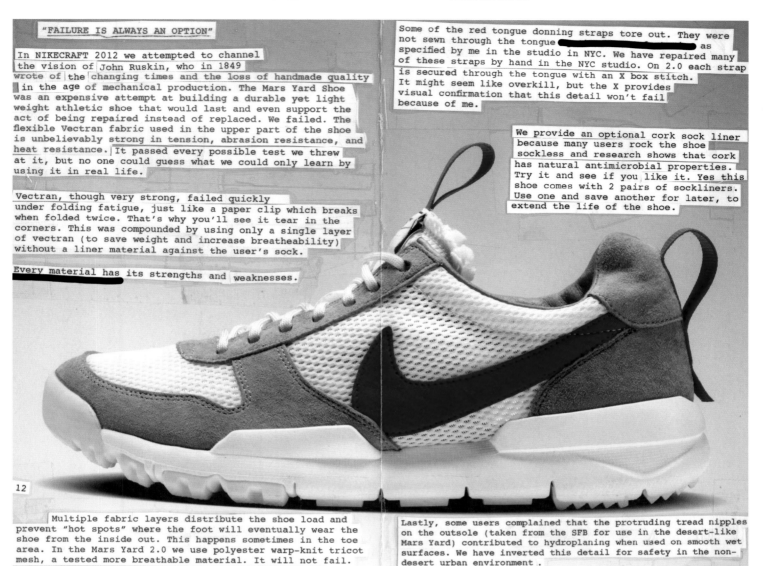

12

Multiple fabric layers distribute the shoe load and prevent "hot spots" where the foot will eventually wear the shoe from the inside out. This happens sometimes in the toe area. In the Mars Yard 2.0 we use polyester warp-knit tricot mesh, a tested more breathable material. It will not fail.

Lastly, some users complained that the protruding tread nipples on the outsole (taken from the SFB for use in the desert-like Mars Yard) contributed to hydroplaning when used on smooth wet surfaces. We have inverted this detail for safety in the non-desert urban environment.

Pages from the *NIKECraft: Mars Yard 2.0* zine   2017

Pages from the *NIKECraft: Mars Yard 2.0* zine   2017

| NIKECraft Transitions Collection | 2020 |

| NIKECraft Mars Yard Overshoe | White/Sport Red-Black-Cobalt Bliss | 2018 |

| NIKECraft Poncho | 2020 |

The NIKECraft Collection debuted on the eve of *Space Program: Mars*, Sachs's 2012 exhibition at New York City's Park Avenue Armory. The imaginary space mission featured the artist and his team wearing the designs, which visitors could purchase in an adjacent retail space. In 2017 the Mars Yard Shoe returned in a 2.0 version, with empirical material updates based on Sachs's wear-testing feedback. The developments were expanded upon a year later in the Mars Yard Overshoe, a wet-weather version of the original.

In 2020 the collaboration revisited apparel with the Poncho, a slimline pack that deploys into rain gear thanks to a trademark release mechanism. The fruit of more than four years of cooperation, the Poncho epitomizes the core of NIKECraft, which is officially branded as a "fifty-fifty enterprise between Nike and Tom Sachs" and is anecdotally defined by Sachs as "a philosophy and an approach to how we do stuff based on transparency and evidence of construction."

| React LW WR Mid iSPA | Summit White/Off White-Light Crimson | 2018 |

| iSPA Air Max 720 | Summit White/Black/White | 2020 |

Improvise. Scavenge. Protect. Adapt. The four pillars of the iSPA series evidence an ever-evolving design perspective defined by the inescapable flux of the built environment (i.e., modern life in a big city, where inhabitants are perpetually on their feet and exposed to the elements). The series, which debuted in 2018, is led by a dedicated team within Nike Sportswear that synthesizes creative insights from external collaborations and internal teams with proprietary innovations to create function-first designs with radical forms. In philosophy, iSPA follows product-agnostic design principles to solve problems for urban athletes. Experimental yet pragmatic expressions combine available materials with what the iSPA manifesto details as "a little inspiration." The provocative nature of the label's offerings is the direct by-product of these seemingly simple constraints: only Nike designers possess the access to and deep knowledge of Nike's unique materials and innovation libraries. Combined with creative free rein and a remit to illustrate the future, iSPA has given rise to an entirely new profile of Nike design.

BUILDING/SECTION

WHQ / KG-3

+1(503) 671-6453 | 1 One Bowerman Dr. Beaverton. OR 97005

ABOUT I.S.P.A.

IMPROVISE / SCAVENGE / PROTECT / ADAPT

Functional, versatile and adaptable footwear and apparel informed by the built environment prioritizing performance and utility.

—

Within the built environment, we live in a constant state of evolution. The updates to it — particularly in movement in and around it — force a constant reappraisal of what it means to be human. *ISPA* is a response to, and solution for, the shifting variance of this change. It is a declaration of communication with and awareness of the perpetual challenges.

— — — — —

ISPA is a philosophy. A set of design principles that represents a pinnacle, experimental expression of Nike design across all categories, including the latest innovations and established creations. It is product-agnostic, driven by experimentation and targeted toward solving problems for unique athletes.*

ISPA is a belief that, with a little inspiration, any problem can be solved with the materials at hand.

Part of *ISPA*'s philosophy is manifest by a guide. See below:

I	*[never be blocked by the first answer to a problem, **IMPROVISE** to see if it can be improved]*
S	*[to find the materials you need, **SCAVENGE** and pull together the best available options to solve the problem]*
P	*[your solution must **PROTECT** against the problem]*
A	*[**ADAPT** all solutions to fit their broadest potential]*

* Unique athletes are people who push themselves and their bodies as part of their own idiosyncratic routines. ISPA treats these athletes the same as any pinnacle athlete, recognizing that, just as solving for Breaking2 realized a new design, tackling the niche problems faced by city dwellers can do the same.

PACK

3

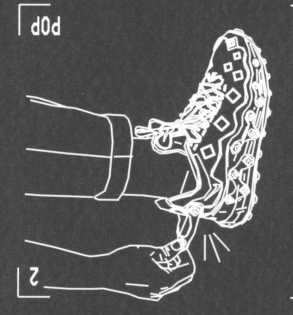

POP

2

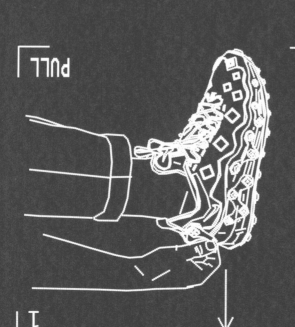

PULL

1

CONTAINS
HIGH PRESSURE
NITROGEN

IMPROVISE SCAVENGE PROTECT ADAPT
CRÉER RECUPÉRER PROTÉGER MODIFIER
IMPROVISAR RECUPERAR PROTEGER ADAPTAR
IMPROVISIEREN DURCHSTÖBERN SCHÜTZEN ANPASSEN
即興で作る 収集する 保護する 適合させる

| iSPA Joyride Envelope | Black / Metallic Silver / White | 2019 |

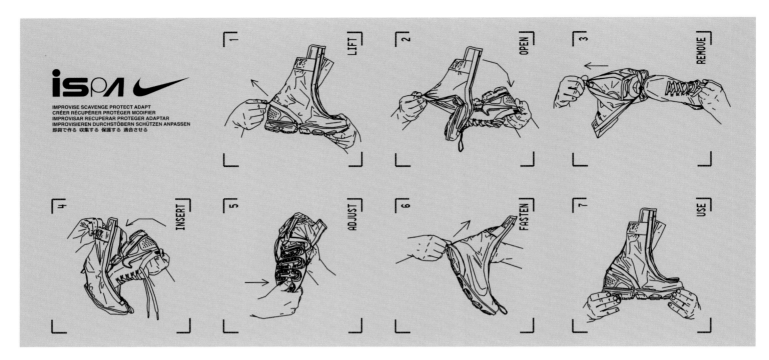

Air VaporMax Flyknit 3	Black/Black-Black	2019

Air VaporMax Flyknit Gaiters iSPA	2019

Air VaporMax Flyknit Gaiters iSPA and Air VaporMax Flyknit 3	Metallic Silver/Black/White/Metallic Silver	2019

DRIFTER - FREE

DRIFTER - FREE UTILITY

MASH-UP

ROAD WARRIOR

GRAM SHAVER

FUTURE NO-FOAM

SPSU2020   COLLECTIVE COMMUNE   CREATIVE LAUNCH   18.03.12   COLLECTIVE COMMUNE   SPSU2020   COLLECTIVE COMMUNE   CREATIVE LAUNCH   COLLECTIVE COMMUNE   18.03.12   KEEP IT TIGHT   29

AESTHETIC - FORM STUDIES

BASED IN ISPA DESIGN PHILOSOPHY.
INTEGRATED SUSTAINABILITY.

iSPA internal design presentation   2018

| *iSPA* zine collage | 2020 |

Working three seasons ahead and guided by culturally inspired narratives, such as "State of Emergency," iSPA's provocative designs invariably force a reckoning of accepted design practices and aesthetics. The label's first release, the 2018 React LW WR Mid iSPA, was devised to be quickly adorned in the event of, and adaptable to, either natural or man-made disasters thanks to its unique lightweight, stretchy, water-resistant upper, and cutting-edge sole, which is borrowed from the React Element 87. The 2019 Air VaporMax Flyknit Gaiter iSPA offered a solution for wet conditions by introducing a removable shroud that protects the Air VaporMax Flyknit, while the iSPA Joyride Envelope implanted the Joyride NSW Setter with an easy on-off mechanism. The label's pinnacle apparel release to date, the 2020 iSPA Inflate JKT, translates the iSPA code into outerwear with a manual loft solution for fluctuating temperatures. Uninhibited by tradition, iSPA designs showcase the paradigm-shifting potential of experimentation to address today's everyday performance issues and solve tomorrow's before they arrive.

| iSPA Zoom Road Warrior | Sail / Volt-Spruce Aura | 2020 |

| iSPA Zoom Road Warrior outsole | | 2020 |

| iSPA OverReact Flyknit | Sail/Multi-Color-Barely Orange | 2020 |

| iSPA Drifter | Grey Fog / Black-Olive-Spruce Aura | 2020 |

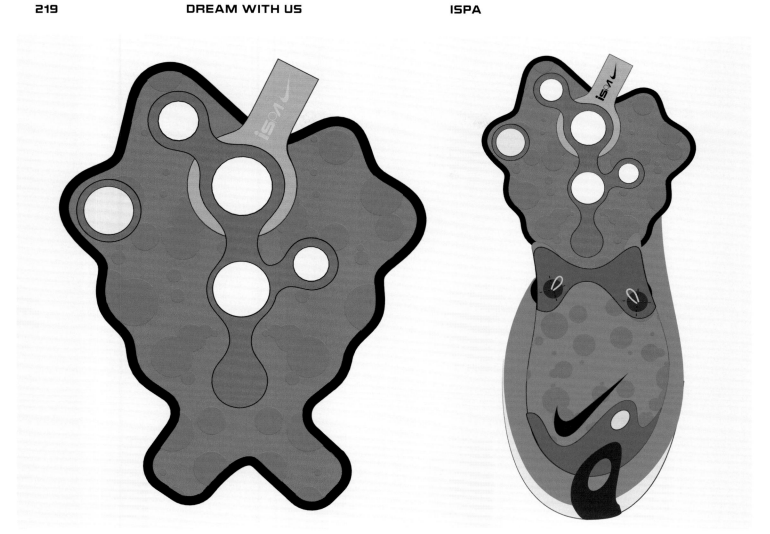

iSPA Flow line art		2018

iSPA Flow 2020	Medium Olive / Persian Volt-Saffron Quartz	2020

iSPA Short	2020

iSPA Inflate Vest	2020

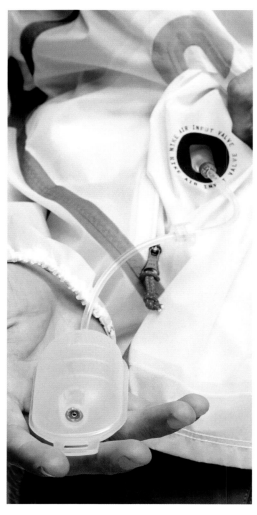

iSPA Inflate JKT and detail	2020

"WE'RE ALLOWED TO FAIL,
AND THOSE FAILURES
BRING SOME REALLY
SURPRISING RESULTS.
WE WANT TO SHOW OFF
THE FAILURES BECAUSE
THAT'S THE HONESTY
BEHIND THE DESIGN."

DARRYL MATTHEWS

4 OPENING THE APERTURE

Air Gauntlet
Air Zoom Drive
Air Presto
LeBron Soldier 8 FlyEase
LeBron Soldier 9 FlyEase
Lebron Soldier 10 FlyEase
Lebron Soldier 13 FlyEase 4

Air Zoom Pegasus 33 FlyEase 4E
Air Zoom Pegasus 35 FlyEase
Air Zoom UNVRS FlyEase
AJI High FlyEase
Air Max 90 FlyEase
Pro Hijab
Victory Swim Collection

Sole
(M) Swoosh Bra
Nike × MMW 2.0 AeroAdapt Bra
Pro Luxe Tight
Nike × Gyakusou Knit Hoodie
CruzrOne

Few people in Nike's history are more legendary than Jeff Johnson, who—even in retirement—retains the unofficial title of "employee number one." Johnson met Phil Knight at Stanford in the early 1960s and in 1965 became the first official hire of Blue Ribbon Sports. He not only led sales and helped set up the company's first factories, R&D facilities, and stores, but in 1971 he even gave it its new name. So in 2004, when the lifelong runner suffered a debilitating stroke that left the right side of his body numb, Knight and Mark Parker offered to help in any way they could.

Constrained by his newly limited mobility, Johnson found that the once incidental task of getting in and out of his Nikes had become a significant challenge. Parker leaned on Tobie Hatfield, senior director of Athlete Innovation and one of the veteran designers on the Innovation team, to see if he could produce a solution. Hatfield began toying with an alternative enclosure system that would enable Johnson to slide his foot in from the back of the shoe and created a series of one-off prototypes for him. As Johnson pushed through his physical therapy and eventual recovery, Hatfield also kept promoting the idea of shoes that would be easier to get in and out of; in his spare time between other assignments, he continued to experiment with novel approaches to entry, enclosure, and adjustment.

Some years later, another experience further reinforced Hatfield's view that adaptive athletes were being overlooked. In 2011 he met Sarah Reinertsen, an American triathlete who was the first woman to finish the Hawaii Ironman World Championship on a prosthetic leg. During the exchange, Reinertsen walked Hatfield through the hour-long, ad-hoc process of outfitting her carbon-fiber prosthetic blade with a road-ready protective "shoe" (in reality a sole harvested from a regular running shoe and attached to the prosthetic with tape and Velcro). An incredulous Hatfield told her "not only are we going to commit to this, but instead of taking sixty minutes to put on, it will only take six seconds." With the constraints determined by the design of the prosthetic (and the promised adjustment time), Hatfield settled on a minimalist approach, paring down the effort to only what was absolutely necessary. Working closely with Reinertsen, Hatfield conceived the Nike Sole, a lightweight, durable composite sole for use in combination with the Össur Flex-Run carbon-fiber blade. The design includes both an outsole and midsole, as well as a layer of thermal plastic urethane called Aeroply, made from recycled Air units, which sits between the two components. Nylon plastic tabs and a surfboard leash-inspired strap secure the blade in place. The collaboration resulted in the first-ever shoe made explicitly for an athletic prosthetic; but more significantly, it expanded the notion of Nike innovation to benefit an even wider range of athletes.

In the world of sport, Nike reigns by serving the most elite athletes on the planet. For five decades, the company has pushed the envelope of design and innovation to make the best performers in any given field even better. But as much as cofounder Bill Bowerman wanted to win championships, he also believed that if you have a body, you are an athlete. In the 1960s, after a revelatory trip to New Zealand—where he saw noncompetitive "jogging" for the first time—he became instrumental in introducing the concept to Americans with the 1966 publication of *Jogging: A Physical Fitness Program for All Ages* (not necessarily to produce more elite runners but to help people in his community become healthier). This highly participatory, inclusive idea of sport has always been in Nike's DNA and today is finding completely new avenues and expressions. "We are a company that truly cares about everybody," says Hatfield. "Exploring these ideas is opening up this other part of our aperture that's always been there."

"We're looking at how we can provide more access to more people to be active across a broader spectrum," says Parker. "It may start with a specific group, but the solutions to some of those problems are actually relevant to a much broader range of consumers." In practice, this process isn't so different from when Nike collaborates with a top athlete—there are design consultations, wear-tests, insights, and iterations until the product surpasses the expectations of all involved. However, the goal isn't necessarily about breaking world records or winning championships but to create greater access to sport for everyone.

Today FlyEase—a series of easy-entry footwear systems designed to help all users to quickly and easily put on and take off their shoes—is doing just that. The concept first launched in fall 2015 with the LeBron Soldier 8 FlyEase—as Hatfield describes it, a "plug-and-play" version of the popular basketball shoe worn by LeBron James. The designer felt it was important to debut the technology on a pair of shoes that was nearly identical to the "in-line" versions worn by classmates and teammates. As a small design and development team formed to evolve the FlyEase technology further and support rolling it out in other models, they started getting all kinds of feedback they hadn't anticipated. There was excitement and appreciation but also unique counterperspectives from a broad array of people with disabilities and their caregivers.

The experience was reminiscent of an earlier chapter in Hatfield's career where listening deeply to the needs of runners led to a series of nonintuitive innovations that changed Nike's approach to design. "We were making these very complicated cushioning shoes, and I was just seeing multiple layers, multiple layers, multiple layers," Hatfield recalls. After meeting with countless athletes who complained that they just wanted a shoe that was comfortable and fit "right," he began to articulate the front of the shoe from the back and removed as much material as possible from the upper to create something lighter and more seamless. In 1998 the Air Gauntlet debuted the new approach—a single-layer stretch mesh in the forefoot offered lightweight comfort, a deep notch separated the heel from the toe to promote natural movement, and an adjustable steel clip allowed for the wearer to dial in a customized fit. The Air Zoom Drive and Air Presto eventually took the ideas even further and into the mainstream. "It was about the foot being more of a hero than the shoe itself," says Hatfield. "The shoe is just along for the ride." Nowhere is this maxim more apparent than with Hatfield's 2004 Nike Free—a unique articulating design born out of observing runners training barefoot to strengthen their feet.

As Hatfield sees it, innovation doesn't just happen because the company wills it. "For me," he says, "the best thing to do is to actually go talk to our experts, our athletes, our trainers, and our coaches and just ask them what's working and what's not working. Essentially, they are our living, breathing brief. We don't need it on paper—we just need to talk to warm-blooded individuals, and then they'll tell us. We'll figure it out from there."

With FlyEase, the team decided that better ideas would result from involving even more people in the conversation. So in 2016 Nike announced an open innovation competition called the Nike Ease Challenge in search of a big new idea to accelerate problem-solving around putting on, securing, and taking off shoes. Selected from more than five hundred entrants, three finalists flew out to Beaverton to share their prototype designs with a jury of Nike team members and athletes, including Parker; Hatfield; Tatyana McFadden, a seventeen-time Paralympic medal winner; Carl Lewis, a nine-time Olympic gold medalist; and Elena Delle Donne, a six-time WNBA All-Star and 2019 league MVP, among others. The winning design—a hack of the 2016 Hyperdunk—offered a drawbridge-like system where the heel counter of the shoe was hinged to allow easy, one-handed access from behind, while small, lightweight magnets secured the foot in place once the entry point was closed.

Delle Donne, in particular, was taken with the design—and wondered if it could be incorporated into her on-court footwear. The 6-foot 5-inch-tall Olympic gold medalist and two-time MVP has reached the height of achievement in her basketball career, and her older sister Lizzie—who lives with disabilities—has always served as a muse. Delle Donne pushed Hatfield and the team to create a shoe that would not only meet the highest demands of performance on the court but could also be worn by her sister. Based on the principles of universal design, where equitably driven design considerations result in better products for people of all abilities, the Air Zoom UNVRS was the first FlyEase product to be designed from the ground up instead of being adapted from an existing Nike model. As such, it was crucial for Delle Donne and the FlyEase team that the shoe be one anybody would be happy to wear.

Drawing inspiration from the winning design from the Nike Ease Challenge, the team underwent a lengthy design and development period using both Delle Donne sisters as their wear-testers. Getting the opening mechanism right proved particularly troublesome. Instead of using magnets to secure the heel closed, they were placed on the back side of the heel counter, allowing for the user to hitch it to the midsole and prop it open. Velcro covers the entire back of the boot to allow for the one-handed adjustment of an articulated strap that engages Flywire cables to provide a customized fit. A dimensional Flyknit weave covers the upper, which prominently features printed messaging to promote the guiding philosophy behind FlyEase—to "bring inspiration and innovation to every athlete in the world." The designers even snuck in a small Easter egg for the Delle Donne sisters (braille printing reads *Elena* on the right toe cap and *Lizzie* on the left one).

"ALL ATHLETES, ALL ABILITIES, ALL BODY TYPES, ALL NEEDS, AND ALL ASPIRATIONS."

MARK PARKER

"AS OUR CENTER HAS GOTTEN BIGGER, THE OUT-SIDE EDGES HAVE GOTTEN CLOSER. OUR EYES HAVE BEEN OPENED TO PLACES AND PEOPLE THAT ARE YET TO BE SERVED."

MARTHA MOORE

The Air Zoom UNVRS made its debut in August 2019, just in time for Delle Donne to wear a pair in the WNBA Finals. "They feel great, and I won a championship in them," she enthuses. "Can you ask for anything better out of a shoe?" But the star is quick to pivot to her true pride in what the design represents. "Because my sister's deaf and blind, her other senses are really heightened. She can't see the shoe, but she can feel it, and when she first got it, she was running her fingers back and forth over that waffle texture—and then the soft Velcro on the back. She gets to experience this shoe, too, in her own way." The Delle Donne sisters' high-profile story may be unique, but if FlyEase has taught the design and innovation teams at Nike anything, it's that one person's idea of extraordinary is another's version of ordinary. The company is continuing to invest in new and varying approaches to entry, enclosure, and adjustment to make products that aren't simply better for people with disabilities but that provide smarter, better-designed footwear for everyone.

For leadership at Nike, this unique form of open problem-solving is critical to the company's future. While in the past expansion meant taking on entirely new product categories at the macro level, such as golf or football, today chief design officer John Hoke sees an increased role for addressing highly specific problems. "We want to invite more people into the world of sport," Hoke says, "and there are still individual participants or constituents that we haven't brought innovation to, so we're going to turn our muscle there." Even for a company of Nike's scale, commerciality isn't necessarily the essential driver. Hoke, like Parker, understands that tasking designers to solve problems within a tight set of constraints often leads to solutions that can take the company in surprising new directions.

This approach is evident in the company's recent efforts to address modesty. In 2017 Nike introduced the Pro Hijab—the world's first performance-driven hijab designed specifically for sport. Nike designers met with athletes across a range of activities, from weight lifting to figure skating to fencing, to understand their needs—and more often than not, the manifold problems associated with modifying a traditional garment for sport. Ibtihaj Muhammad, champion fencer and the first Olympian to represent the United States in a hijab, typically competed in a model intended for kids so that the covering would be tight enough not to shift or billow. However, the garment was made from a doubled georgette material that was heavy and caused her to "literally bake" under the bright lights of competition. When it became wet, it also became heavy and stiff. Moreover, it completely obstructed her hearing, so she was often penalized for false starts. The Pro Hijab was designed to be lightweight and breathable, framing the face perfectly while remaining as inconspicuous as possible to the wearer. For Muhammad it was life-changing—both for her performance as an athlete and for what it means to her. "To some people," she says, "it may just seem like a piece of fabric, but to me this really transforms lives in meaningful ways. I would love to see a study twenty years down the road of how many people, no matter their age, make a conscious decision to be active because the Pro Hijab [adds] an element of ease to working out."

Enabling access to sport was also the driving force behind Nike's 2019 Victory Swim Collection. As the company's swim division began a push to broaden their business globally, a team of designers—including vice president creative director for Licensed Product Martha Moore—identified a community of women living a modest lifestyle that was completely underserved in the category and began to dig deeply into the problems associated with modest swimwear. Given the lack of available attire, women had been known to wear their street clothes, or some adaptation thereof, into the water. Because of this, "lifeguards would tell us that it was the women, not the little kids, they worried the most about," says Moore. The team also learned that when girls reached the age when they would transition to a more modest lifestyle, that usually meant leaving their aspirations and love of sport behind—especially in competitive swimming, where traditional bathing suits represent the antithesis of modest attire and the few available options were more of a hindrance than a help.

Although the team took insights from Nike staples, such as leggings and bras, to develop their design, the Victory Full-Coverage Swimsuit (consisting of the Victory Swim Hijab, the Swim Tunic Top, and the Swim Leggings) offers the wearer a completely revolutionized experience of swimming— from the moment the wearer begins to put it on until she's out of the water drying off. The form of the garments, loosely conforming to the body and expertly tailored with tapering lines, echoes classic silhouettes from the 1960s and 1970s. The warp-knit fabric is fast-drying, breathable, and lightweight. The hijab was constructed to stay securely in place and also offers an integrated mesh pocket for hair management. The single-layer tunic features a full interior support system that's based on Nike's bra technology and features a series of vents—inspired by fish gills—to allow for optimal flow in the water and drying on land. While the pants are based on running tights, the cut was altered to be more generous while still adhering to the ankle. With one of the initial wear-tests of the final product, the team knew they were onto something. "Shaikha [Al-Saud] came out of the locker room in tears," says Moore, "just crying with sheer joy and delight, and dove right in the pool. I've been here thirty years, and I've worked with a ton of athletes—you don't get crying often." Based on the initial success and feedback, the team is already beginning to look at adapting their findings to other areas, such as running.

Internally at Nike, one of the biggest impacts of the Breaking2 sub-two-hour marathon attempt was to inspire the company's design and innovation teams to look at problems and solutions more holistically— accounting for every element on athletes' bodies, their mental states, and the context and conditions around their athletic experiences. That thinking clearly informed the Victory Swim Collection and with a broader arc is affecting the company's approach to apparel innovation. Led by Janett Nichol, vice president of Apparel Innovation, teams are tasked with developing better materials and production methods that deliver new performance attributes as well as looking for new solutions to the problems faced by an ever-broader array of athletes. "I think some of the best innovations are staring us right in the face," says Nichol, "and we don't see it because we're looking for the big, shiny object. It's usually something very, very simple that people respond to most."

To prove her point, some of the company's biggest advances in apparel have come from examining a basic function of human biology: thermo-regulation—or more commonly, sweating. In 1991 Nike first introduced Dri-FIT, a polyester fabric that disperses perspiration evenly over the surface of the garment so that it evaporates more quickly. Building from this foundation, Nike's designers have even greater technological capabil-ities at their disposal today, including a trove of athlete data (showing everything from where the body sweats to where garments stretch) and computational design and production tools (such as 3-D knitting machines). Introduced in 2019, AeroAdapt demonstrates how these advances are being put to use. The proprietary material features yarns that react to moisture by expanding and allowing for greater airflow (and conversely contracting when dry to better insulate the wearer). Another example is Nike's Therma-FIT technology, an alternative to fleece created through a lofted engineered knit. First released in spring 2020 as part of the Gyakusou running collection, the new technology is designed to com-pletely mitigate body temperature changes before, during, and after activities to keep the athlete at an optimum temperature. Nike Stealth Evaporation Fabric, the latest incarnation of Dri-FIT, is perhaps the most remarkable yet. As the name suggests, the textile was developed to reduce the visibility of awkward patches of sweat that accumulate during sport—a concern specifically cited by women, who told Nike's research-ers that sweat stains were embarrassing and distracting to the point where they affect confidence and performance. Featuring a double-knit construction of moisture-wicking and water-repellent yarns, the novel textile works by quickly dispersing sweat over a greater surface area on the inside of the fabric to keep it from showing through on the face. Congruent with how innovation teams work at Nike, these technologies are being employed across a variety of categories and product lines, while also helping push the business in new directions.

Nike (M), a new apparel collection that adapts to a woman's changing body before, during, and after pregnancy, offers a window into how Nike is adapting its apparel capabilities to new contexts. In development since 2017, the four-piece collection required nearly three years of detailed research, testing, and design to ensure that it would meet the needs of mothers at every stage of pregnancy—in the same way that the company might design for an athlete on the field. Part of this research involved the analysis of 150,000 comparison scans of nonpregnant women against those of pregnant women to demonstrate how the body grows from a size XS to XL over the gestation period. To create garments that would accom-modate such intense shifts, the team started with existing products in the Nike catalog but imbued them with dramatic new qualities. An expanded waistband on the tights literally grows and shrinks with the belly (testing demonstrated that even after being stretched to 100 percent, the fabric returns to its original form). The poncholike pullover and tank top were both conceived with nursing in mind, allowing for easy access, while special attention was paid toward making any seams as flat and smooth as possible to avoid irritation. The bra not only features a slider to help scale the garment as the rib cage expands during pregnancy but was designed with three overlapping layers of Stealth Evaporation Fabric to reduce visibility of the inevitable leakage that occurs while nursing. Paired with the company's state-of-the-art technology and fabrication techniques, the (M) collection represents a more empathetic and holistic approach to problem-solving that has redefined performance as much through the lens of transformative life experiences as sport.

A similar notion informed the design of the CruzrOne, Nike's first shoe created specifically for "really slow running." Aimed at the generation of hard-core runners who may have grown up with Nike in the 1970s and 1980s, the CruzrOne resulted from a conversation between Nike cofounder Knight and vice president of Creative Concepts Tinker Hatfield, in which the eighty-two-year-old Knight protested that he didn't go out for walks, just really slow runs. Hatfield turned the jocular comment on its face and responded with a design that acknowledges the nuanced difference between the two activities. At slower speeds, the heel strikes the ground with more impact, so the CruzrOne offers a rocker-shape sole that assists in naturally propelling the wearer forward to complete the heel-to-toe motion. A padded collar lined with shearling and a two-way stretch upper make for greater comfort and easier on and off than your typical running shoe. With more offerings based on the idea of slow running in the works, Hatfield feels like a whole new category could emerge.

Although some of these ideas may seem like they are on the outer fringes of the Nike universe, as the company continues to grow, there are seemingly unlimited directions to explore. "Thirty years ago, I never thought I'd be working on product like this," explains Moore of the Victory Swim Collection. "We never even considered this community of people as a focal point for us. But as our center has gotten bigger, the outside edges have gotten closer. Our eyes have been opened to places and people that are yet to be served."

While Nike's future will undoubtedly be rooted in helping the best athletes on the planet perform even better, increasingly the company also sees itself taking a more critical role to inspire and enable everyone to participate in sport. In the past this might have meant addressing entirely new categories, such as golf or tennis, but today it means looking for opportunities to serve audiences for whom—by virtue of their ability, age, culture, gender, or otherwise—access to sport has been limited or nonexistent. Doing so hasn't only improved the lives of typically overlooked constituents; it is also driving a design strategy in which solving new kinds of problems in new ways leads to innovations that stand to benefit everyone. "This is bigger than winning championships and winning gold medals," says Tobie Hatfield. "Quite frankly, I think this will be the most important thing Nike does in the history of Nike."

| Air Gauntlet | White/White/Red/Black | 1998 |

| Air Zoom Drive | Silver/Teal/Black | 1999 |

Designer Tobie Hatfield's oeuvre ranges from the Free to the Sole, a tooling system for prosthetic running blades. Despite their diversity, each design embodies the company's commitment to "listen to the voice of the athlete." Fittingly, this pledge is attributed to Nike cofounder Bill Bowerman, who also coached Hatfield while he was studying at the University of Oregon and who introduced the then-young pole vaulter to the power of athlete–designer relationships by crafting him a pair of custom spikes. At Nike, Hatfield has continuously upheld and evolved Bowerman's legacy. Famously, in 1996 he answered demands for better-fitting, more comfortable footwear with a prototype featuring a V notch near the ankle. The design birthed a lineage of running silhouettes, eventually leading to the revelatory Air Presto, billed as a "T-shirt for the foot."

ALL KNIT, NO' QUIT

Nike Air Presto Ultra Flyknit

We've never liked quitters. So we made the Presto's Flyknit
material so soft and comfortable that once they're on,
you'll never want to stop.

Air Presto advertisements and ephemera   2000–16

| Air Presto "Brutal Honey" | Black/Neutral Grey-Yellow Streak | 2000 |

| Air Presto "Orange Monk" and outsole | White/Orange Peel-Black | 2000 |

| Air Presto "Rogue Kielbasa" and outsole | Comet Red/White-Black | 2000 |

| LeBron Soldier 8 FlyEase | White/Metallic Silver-Black | 2015 |

| LeBron Soldier 9 FlyEase | Obsidian/Metallic Gold | 2016 |

| Lebron Soldier 10 FlyEase | White/White-Metallic Silver-Ice Blue | 2017 |

| Lebron Soldier 13 FlyEase 4 | Thunder Grey/Bright Crimson-Electric Green | 2019 |

In 2015 Hatfield's ability to translate athlete insights into eloquent designs materialized as the LeBron Soldier 8 FlyEase, an easy-entry shoe with a wraparound zipper closure designed for athletes of all abilities and ages. The novel system had its genesis in an innovation that Hatfield began developing in 2004 after Jeff Johnson, Nike's first employee, suffered a stroke. In response, Hatfield created a set of one-off prototypes that would cater to Johnson's temporarily diminished motor skills. The specification of the appeal led Hatfield to fully reexamine the foundational functionality of footwear, eventually precipitating FlyEase. Debuting on LeBron James's signature shoe, the breakthrough system was soon adapted across the Nike range and has since evolved to incorporate insights from adaptive athletes. Moreover, FlyEase affirms a set of design principles that has enabled the creation of superior shoes for all athletes.

| Air Zoom Pegasus 33 FlyEase 4E | Black/White-Anthracite-Cool Grey | 2016 |

| Air Zoom Pegasus 35 FlyEase | Barely Grey/Hot Punch | 2018 |

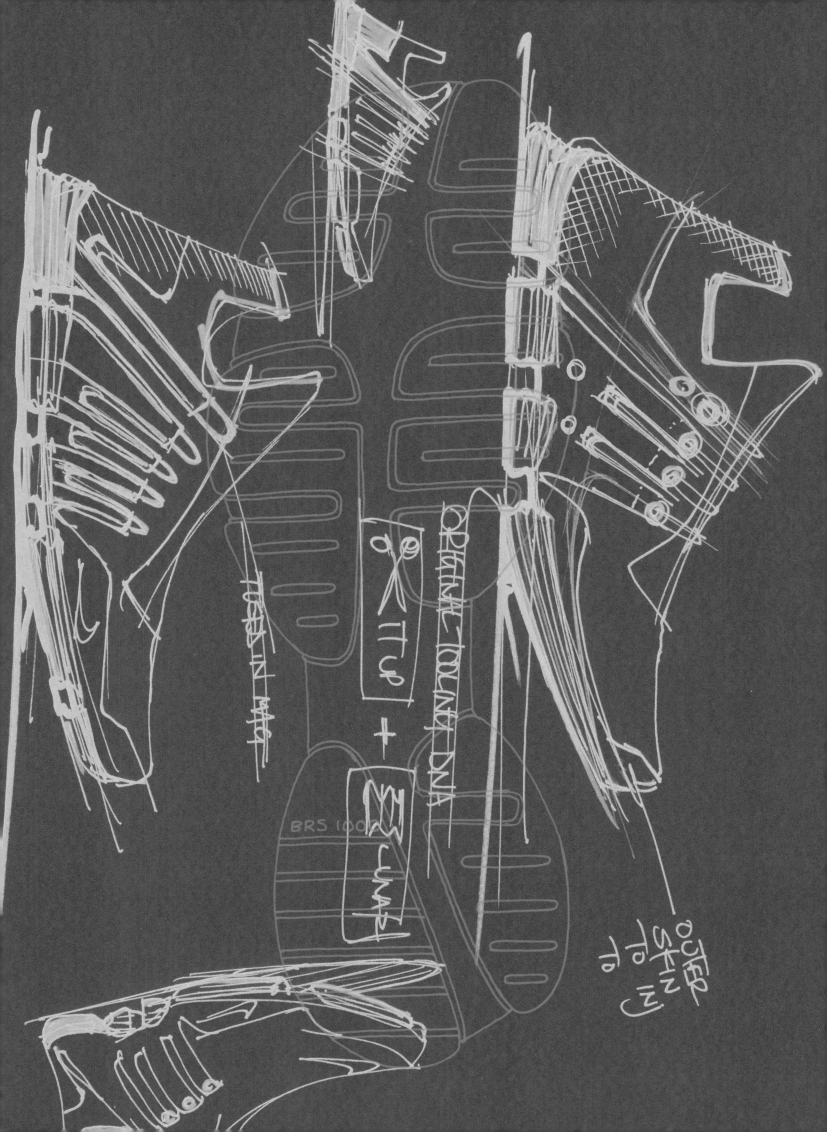

ORIGINAL TOOLING DNA

CUT IT UP + REUSE

TUCKS IN MFG

BRS 1000

OUTER SKIN TO IN TO

"I WANT THIS TO BE A SHOE FOR EVERYONE, WHETHER YOU'RE MALE OR FEMALE, WHETHER YOU'RE AN ATHLETE OR AN ADAPTIVE ATHLETE."

ELENA DELLE DONNE

Nike Ease Challenge winning design | 2017

Details of the Nike Ease Challenge winning design's magnetized rear-entry and lacing systems | 2017

The arrival of the LeBron Soldier 8 FlyEase elicited responses that both validated its existence and illuminated the need to further develop the innovation. In addition to incorporating much of the feedback into the FlyEase line, Nike sought to expand the dialogue with the 2016 Nike Ease Challenge. The open-call contest invited designers, engineers, makers, and innovators to advance and reinvent footwear for athletes of all abilities. After considering entries from across the United States, the challenge's judges selected a rear-entry solution as the winner. Taking cues from the 2016 Hyperdunk support system, the design employed powerful, lightweight magnets to transform the shoe's heel into a "drawbridge" with a simple, wide entry-and-exit area.

| Air Zoom UNVRS FlyEase | White/Sport Red | 2019 |

| Air Zoom UNVRS FlyEase articulated strap | | 2019 |

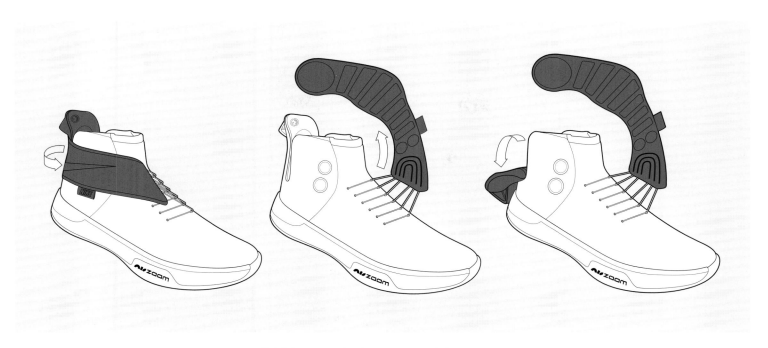

Air Zoom UNVRS FlyEase closure system with articulated strap and integrated Flywire cables | 2019

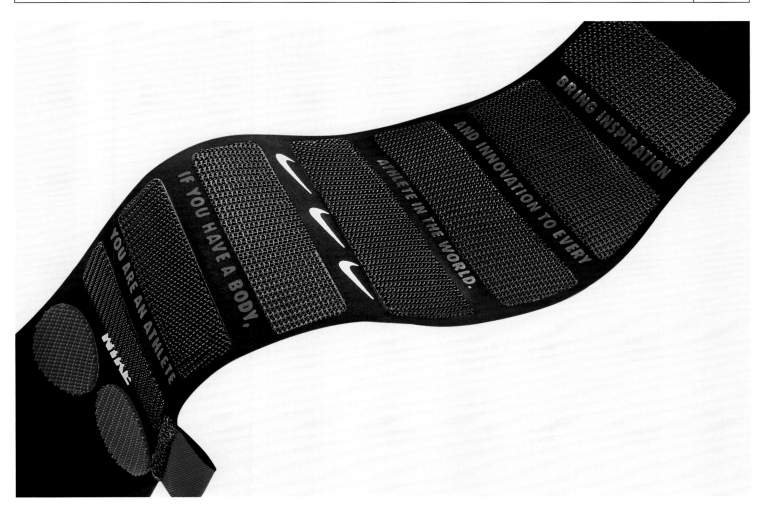

Detail of the Air Zoom UNVRS FlyEase articulated strap | 2019

In August 2019 Elena Delle Donne unveiled the Air Zoom UNVRS FlyEase during the WNBA finals. Based on the Nike Ease Challenge-winning design, the shoe introduced a new FlyEase system comprising a fold-down magnetized heel, which connects to the midsole for easy, hands-free entry and exit. An articulated strap engaging Flywire cables further enhanced the shoe's performance by enabling a one-handed, two-motion customized, secure fit. Delle Donne's decision to introduce the shoe wasn't incidental. The basketball star, who had been one of the challenge's judges, was personally invested in the design. Her older sister Lizzie lives with disabillities, which fueled Delle Donne's advocacy for a shoe that would serve both her sister's needs and her own on-court demands. The shoe's function directly responds to this petition, while design details honor its muses. Braille on the toe caps spells *Elena* on the right side and *Lizzie* on the left, and Nike's mission statement—to bring inspiration and innovation to every athlete in the world—is one of two concealed messages printed on the underside of the strap.

AJI High FlyEase	Black/Gym Red/White/Black	2019

Details of the AJI High FlyEase closure system | 2019

| Air Max 90 FlyEase | White/White/Deep Royal Blue/Hyper Pink | 2020 |

| Air Max 90 FlyEase outsole | | 2020 |

As with all Nike innovations, FlyEase is in a constant state of evolution, with new systems and silhouettes inspired by insights from adaptive athletes and underpinned by clearly defined criteria: FlyEase footwear must be easy to open and close, it must be easy to put on and take off, and it must accommodate different foot shapes. Along with birthing wholly new silhouettes, such as the Air Zoom UNVRS, these guidelines have generated easy on-off versions of a number of the company's hallmark shoes, including the AJI High FlyEase, Air Zoom Pegasus FlyEase, and Air Max 90 FlyEase. The latter shoe also marks the Hatfield brothers' first Nike Sportswear collaboration, combining Tinker's iconic design with Tobie's FlyEase technology.

Ibtihaj Muhammad (top) and Zeina Nassar (bottom) in the Pro Hijab | 2017

Pro Hijab	2017

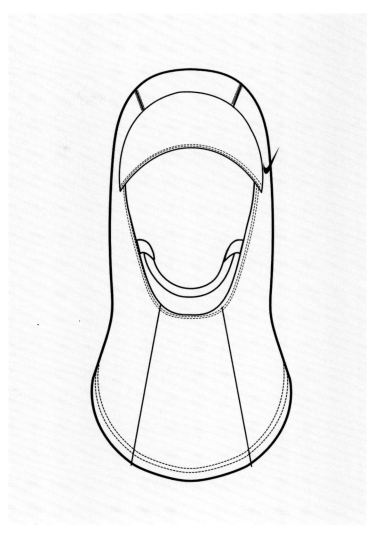

Pro Hijab design exploration sketch	c.2016

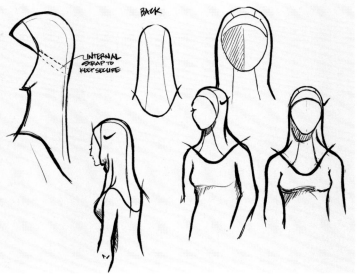

Pro Hijab design exploration sketches	c.2016

After more than thirty years of creating performance footwear and apparel, Nike—while always striving for improvement—had ostensibly mastered the basics; its offerings graced the world's top competitors and legions of everyday athletes. But just as Nike's FlyEase systems highlighted a gap in the company's offerings, so too did insights from female Muslim athletes, such as Team USA Olympic fencer Ibtihaj Muhammad, who detailed the need for a better sports hijab. Signed as a Nike athlete in 2016, Muhammad communicated to the company her inability to find an adequate garment. As a result, she recounted, she was inhibited by sweat and her hearing was impaired, which often cost her penalty points for false starts. Hijabi athletes from around the globe validated her experience. Combining observations and requests from weight lifters, figure skaters, boxers, runners, and others, Nike designers created the 2017 Pro Hijab, a light, breathable, and soft head covering that met cultural standards and invited a new global constituent of women to participate in sport.

| Victory Swim Collection design exploration sketches | 2019 |

Passionate public responses to both FlyEase and the Pro Hijab provoked within Nike a progressive vision of product innovation that went beyond supporting athletic achievement to enabling basic access to sport. The 2019 Victory Swim Collection, the company's first modest swimwear line, proudly expressed this advanced ambition. Led by vice president creative director for Licensed Product Martha Moore, the four-piece collection comprised the Victory Full-Coverage Swimsuit, the Victory Swim Hijab, the Victory Swim Tunic Top, and the Victory Swim Leggings. Each piece combined advanced materials and fit innovations into streamlined swimwear for female athletes seeking full coverage and unconstrained motion in the water. Victory Swim's success swiftly prompted Nike to begin adapting the collection's insights and innovations to running and other sports traditionally deprived of modest performance garments.

Victory Swim Collection campaign imagery   2019

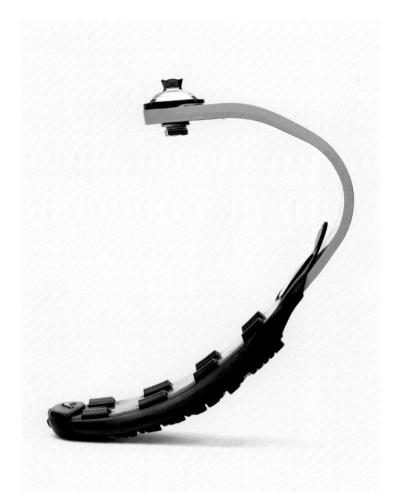

Össur Flex-Run prosthetic blade with Sole	2012

Sole	2012

While Nike's commitment to serving all athletes has increasingly gained external awareness, its presence within the company's innovation pipeline isn't new. Nike has routinely created custom products for Special Olympians and Paralympians, partnering with these athletes to meet highly specific equipment demands. In 2012 the collaborating athlete was amputee triathlete and world-record holder Sarah Reinertsen. Due to limited industry innovations, Reinertsen had been forced to cobble the outsole of a traditional running shoe onto her competition prosthetic, a suboptimal and unstable solution. To resolve the issue, Tobie Hatfield joined forces with Reinertsen to create Sole, a lightweight, durable composite sole designed to pair with the Össur Flex-Run prosthetic blade. Beyond providing amputee athletes with a much-needed innovation, Sole cemented Reinertsen's relationship with Nike, where she is now a senior manager for FlyEase Innovation.

Sarah Reinertsen wear-testing the Össur Flex-Run prosthetic blade with Sole   c.2011

| (M) Swoosh Bra | 2020 |

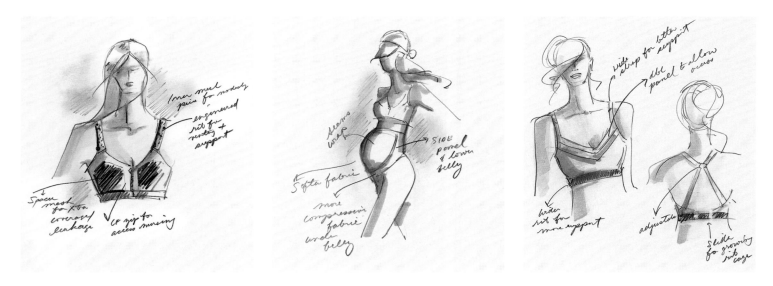

| (M) collection design exploration sketches | 2020 |

In 2020 Nike apparel innovation literally took on a new shape with the launch of the (M) collection maternity line, a tightly edited series of garments for athletes carrying future athletes. In trademark Nike fashion, its designers worked from empirical data to construct four essential clothing items that would optimally support female athletes from pregnancy to postpartum. More than seventy materials were analyzed for compression and stretch, with seven eventually selected and transformed into a sports bra, tank top, poncholike pullover, and leggings. Each garment anticipates and addresses its wearer's changing physicality, whether it be accommodating her fluctuating shape or serving nursing needs with accessible panels and the company's Stealth Evaporation Fabric.

(M) collection sketches	2020

  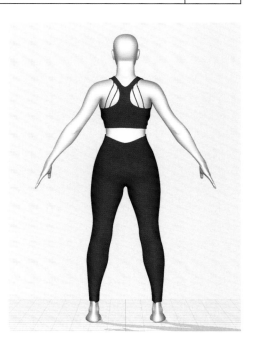

(M) collection including One (M) Tight, (M) Swoosh Bra, (M) Tank, and (M) Pull Over	2020

Nike × MMW 2.0 AeroAdapt Bra | 2019

Details of AeroAdapt fabric | 2019

When Dri-FIT arrived in 1991, it introduced an advanced breed of performance textiles that wicked sweat away from the skin to the fabric's surface, where it could rapidly evaporate. The technology's suffix spoke to this advancement: Functional Innovative Technology. True to its name, over the next nearly thirty years Dri-FIT continuously pushed the edge of innovation, eventually leading to AeroAdapt, a 2019 technology designed to maintain an athlete's optimal body temperature from warm-up to cooldown. Upon sensing sweat, the proprietary material's moisture-reactive yarns open to release body heat and permit airflow. As the athlete cools down, the vents close, minimizing post-workout chills. This smart process is both sensorial and visual: the fabric appears flat when dry; when wet, its yarns contract, imparting a crinkled appearance.

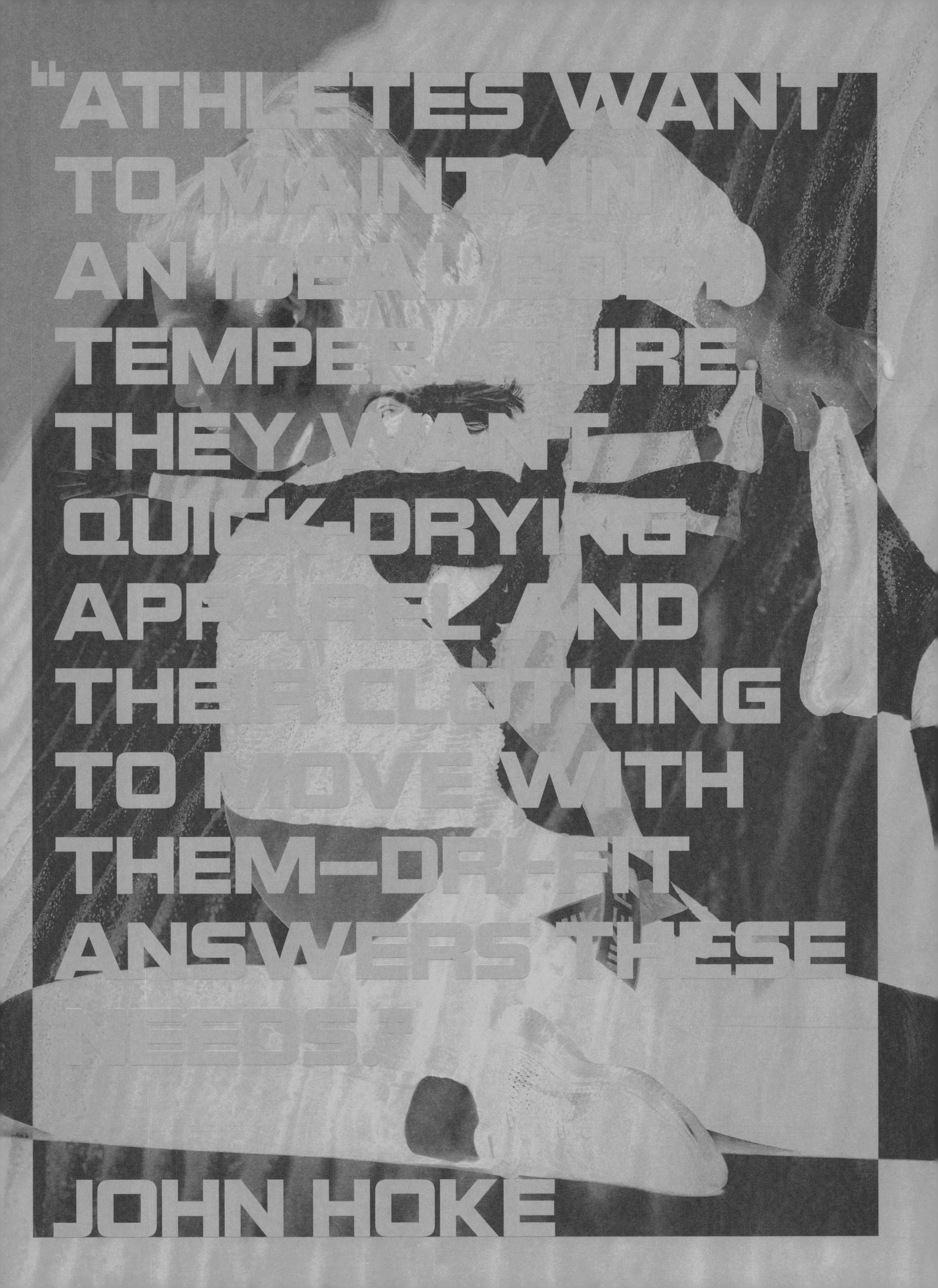

"ATHLETES WANT TO MAINTAIN AN IDEAL BODY TEMPERATURE. THEY WANT QUICK-DRYING APPAREL AND THE CLOTHING TO MOVE WITH THEM—DRI-FIT ANSWERS THESE NEEDS."

JOHN HOKE

MOISTURE VAPOR
PASSES THROUGH
HYDROPHOBIC FACE FABRIC

SKIN

SWEAT

ART DIRECTION: OKSANA ANI
PHOTOGRAPHER: BRENDAN COUGHLIN
LOCATION PRODUCER: SHAUN DALEY
NIKE NXT F-18

MOISTURE ABS
INTO HYDROPH
YARN SIDE ONL

MOISTURE WICK
OFF OF SKIN

Pro Luxe Tight	2020

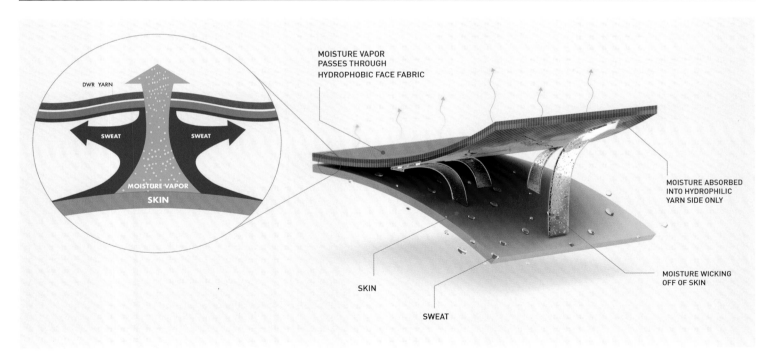

Computer rendering illustrating Stealth Evaporation Fabric technology	c.2019

As a rule, Nike eschews a one-size-fits-all approach to creation, believing that hyper-specific problem-solving unlocks greater innovation. Stealth Evaporation Fabric demonstrates how these seemingly contradictory aims intersect. The 2020 technology was developed in response to the requests of female athletes to hide visible signs of sweat. Building on the Dri-FIT platform, the fabric uniquely combines moisture-wicking yarns and durable water resistant yarns in a double-knit construction that manages sweat and disperses it over a greater surface area on the inside of the fabric, minimizing its appearance on the outside. The technology debuted on women's Pro Collection base garments but was quickly appropriated for use in unanticipated ways, such as mitigating leaks in the (M) Swoosh Bra.

| Nike × Gyakusou Knit Hoodie | 2020 |

| Details of Therma-FIT fabric | 2020 |

Just as Dri-FIT paved the way for the creation of AeroAdapt, the evolution of another member of the original FIT family, Therma-FIT, demonstrates Nike's dogma of constant progress. Upon its debut in 2020, Therma-FIT introduced a patented technology that kept athletes warmer without significantly increasing the weight of their garments. For the first time, the breathable, engineered technology incorporated zoned warmth and airflow into one responsive, lightweight knit fabric. The material aimed to maintain its wearer's optimal performance temperature, which Nike Sport Research Lab (NSRL) data posited felt like 74 degrees Fahrenheit (23 degrees Celsius) and sunny. This new class of Dri-FIT launched as part of the Gyakusou Spring 2020 Collection on a knit running hoodie and pants.

| CruzrOne | Bright Crimson/White-Black-Electric Green | 2019 |

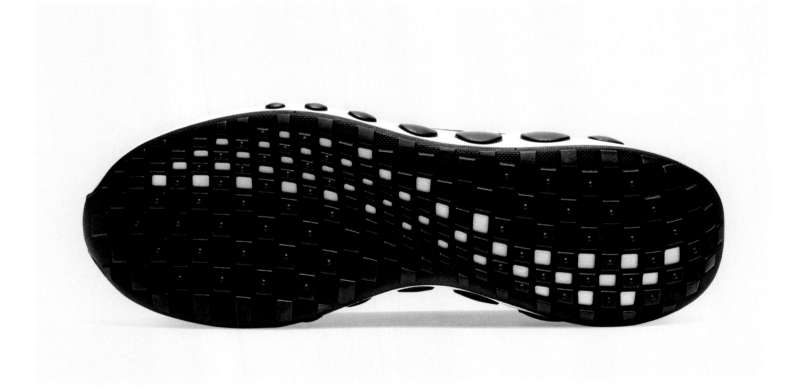

| CruzrOne outsole | | 2019 |

Whether enhancing athletic performance, democratizing sport, or both, Nike innovations catalyze a chain reaction: they enable human potential, which leads to more insights, which advances innovation, which provides access to even more athletes. Enter the 2019 CruzrOne, Nike's first running shoe designed for really slow runs—or "cruises," as its designer Tinker Hatfield calls them. Although the shoe targets a new demographic for Nike, it takes inspiration from the company's cofounder Phil Knight, who at eighty-two years old defined his daily 8-mile (13-kilometer) workouts not as walks but as "really slow runs." To better address the physical nuances of cruising, Hatfield united a naturally propelling, rocker-shape sole and flexible, segmented outsole with a comfortable, easy-to-don, two-way stretch upper and padded, shearling-lined collar.

CruzrOne campaign patches

2019

"I DON'T WALK.
I RUN !
JUST REALLY,
REALLY SLOWLY."

PHIL KNIGHT

5 PLAYGROUND EARTH

Air Max 1	Air VaporMax Flyknit Be True	Air VaporMax Flyknit Random 2
Air Max 90	ZoomX Vista Grind	FE/NOM Flyknit Bra
Air Max 180	Considered Boot	Zoom Vaporfly Elite Flyprint
Air Max 93	Considered Mowabb II	Flyleather Cortez
Air Max 95	Considered Humara	Flyleather Air Force 1 SE
Air Max 97	Considered Tiempo	Flyleather Jordan 1 SE
Air Max Plus	Considered Gem Shoe	Flyleather Air Max 90 SE
Air Max 360	Considered BB High	Flyleather Cortez SE
Air Max 2015	Considered Rock Shoe	Space Hippie 01
Air VaporMax Flyknit	Flyknit Trainer	Space Hippie 02
Air Max 270	Flyknit Racer	Space Hippie 03
Air Max 720	Flyknit Racer Be True	Move to Zero Collection
Air VaporMax CS	Flyknit Air Max	Team USA Medal Stand Collection
Air VaporMax 2019	Mercurial Superfly FG	
Air VaporMax Flyknit 2.0	Free Flyknit 3.0	

"It is a well-provisioned ship, this on which we sail through space," Henry George wrote in 1879's *Progress and Poverty*. "If the bread and beef above decks seem to grow scarce, we but open a hatch and there is a new supply, of which before we never dreamed." While his view of the earth as a single life-sustaining vessel in the vast reaches of space was astute, over the course of the following century, we as its passengers have come to understand the folly of believing the supplies were limitless and the ship itself required little upkeep. "We have not been seeing our Spaceship Earth as an integrally designed machine," cautioned visionary designer Buckminster Fuller, furthering the analogy in 1969's *Operating Manual for Spaceship Earth.* "You're either going to have to keep the machine in good order or it's going to be in trouble and fail to function."

As we sail toward the second quarter of the twenty-first century, the machine's warning lights are flashing red. Temperatures are rising. Weather patterns are changing. Oceans are warming. Biomes are threatened. Resources are depleting. Despite the fact that we now possess incredible scientific understanding of the interplay and interdependence of our planet's complex natural systems—and the effects of human activity upon them—obfuscation, ignorance, and inertia remain an acceptable solution in some quarters. There is an ever-tightening window within which to stave off catastrophic disaster, and doing so will require upending a way of life that has evolved without taking the planet's limitations into account. Alarmist though it may sound, the future of our species— projected to grow in number to ten billion by 2050—is not assured.

Dating at least back to the 1990s, executives at Nike saw the writing on the wall: a future without a planet is a future without sport. During a period when the company faced intense pressure to address labor issues in its supply chain, Nike also began to formulate a complementary strategy to lessen its environmental footprint. This didn't happen because customers demanded it but because the company knew it was the right thing to do, and the only way it could ensure a sustainable future—one where athletes everywhere would have access to safe places to play and train. In the early 2000s the company laid out goals for 2020 that included eliminating waste in product design, eliminating substances that are known or suspected to be harmful to human health, taking responsibility for the entire life cycle of products, and developing new financial models to reflect the full cost (environmental, social, and otherwise) of doing business. By 2016, when Nike released its biannual Sustainable Business Report, these had evolved to encompass doubling the business while halving the impact. Scaling sustainability throughout Nike's entire value chain was, and is, the intended goal. As a side effect, the relentless challenge of searching for new, more environmentally attuned solutions— and of working within the strict confines of the stated targets—unlocked game-changing innovations that transformed how the company, and its consumers and competitors, view footwear and sportswear design. In other words, sustainability at Nike isn't just an extra talking point; it's integral to the future of the business.

For example, look no further than Nike Air, the iconic technology at the heart of the company's most successful designs. Utilized by Nike as a form of shock-absorbent cushioning since the late 1970s, Air was the brainchild of aerospace engineer Marion Franklin Rudy, who had envisioned placing tiny air units in the soles of athletic shoes to soften impact and provide a smoother ride. Initially the Air bladders were filled with perfluoroethane gas (Freon 116), which, after being discontinued by chemical company DuPont in 1989, was replaced with sulfur hexafluoride (SF_6). Both gases worked because they were stable, nonflammable, and, most important for the design and longevity of the Air units, made up from large molecules that were easily contained. But when *StiftungWarentest*, a German consumer magazine, ran an article about the warming effects of greenhouse gases, SF_6 was included among the culprits. Although few nations were regulating against it, Nike determined that it needed to find an alternative to protect the future of the franchise—and the planet.

At the outset no one suspected that the search would entail more than a decade of research and development from an internal innovation and engineering team, consultations with sixty experts from more than fifty external organizations, and a massive capital investment in customized equipment for testing and analysis. "I thought I was going to get fired for being the guy who took the air out of Nike Air," recalls former chief operating officer Eric Sprunk, who at the time led the footwear division. The search for a sustainable alternative for Air led the team to nitrogen, a benign gas that met Nike's performance standards without contributing to global warming. The problem was that nitrogen has a much smaller molecular structure than SF_6 and was therefore harder to encapsulate. "We probably had 200 different trials," recalls Sprunk, "and 199 of them didn't work."

Undaunted, the team pushed forward with a proprietary process of extruding thermoplastic polyurethane (TPU) pellets into large sheets from which the Air units are made. To contain the nitrogen molecules, each sheet contains seventy-four micro-layers running in alternating directions with a barrier layer the thickness of a human hair at its core. The new approach also led the team to develop a new kind of encapsulation technology called thermoforming, which allows for the manufacture of hollow or double-walled 3-D Air units. The innovation, which remains one of the company's most coveted trade secrets, unlocked a variety of new possibilities for Air—including bigger, better, more responsive Air units. The Air Max 360 was the first shoe produced with the process, and it was not a coincidence that it was the first to be fully cushioned by Air from heel to toe.

By 2006 the company had transitioned entirely from SF_6 and was working to further eliminate waste from the Air manufacturing process. Today, at Nike's three Air Manufacturing Innovation (MI) facilities, more than 90 percent of waste is recycled back into the product. Innovations such as the super-responsive Zoom Air cushioning system, in which tightly stretched tensile fibers are knit inside a pressurized Air unit; the best-selling Air VaporMax shoe, and the huge colored Air units of the Air Max 270 have only been possible because of technological advances that resulted from the transition to nitrogen. Sprunk explains, "We were spending the entire innovation budget on something that ultimately might not even be appreciated by the consumer! But it was a great challenge that eventually taught us that sustainability can be a catalyst for innovation."

Hannah Jones—who was appointed as Nike's first chief sustainability officer in 2004 and is now president of Nike Valiant Labs, the company's new business incubator—was instrumental in Nike's acceleration of sustainability as a driving force for innovation and growth. Jones joined Nike in the late 1990s. "It was not a very good career move or social maneuver at the time," she recounts, "but I felt convinced that if my platform was about social and environmental impact, and I could go work for a major company that was in a crisis but wanted to change—then that was a bet worth taking." Her early efforts working with factories, community groups, employees, and business leaders taught her that the issues at hand were inseparable and could only be addressed through holistic, systemic change—and that Nike's innovation and design teams would be integral to the process. She found willing partners in chairman Mark Parker and chief design officer John Hoke, who pushed for each of Nike's designers to become advocates and champions for sustainability.

At the outset Jones and her nascent team had no shortage of white space to operate within. "Sometimes the really important part of innovation and design is the unsexy bit, which is actually finding evidence and truth to inform what your constraints should be," she explains. To that end they spent six years and millions of dollars to perform an environmental analysis on each of the seventy-five thousand entries in Nike's materials library and built a database with their findings. The work was crucial to any future efforts, because materials are estimated to account for 63 percent of the environmental impact during the life cycle of a pair of shoes, from raw materials through the end of a product's useful life. Utilizing their database, the team developed a tool to provide designers with more informed choices (and alternatives) during the design process, and to rank every Nike product with a sustainability score based on specific environmental impact areas of chemistry, energy, water, and waste, as well as whether the materials in the given product use recycled or organic content. Subsequently Jones's team transformed this data into the Nike Materials Sustainability Index (MSI), one of a handful of indices—the others being for footwear, apparel, manufacturing, and risk—that offer the company accurate metrics of success.

As Nike invested more of its resources into the effort, leadership realized that if the ultimate goal was change at scale, then it made sense to share as much of their work as possible. "We're very competitive, so we want to protect our innovations and intellectual property," says Parker. "But this is one of those areas where I think it's important to collaborate more and team up with the right other groups, industries, and academic partners. Not only to lessen our own footprint but to make a bigger impact."

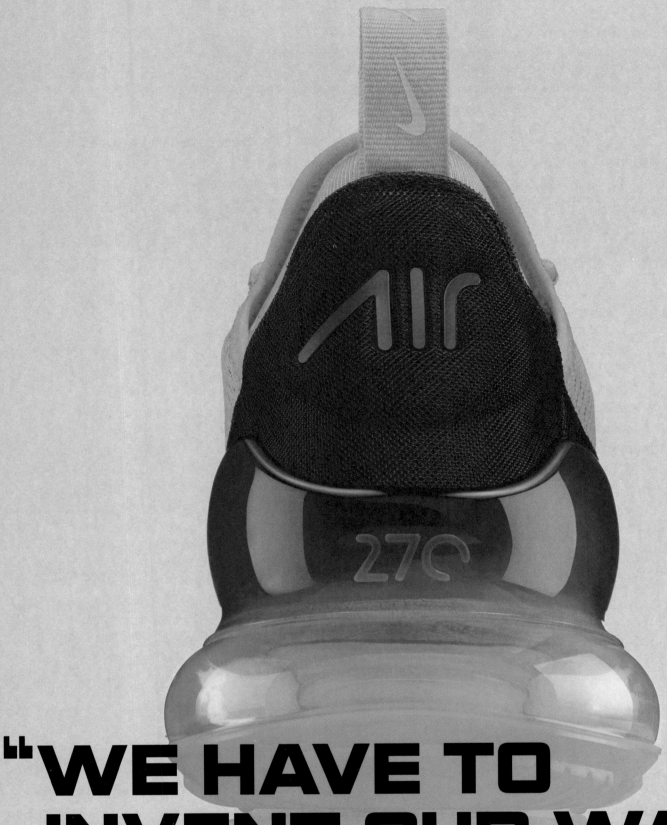

"WE HAVE TO INVENT OUR WAY INTO THE FUTURE."

HANNAH JONES

50% RECYCLED MATERIALS

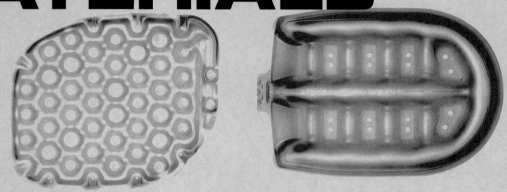

PRODUCED WITH 100% RENEWABLE WIND ENERGY

"Even though we're really large, we're only one small part of an industry that's entirely codependent on the same resources," Jones adds. "If we don't work together, the supply chains won't change." While a lot of that collaboration happens behind the scenes in what Jones refers to as a "pre-competitive" environment, other Nike efforts to share its work have been far more public. In 2013 the company debuted the MAKING app, a free educational tool for designers that integrates data from the MSI to help inform smarter materials choices. Select from one of forty-five materials categories, and it instantly serves up comparisons with suitable alternatives based on chemistry, energy use, water use, and waste.

While the work behind the MSI and MAKING app were indicative of the operational effectiveness that Jones and her team built up within the organization so they could scale sustainable practices globally, the roots of sustainability at Nike extend back even further. In 1993 Nike employee Steve Potter began experimenting with shredding old shoes to see if he could create a useful material out of one of the company's most abundant forms of waste. By separating the shoes into their component parts, breaking them down into small granules, and reconstituting them, Nike began to produce a variety of shock-absorbent surface materials that could be used in a variety of applications, including playgrounds and athletic fields. Annually, Nike Grind (as these recycled materials became collectively known) utilizes tens of millions of pounds of manufacturing scraps, unsold merchandise, and postconsumer goods collected through Nike's Reuse-A-Shoe program (through which Nike retailers collect any old sneakers—of any brand—to recycle). Starting with a single basketball court in 1994, the program has since recycled more than 120 million pounds (nearly 55 million kilograms) of footwear factory material, equivalent to the weight of approximately seven hundred jumbo jets, and transformed thirty million pairs of athletic shoes—material that would otherwise have been considered "waste"—into running tracks, games courts, playgrounds, and other surfaces. Notably, the Grind materials from Nike products are even recycled back into the brand's own products, including footwear, apparel, and various synthetic textiles and yarns.

It's no coincidence that the approach is reminiscent of the closed-loop upcycling model proffered in *Cradle to Cradle: Remaking the Way We Make Things*, Michael Braungart and William McDonough's highly influential 2002 treatise on sustainable manufacturing. McDonough gained prominence in the 1990s with a pioneering approach to environmentally effective architecture that informed the United States Green Building Council's LEED certification program. In 1997 Nike engaged his firm to design its European headquarters in Hilversum, the Netherlands. The following year McDonough and Braungart—a chemist by training—were contracted to help Nike adopt their Cradle to Cradle (C2C) approach. As outlined in Nike's first corporate responsibility report from 2001, the pair helped set the company on a path to "ultimately design products of consumption that can be safely returned to the earth, and products of service that remain in technical cycles, using technical nutrients."

Nike's goal was to embed sustainably focused principles into every stage of the value chain, and designers took it upon themselves to help lead the way. Designed by Mike Aveni in 2000, the Air Woven featured a unique upper woven from strips of nylon and rubber to cut back on material waste, stitching, and adhesives. The Presto Clip, conceived by retired Nike designer Bruce Kilgore in 2003, offered a novel construction whereby the upper snapped into the midsole without the use of glues. In 2005 these initial efforts came to a head with the Considered line, the company's first consolidated attempt to design footwear within the explicit boundaries of a C2C approach—and to concertedly manifest that effort in the product through a deliberate aesthetic. It was also an effective strategy to bring sustainable design into the mainstream. That same year, Toyota's instantly recognizable Prius hybrid rose to prominence by empowering consumers to openly declare their values through their choice of vehicle. Spearheaded by design lead Richard Clarke, the Considered line's vocabulary of veg-tanned leather, woven hemp, cotton canvas, and recycled rubber containing Grind stood in sharp contrast to the more technical, futuristic approach commonly associated with the brand and gave consumers a platform to express their ideals. But Considered also walked the walk. With fewer production steps, less stitching, and discrete components, the line reduced solvent use by 80 percent, required 37 percent less energy use to manufacture, and created 63 percent less waste than comparable Nike products. Even though Considered never achieved massive mainstream success, internally it continues to be viewed as an influential turning point for Nike's approach to sustainable materials and methods of making—a tool kit for the future.

Going forward, Nike's innovation and design teams realized that if they wanted to design the products of the future, their manufacturing methods would have to be redesigned as well. Traditionally shoes have been made by stitching together cutout pieces of materials in what could be described as a reductive process. With Considered, certain parts of the uppers were woven from a single shoelace, using only the length of material required—an additive process. "Instead of buying a textile and cutting it and stitching all the constituent pieces together," explains Michael Donaghu, vice president of Innovation, "it's about bringing the right ingredients together to produce what you need in real time on the manufacturing floor."

The other critical factor driving Nike's approach was to ensure that it was leading with innovations that mattered most to the customer. "I don't think people buy solely for sustainability," says Jones. "When they go into the store, they make a choice based on performance, or aesthetic, or price, depending on where they're coming from. And that's OK because I think that you should be able to have your cake and eat it. This false promise that was made by the sustainability movement—that people will buy sustainability and they'll be willing to compromise on those other things—was lazy thinking." Instead, Jones and her team recognized that the tipping point for the movement would come when the sustainable option represented the better choice precisely because of its ability to meet all of those other criteria.

These premises soon coalesced into a singular strategy that has propelled Nike from one disruptive innovation to the next. By harnessing, developing, and inventing new capabilities to deliver designs that are higher-performing, aesthetically pioneering, and covetable—*and* just so happen to be better for the planet—the company has achieved exponential success by addressing the uncertainties of running a twenty-first-century global business head-on.

Take the example of Flyknit. In 2001 an innovation team at Nike were asked to respond to an internal design brief that sought to eliminate the conventional methods of combining footwear components, and began to experiment with the possibility of knitting the entire upper of a shoe in real time (on the fly, so to speak). After years of trial and error, they eventually adapted and hacked commercial knitting machines to knit recycled polyester filaments into a workable prototype. Driven by computational design, each stitch in a Flyknit pattern is micro-engineered in sequence, opening up new worlds of aesthetic possibilities for pattern, texture, and color, and allowing for the designer to define optimal zones of flexibility, tension, porousness, and breathability around the foot to enhance fit, comfort, and performance. When Nike debuted its Flyknit Racer in the summer of 2012, it not only looked like nothing that had come before but was also significantly lighter than Nike's most comparable cut-and-stitch model. By virtue of its construction, Flyknit also utilizes a high percentage of recycled content while offering on average 60 percent less waste than traditional upper manufacturing. Because the technology was integrated throughout Nike's various lines, from running to basketball to lifestyle to apparel, the environmental benefits accrued accordingly.

One of the most startling uses of Flyknit, and one that demonstrates Nike's commitment to iterative design exploration, is 2017's FE/NOM Flyknit Bra. Bras, which can boast up to forty-one pieces and twenty-two seams, have traditionally been one of the singularly most wasteful and energy-consuming garments in production. Nike senior creative director for Bra Design and Innovation Nicole Rendone and her team began to collaborate with the footwear teams with the goal of taking Flyknit from the foot to the body for the first time, not only to address the environmental impact but also to create a superior product. Based on more than six hundred hours of rigorous biometric testing and interviews, FE/NOM was created specifically to address the problems of athletes with larger cup sizes. Flyknit's dimensionality allowed the designers to micro-engineer optimum compression, comfort, breathability, and support throughout the garment. Featuring only two knit panels and a binding, it generates less waste than typical Nike sports bras while also using fewer resources to produce.

At Nike, one good innovation always begets another. The ongoing success of Flyknit led the company to double down on its strategy of working further and further upstream in the product cycle. In 2016 the company opened the Advanced Product Creation Center (APCC) on its Beaverton, Oregon, campus to give designers easy access to a wide range of production methodologies and manufacturing tools. Now, instead of waiting weeks for samples to come back from an overseas supplier, a designer can walk across campus to make and test a new prototype in a matter of hours. The APCC also acts like something of an industrial playground to enable critical exploration, experimentation, and invention—spurring on such advances as Flyprint, Nike's first 3-D-printed textile upper. With Flyprint, TPU filament is unwound from a coil, melted, and laid down in layers, allowing designers to translate athlete data into new, never-before-seen textile geometries while eliminating weight, additive glues, and stitching. It's already being used to create some of the most advanced shoes in Nike's lineup, including the Zoom Vaporfly Elite Flyprint.

The directive to work further upstream in the design process propelled the company to reexamine another classic but environmentally challenging material. Before the invention of advanced performance textiles such as engineered mesh and Flyknit, leather was the go-to material of choice for athletes, and is still deemed irreplaceable for products like football boots and baseball cleats. However, its manufacture is energy-intensive, requiring a lot of chemicals during the leather tanning process and resulting in a great deal of leftover scrap material. Born from a challenge to evolve leather into a modern performance material while simultaneously reducing its carbon footprint, Flyleather is an engineered leather that is made up of at least 50 percent leather fiber—including leftover leather scraps—along with synthetic fibers and a fabric infrastructure. Flyleather mimics full-grain leather from fit to touch and smell, but because it comes on a roll (and not in the shape of a cow), it offers a much higher degree of efficiency and consistency.

While each step Nike takes toward embedding sustainability across the company is significant, it is still on a journey to circularity—where, as Cradle to Cradle outlines, organic nutrients are returned to the earth and technical nutrients are returned to the production cycle. "You can't be an employee of a big consumer-product company and think the way we do things is OK," Donaghu declares with urgency. "This has to be one of the most vexing issues that any company that gives a damn is working on." One of the company's newest collections was created as a means of establishing just how far Nike could push sustainability in the here and now. Space Hippie, so named for its combination of outer-space survivalism and communal optimism, is thus far as much a collection of four sneakers as a completely revolutionary mind-set toward product design. The brainchild of a small team of designers within the NXT Space Kitchen tasked with next-generation sustainability, the collection originated with a deep dive into Nike's materials science data. The breakthrough came from discovering that all the remnants of existing products had already been accounted for statistically. Using only the leftovers as a starting point for the design led the team to think differently about why a product should be what it is and look the way it does. Some of the familiar Nike design vocabulary is there—Flyknit, ZoomX, Grind—but Space Hippie reimagines these through the constraints of a lower carbon footprint (the shoes in the collection contain at least 25 percent recycled content by weight) with wholly original results. The flecked gray yarn, a random blend of post-consumer waste, including T-shirt textiles and water bottles; the chunky blue foam, a result of running recycled material back into the machines that make soles all day; the unrefined glue marks and finish details, a determination to expend less energy in production. As the march toward circularity continues deep within Nike's innovation laboratories, the Space Hippie ethos will manifest across Nike in new and surprising ways.

Nike's decades-long aspiration to become one of the world's most sustainable brands may not exactly be obvious to the casual observer, which is by strategy. "What we're not interested in is doing one-off collections here and there and pumping out some PR around this or that green product," says Parker. "It's a huge, core area of focus for us, embedded in all of the aspects of our business, the whole value chain, end to end, enterprise-wide." And the numbers—whether you look at manufacturing, materials, waste, water use, renewable energy, toxins, and reuse—are there to back him up.

"We're not doing it because it's cute," says Jones. "We're setting ourselves up to be a twenty-first-century business that can thrive." None of what's happened at Nike over the last two decades is magic pulled from a hat. The company's path to becoming sustainable has been hard-won and methodical, resulting from intense scenario planning and dogged, incremental improvement toward an ultimate goal. Noel Kinder, who was named chief sustainability officer when Jones moved into her new role, confirms the company's deliberate approach. "I am building on an incredible legacy of sustainability at Nike. Across the enterprise we've strategically integrated teams with sustainability at their core to help us accelerate our efforts in achieving our future goals," he says, pointing to how this drive has impacted almost every aspect of the business, from innovation and design to manufacturing, retail, facilities, communications, and procurement. "One of the things that inspires me most about this role is that I get to figure out how to harness the energy of thousands of employees who all care about this really, really intently. A lot of times we just have to provide the spark, enable the passion and power that exists here, and direct it in ways that help us to achieve our targets and the ambition to move to zero." For the company to reach its stated goal of zero carbon and zero waste, Kinder is mobilizing a broader team effort.

William Gibson, the cyberpunk science fiction author, once said, "The future is already here—it's just not very evenly distributed," and that's precisely how Nike's sustainability teams have been able to see around corners. Looking at macro forces and micro trends in society, politics, economics, climate, resources, and consumption has led them to envision the world where the company needs to be tomorrow, as well as ten years from now. When it comes to sustainability, there are no easy answers, no time-outs, and no finish lines. As Jones says, "We have to invent our way into the future."

| Air Max 1 and Air unit | White/Light Neutral Grey/Light Royal Blue | 1987 |

| Air Max 90 and Air unit | White/Zane Grey/Concord-Fluorescent Pink | 1990 |

| Air Max 180 and Air unit | White/Sapphire/Hot Lime | 1991 |

| Air Max 93 and Air unit | White/Laser Lime/Royal Blue | 1993 |

| Air Max 95 and Air unit | White/Wild Grape-New Green | 1995 |

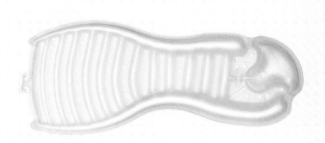

| Air Max 97 and Air unit | Metallic Silver/Polar-White-Obsidian | 1997 |

| Air Max Plus and Air unit | Machine Grey/Ceramic-Midnight Navy | 1998 |

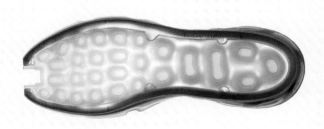

| Air Max 360 and Air unit | Metallic Silver/True White-Deep Royal | 2006 |

| Air Max 2015 and Air unit | Light Iron Ore/White-Tumbled Grey-Bright Crimson | 2015 |

| Air VaporMax Flyknit and Air unit | Pure Platinum/University Red-Wolf Grey | 2017 |

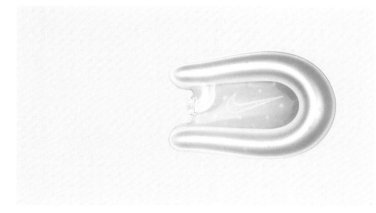

| Air Max 270 and Air unit | Barely Rose/Elemental Rose/White/Vintage Wine | 2018 |

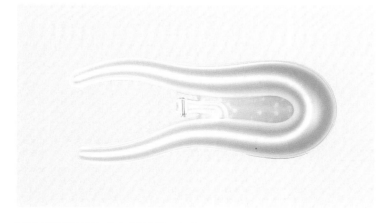

| Air Max 720 and Air unit | Hyper Grape/Black-Hyper Pink | 2019 |

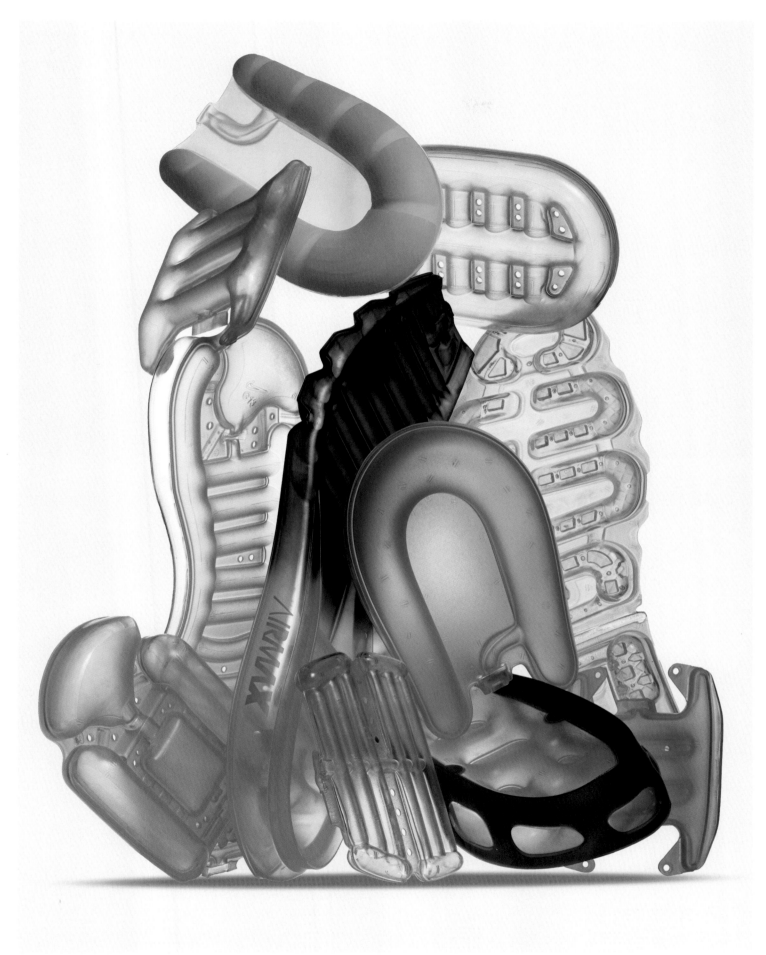

When the show-and-tell aesthetic named Visible Air entered the public lexicon in 1987 with the arrival of the Air Max 1, it featured Air units filled with sulfur hexafluoride (SF_6), which five years later was exposed as a greenhouse gas. The news prompted an internal race at Nike to replace the pollutant without conceding performance or aesthetic.

A decade of trial and error led to a proprietary manufacturing process using nitrogen that unlocked Nike's ability to create the bigger, more responsive Air units that have continuously evolved the Nike Air line. Moreover, the nitrogen-base bags established sustainability as a springboard for future-forward innovation.

Air unit production	Air Manufacturing Innovation facility, Nike World Headquarters, Beaverton, Oregon	c.2019

Nike's first sneaker to cushion the entire sole with a bed of Air, the 2006 Air Max 360 introduced a new Air era. Specifically, it leveraged the company's updated Air manufacturing process, which extruded thermoplastic polyurethane (TPU) pellets into large sheets that contained nitrogen molecules and introduced an encapsulation technology called thermoforming, facilitating the creation of double-walled 3-D Air units and the partition of individual Air bubbles. This capability allowed Nike designers to replace traditional foam with rubber caging, providing more comfort with less weight and advancing the company's dream of enabling athletes to run exclusively on Air.

| Air Max 360 | Metallic Silver/White-Anthracite-Varsity Red | 2006 |

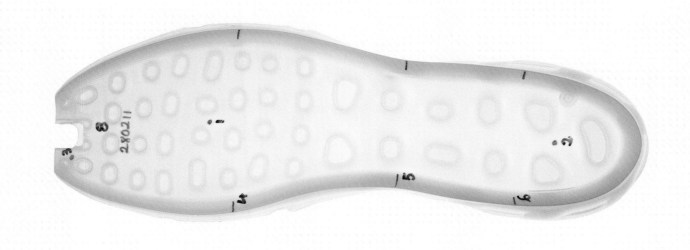

| Air Max 360 Air unit | 2006 |

| Air Max 360 outsole | 2006 |

| Air VaporMax Air unit | 2016 |

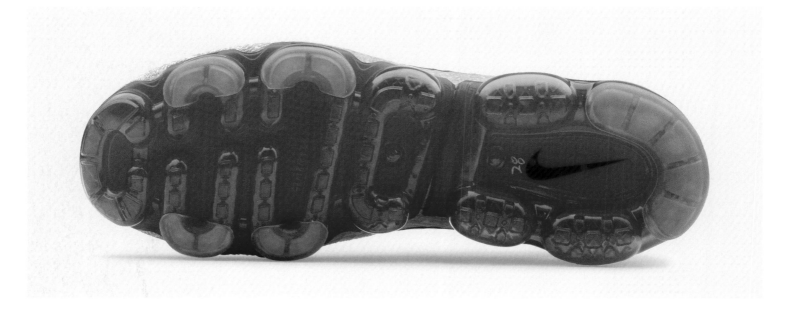

| Air VaporMax outsole | 2016 |

| Air VaporMax outsole | 2017 |

More than forty years into the Air legacy, the Air VaporMax paid off the promise of a stand-alone Air outsole. Its advanced technologies eliminated the need for Air units to be encapsulated in a secondary protective, durable rubber layer. They also discarded the requirement for inflexible structural areas that defined past Air silhouettes. Allowing for greater elasticity and amplified geometries, it placed even more Air underfoot and completely disposed of a traditional foam midsole. Reduced waste was a purposeful by-product of the evolved manufacturing method—an outcome augmented by the design's Flyknit upper, which further diminished its weight and environmental footprint.

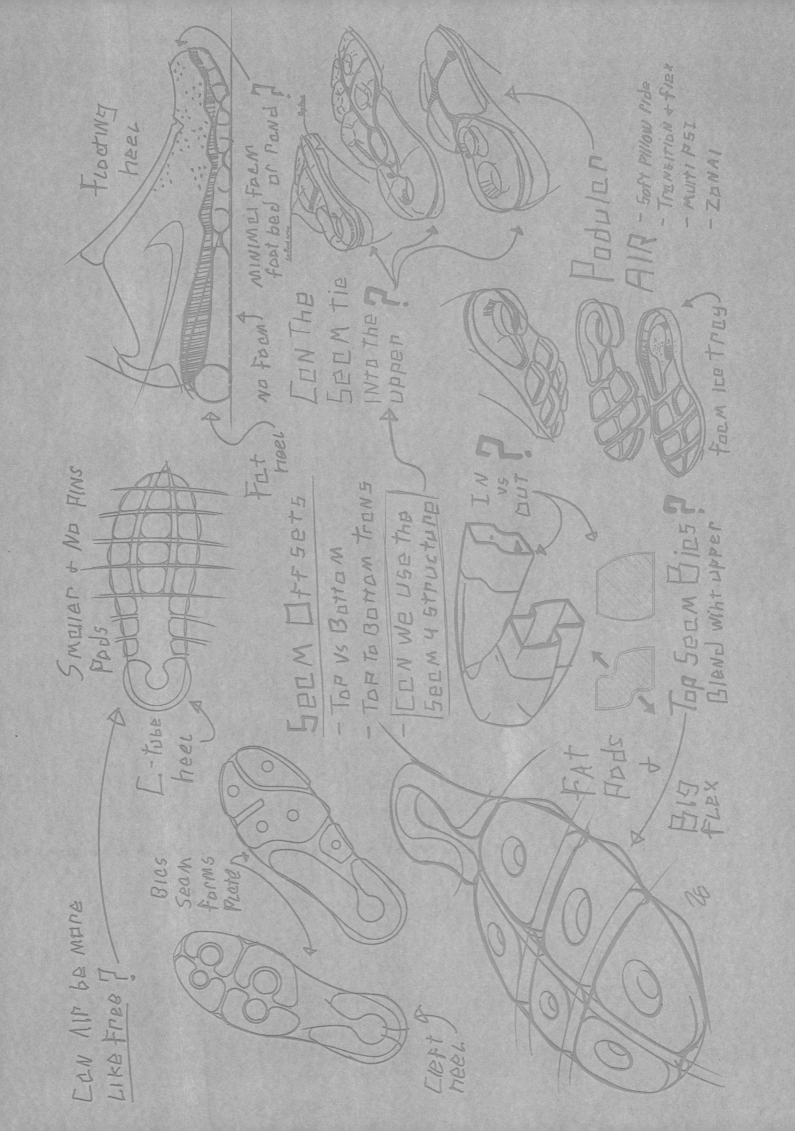

Can Air be more
like Free?

Smaller + No Fins
Pods

C-Tube
heel

Bies Seam
Forms Plate?

Cleft
heel

Floating
heel

no Foam↑
Fat
heel

Minimal Foam
foot bed or Pond?

Can The
Seam Tie
Into the
upper ?

Seam Offsets
- Top vs Bottom
- Top to Bottom Trans
- Can we use the
Seam 4 structure

IN
vs
OUT
?

Fat
Pods
+

Big
Flex

Top Seam Bies?
Blend wiht upper

Podular

AIR - Soft Pillow Ride
- Transition + Flex
- Multi PSI
- Zonal

Foam ice Tray)

"THE FALSE MATH IS THAT IF YOU'RE SUSTAINABLE, YOU'RE GOING TO BE MORE EXPEN-SIVE AND YOU'RE GOING TO PERFORM LESS WELL. GO TELL THAT TO THE ATHLETES WHO WON GOLD IN FLYKNIT."

HANNAH JONES

Air VaporMax CS	Black/Black-Black-Anthracite	2017

Air VaporMax 2019	Black/Black-Black	2019

Air VaporMax Flyknit	Hyper Punch/Pink Blast	2017

Air VaporMax Flyknit	Pure Platinum/White-Wolf Grey	2017

Air VaporMax Flyknit	Sample colorway	2016

Air VaporMax Flyknit	White/Neutral Grey-Ice Blue	2017

Air VaporMax Flyknit 2.0	Black/Hot Punch-White-Dusty Cactus-Aluminum-Anthracite	2018

Air VaporMax Flyknit Be True	Deep Royal Blue/Concord-White-Pink Blast	2017

Air Max 270	Black/Coal Black/White/Sun Red	2018

Air Max 270	White/White-Volt	2018

Air Max 270 Be True and outsole	Purple Dawn/Pink Blast/Multi-Color-Black	2018

Air Max 270 and outsole	White/White-Hot Punch	2018

Air Max 270	Elemental Gold/Black-Light Bone-White	2018

Air Max 270	Black/University Gold-Hot Punch-White	2018

Air Max 720	Team Crimson/Met Red Bronze/Gym Red	2019

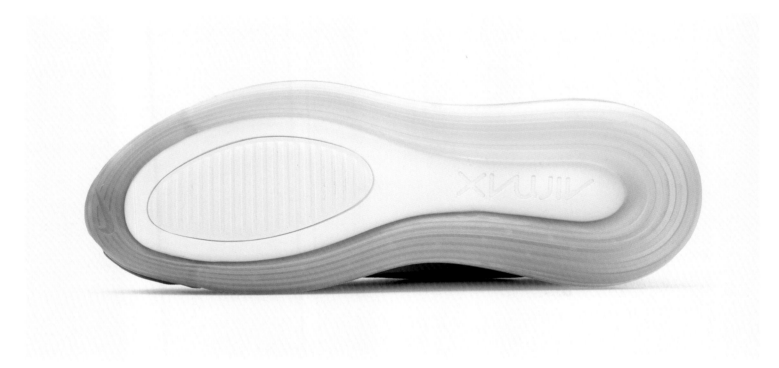

Air Max 720 outsole		2019

Uniting manufacturing upgrades with the company's iterative ethos, Nike designers continuously explore the shape of Air. Infusing even more volume and incorporating even more recycled manufacturing waste into Air units, they have conscientiously developed the performance innovation for a spectrum of activities. The Air Max 270 and Air Max 720 exemplify this progression.

Upon its 2018 arrival, the Air Max 270 billed itself as the first 100 percent lifestyle Air shoe. Whereas past lifestyle Air models—starting with the 1987 Air Safari—incorporated Air units originally created for running, the Air Max 270 introduced an entirely new design. Measuring 1¼ inches (32 millimeters) high, the heel bag was—at the time of its reveal—the tallest in Air unit history, promising maximum cushioning and comfort. The Air Max 270 silhouette also notably nods to the greater Air legacy: its name comes from an internal Nike moniker for the Air Max 93, referencing the 270 degrees of visibility provided by its Air unit, whereas its socklike upper takes inspiration from the Air Max 180.

The Air Max 720 arrived just one year later, in 2019, overtaking the Air Max 270 with an unprecedented 1½-inch (38-millimeter) heel-to-toe Air unit that earned it accolades as the first full-length lifestyle Air Max unit. Its 360-degree form creates a cradle for the foot and prompted the silhouette's name. The number 720 expresses the idea that the Air unit is visible in 360 degrees times two: horizontally and vertically. The extreme unit's volume boasts the additional achievement of containing more than 75 percent of manufacturing waste. From creation to reinvention, the ongoing evolution of Air evidences Nike's belief that steady momentum, not just the occasional standout moment, ultimately transforms the game.

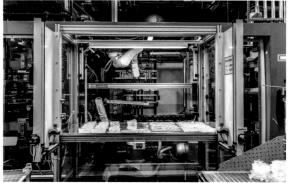

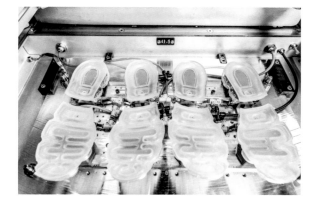

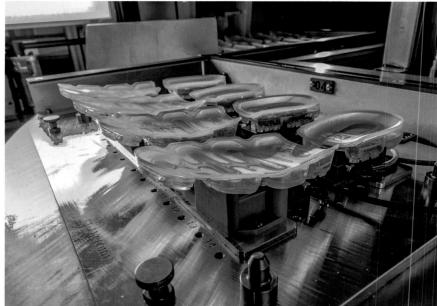

Air unit production	Air Manufacturing Innovation facility, Nike World Headquarters, Beaverton, Oregon	2017

Nike continues to expand the possibilities of Air from its Air Manufacturing Innovation (MI) facilities in Beaverton, Oregon; St. Louis, Missouri; and Goodyear, Arizona. Each endeavors to develop sustainable materials and new methods that decrease environmental impact and increase performance by recycling 90 percent of manufacturing waste back into the product and requiring a minimum of 50 percent recycled materials in all Air unit innovation. This commitment extends beyond the Air units into the facilities themselves, which divert more than 95 percent of their manufacturing waste from landfills and, as of December 2019, are run exclusively on renewable wind energy.

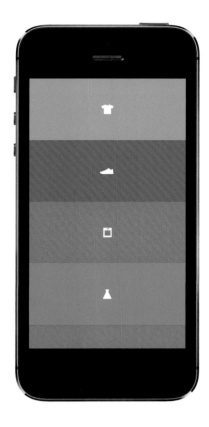

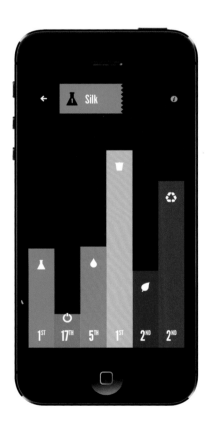

MAKING app	2013

In 2004, led by Nike's first chief sustainability officer, Hannah Jones, and driven by stats suggesting that materials account for approximately 63 percent of a shoe's life-cycle environmental impact, Nike embarked on a six-year mission to audit all 75,000 entries in its materials library. In 2013 the resulting Materials Sustainability Index (MSI) was integrated into the MAKING app. The free educational app empowers designers to replace traditionally manufactured materials with sustainable, functionally suitable alternatives analyzed for chemistry, energy use, water use, and waste. It also evidences Nike's proactive and prominent role in revolutionizing global supply chains.

| Nike Grind processing facility (above and opposite) | Memphis, Tennessee | 2013 |

"Progress in both innovation and design," says Hannah Jones, "is about rechallenging mental models. If you challenge the mental model of what materials are, suddenly the world is your oyster." Nike Grind proves this premise. The brainchild of Nike employee Steve Potter, who in 1993 imagined shredding shoes into reusable materials, Grind is a palette of rubber, foam, fiber, leather, and blended textile granules created from athletic shoes' component parts. The materials were initially transformed into sport surfaces, beginning with an indoor basketball court for the Boys & Girls Club at the Brooklyn Navy Yard, in New York City, that debuted in 1994.

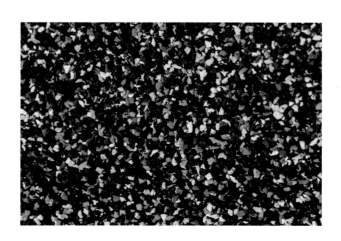

| Nike Grind processing facility and products from the Circular Innovation Challenge | Memphis, Tennessee | 2013–18 |

ZoomX Vista Grind	Barely Volt/Electric Green/Starfish/Black	2019

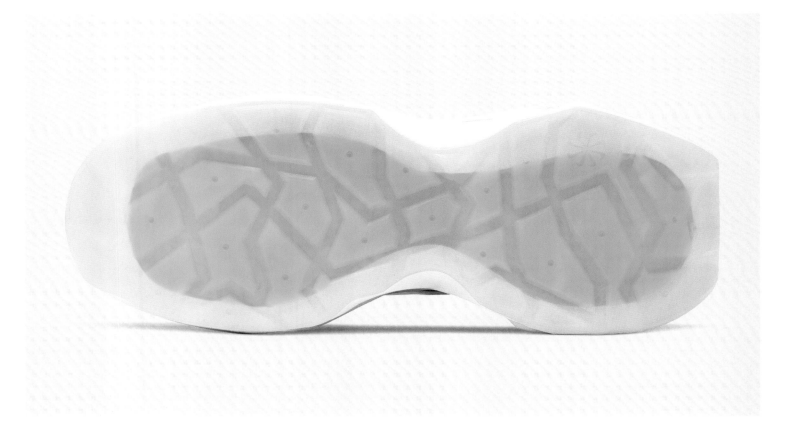

ZoomX Vista Grind outsole		2019

As Nike's sustainability goals progressed, so did its vision for Grind. The repurposed material became an element of global sport surfaces, a commercial carpet padding, and, via the 2018 Circular Innovation Challenge, evidence of the company's ambition for a circular future. Inviting innovators worldwide to prototype promising new uses for Grind, the challenge saw the pellets reconstituted as yoga mats, therapeutic mattresses, and climbing wall holds. In 2019 Nike's own designers advanced the exploration, fusing production scraps from ZoomX running shoes into the ZoomX Vista Grind's midsole— a bold expression of Grind, its revolutionary ethos, and its potential future applications.

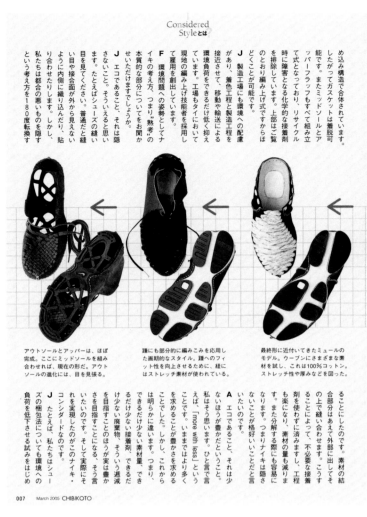

Considered Styleとは?

デザインにも環境配慮にも妥協しない

究極を目指す、改革の過程

ナイキ イノベーション

007 March 2005 CHIBIKOTO

CHIBIKOTO March 2005 006

SOTOKOTO

Considered Style宣言!

For Considered Lifestyles

Considered Styleとは?

"Considered Style!" Japanese-language advertisement for the Considered Collection | c.2005

If Grind was Nike's first attempt to turn trash into treasure, the Considered line was its original case study for creating sustainable performance products. The line's designers were directed to analyze materials and manufacturing with the goal of reducing waste, eliminating toxic substances, and employing environmentally preferred materials. Accordingly, the 2005 launch collection reduced solvents by 80 percent, manufacturing energy use by 37 percent, and waste by 63 percent when compared to other Nike designs. In 2007 the Considered Index—an internal resource that provided usable metrics for design teams to measure the environmental sustainability of individual Nike products—shared the line's production catalog company-wide and was subsequently lauded for precipitating the game-changing sustainability breakthrough Flyknit.

Considered Boot	Baroque Brown/Iron	2005

Considered Mowabb II	Brown/Beige	2005

Considered Humara	Brown/Orange	2005

Considered Tiempo	Brown/Brown/Beige	2006

Considered Gem Shoe	Brown/Beige	2005

Considered BB High	Brown/Green/Beige	2005

Considered Gem Shoe	Classic Olive/Khaki-Sable Green	2005

Considered Rock Shoe	Brown/Beige	2005

Flyknit development   c.2009–12

On February 21, 2012, in New York City, Nike chairman Mark Parker formally introduced an unprecedented shoe. He declared, "Today we've unveiled a technology we believe has the potential to change sport performance. . . . The Nike Flyknit upper redefines the idea of running footwear." True to Parker's words, the marathon shoe being displayed was unlike anything the sport world had ever seen. Its socklike upper was formed of recycled polyester threads, woven by hacked commercial knitting machines programmed to microengineer each stitch for optimized fit, comfort, and performance. Its variegated exterior was almost lenticular. An embodiment of the Nike design maxim that form must follow function, Flyknit began with a 2001 internal brief to "create alternative textiles for a footwear upper using textile manufacturing methods, thereby eliminating the conventional method of combining footwear components." This seemingly simple instruction snowballed into more than a decade of multidisciplinary research and development, ultimately delivering a uniquely sustainable technology that continues to propel performance textile manufacturing.

| Flyknit Trainer, London 2012 Medal Stand sample | Volt/Black/Sequoia | 2012 |

| Flyknit Racer | Volt/Black/Sequoia | 2012 |

Flyknit prototypes   c.2008

Flyknit upper pegboard   c.2010

Upon its unveiling in the summer of 2012, the Flyknit Racer turned the footwear industry upside down. Its digitally engineered upper presented an entirely new way of constructing performance shoes that was as eccentric as its variegated appearance. The shoe's instant success and subsequent cultural cachet triggered the technology's adoption across sportswear and performance categories. On football fields, fluorescent Flyknit boots overtook staid leather styles. On basketball courts, sleek Flyknit high-tops dethroned their bulky predecessors. Across the globe, the multi-hued shoes became synonymous with savvy urbanites. In 2018 Nike introduced an advancement to its Flyknit manufacturing process that enabled it to microengineer 360-degree anatomical forms—instead of flat panels—which afforded an even more precise fit according to the support, texture, and breathability requirements of each sport.

Flyknit sketch   c.2009

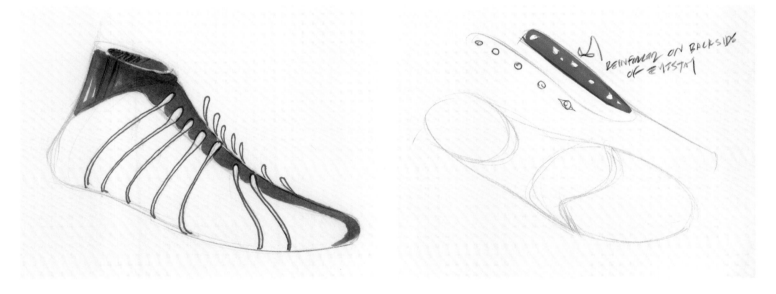

REINFORCE ON BACKSIDE
OF EYESTAY

Flyknit sketches   c.2008–9

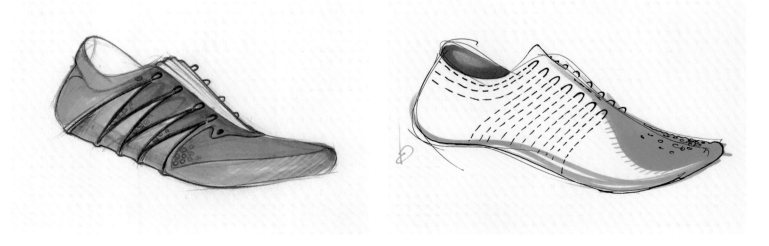

Flyknit sketches   c.2008

Flyknit Trainer	Black/White/White	2018

Flyknit Racer Be True	White/Multi-Color-Black-Pink Blast	2017

Flyknit Air Max	Black/Chlorine Blue-Total Orange-White	2015

Flyknit Air Max	Black/Sail-Atomic Orange-Volt	2014

Mercurial Superfly FG and outsole	Hyper Punch/Volt/Metallic Gold	2014

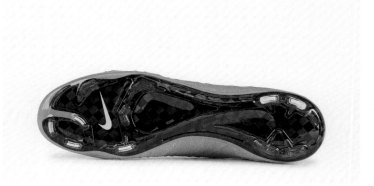

Free Flyknit 3.0 and outsole	White/Volt/Laser Orange	2014

Air VaporMax Flyknit Random 2	Multi-Color/Multi-Color-Multi-Color-Hyper Punch	2019

Air VaporMax Flyknit Random 2	Multi-Color/Multi-Color-Multi-Color-Hyper Punch	2019

| FE/NOM Flyknit Bra | Black/Dark Grey | 2017 |

Flyknit first moved from foot to body in 2017 with the arrival of the FE/NOM Flyknit Bra. Combining the technology with six hundred hours of biometric testing, Nike delivered a design that cut the approximately forty-one pieces and twenty-two seams of traditional sports bras to two panels and one binding, resulting in a 30 percent reduction in weight. Targeted engineering further enabled structural encapsulation and compression—providing better support for a wider range of cup sizes, revolutionizing the garment's appearance, and setting the stage for Flyknit innovation across apparel.

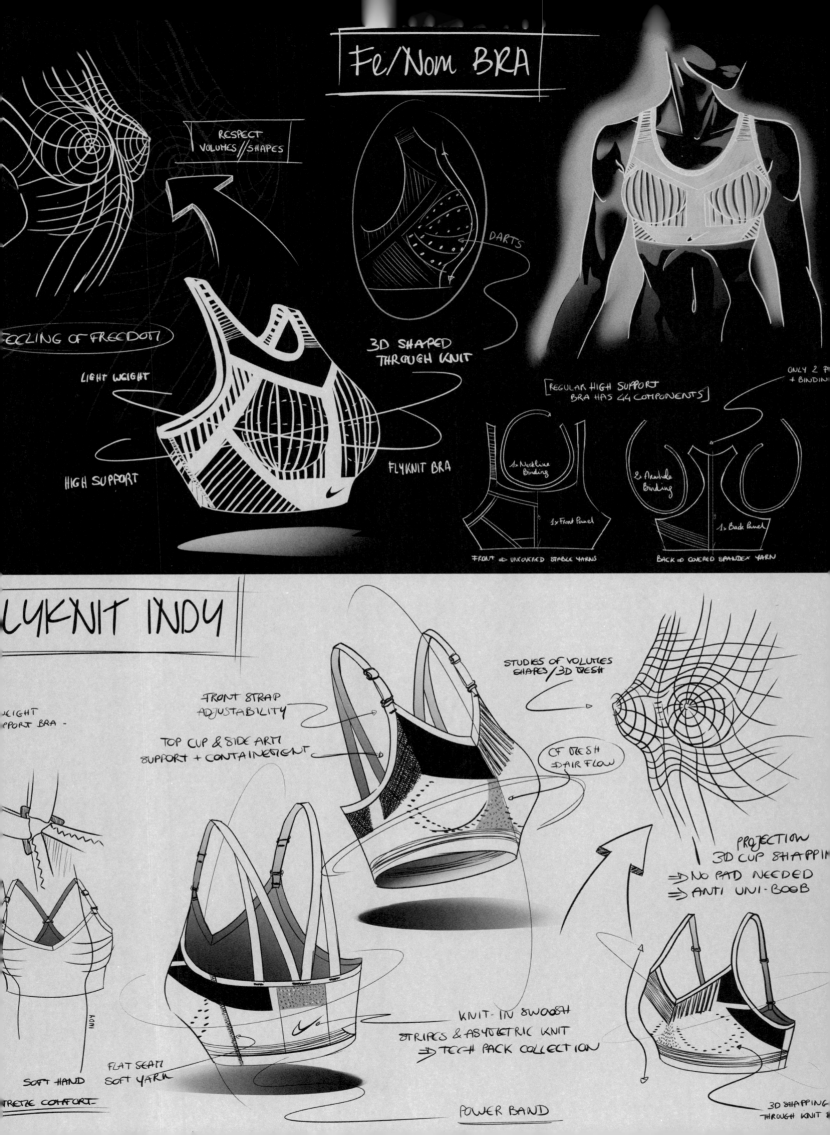

Fe/Nom BRA

RESPECT VOLUMES // SHAPES

DARTS

3D SHAPED THROUGH KNIT

FEELING OF FREEDOM

LIGHT WEIGHT

HIGH SUPPORT

FLYKNIT BRA

[REGULAR HIGH SUPPORT BRA HAS 44 COMPONENTS]

ONLY 2 P + BINDIN

1x Neckline Binding

2 Armhole Binding

1x Front Panel

1x Back Panel

FRONT ⇒ UNCOVERED STABLE YARNS

BACK ⇒ COVERED SPANDEX YARN

FLYKNIT INDY

WEIGHT PPORT BRA -

FRONT STRAP ADJUSTABILITY

TOP CUP & SIDE ARM SUPPORT + CONTAINEMENT

STUDIES OF VOLUMES SHAPES / 3D MESH

CF MESH AIR FLOW

PROJECTION 3D CUP SHAPPIN

⇒ NO PAD NEEDED
⇒ ANTI UNI-BOOB

KNIT-IN SWOOSH

STRIPES & ASYMETRIC KNIT ⇒ TECH PACK COLLECTION

SOFT HAND

FLAT SEAM SOFT YARN

STRETCH COMFORT

POWER BAND

3D SHAPPING THROUGH KNIT

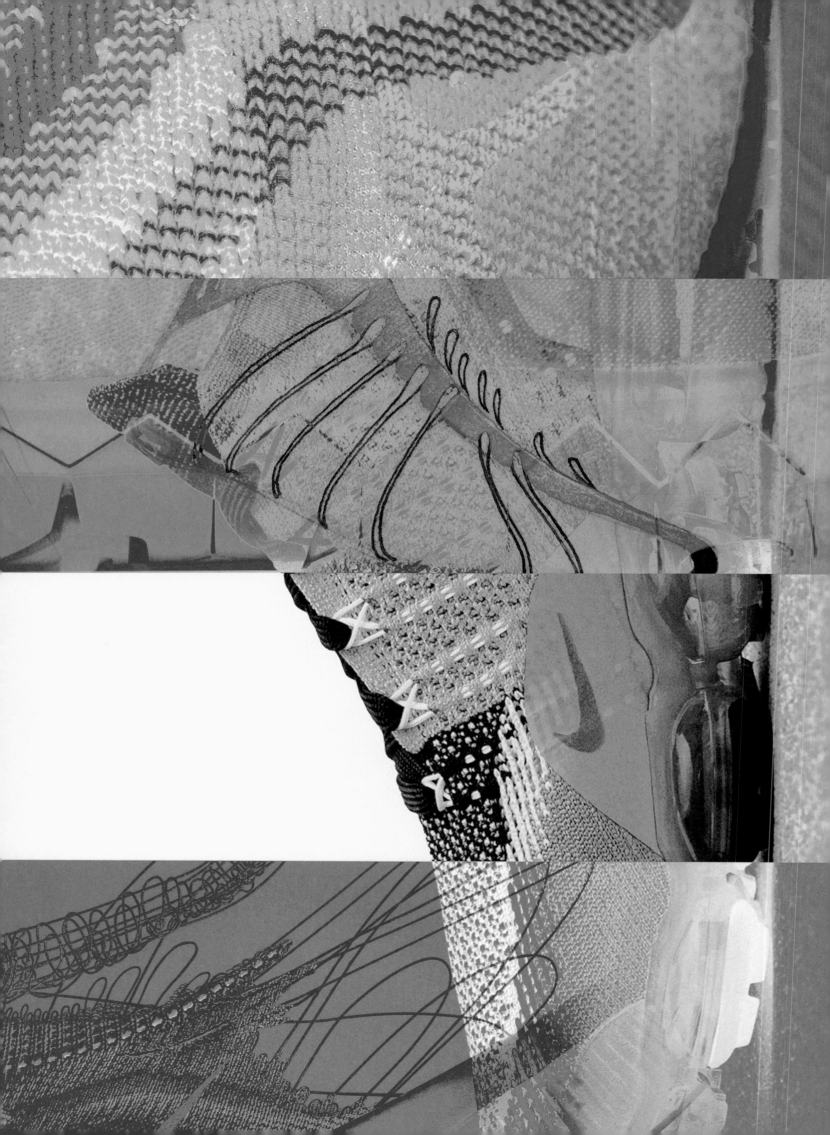

| Flyprint 3-D-printed textile uppers | 2018 |

| Zoom Vaporfly Elite Flyprint, worn and autographed by Eliud Kipchoge | Multi-Color/Black | 2018 |

Ever advancing the intersection of sustainability and performance, Nike introduced Flyprint in 2018. The first 3-D-printed textile upper in performance footwear, the engineered fabric translates athlete data into novel geometries. It unwinds TPU filament from a coil, melts it, and applies it in layers that can be programmed to serve a specific athlete or function. Moreover, the pioneering process hastens design iteration from days to hours and can be combined with Flyknit yarns, which, when engineered to thermally bond with Flyprint, eliminates additive glues or stitching. Flyprint is also lighter and more breathable than Nike's previously employed textiles. The innovation suitably debuted on Eliud Kipchoge, who wore custom Zoom Vaporfly Elite Flyprint shoes to win the 2018 London Marathon.

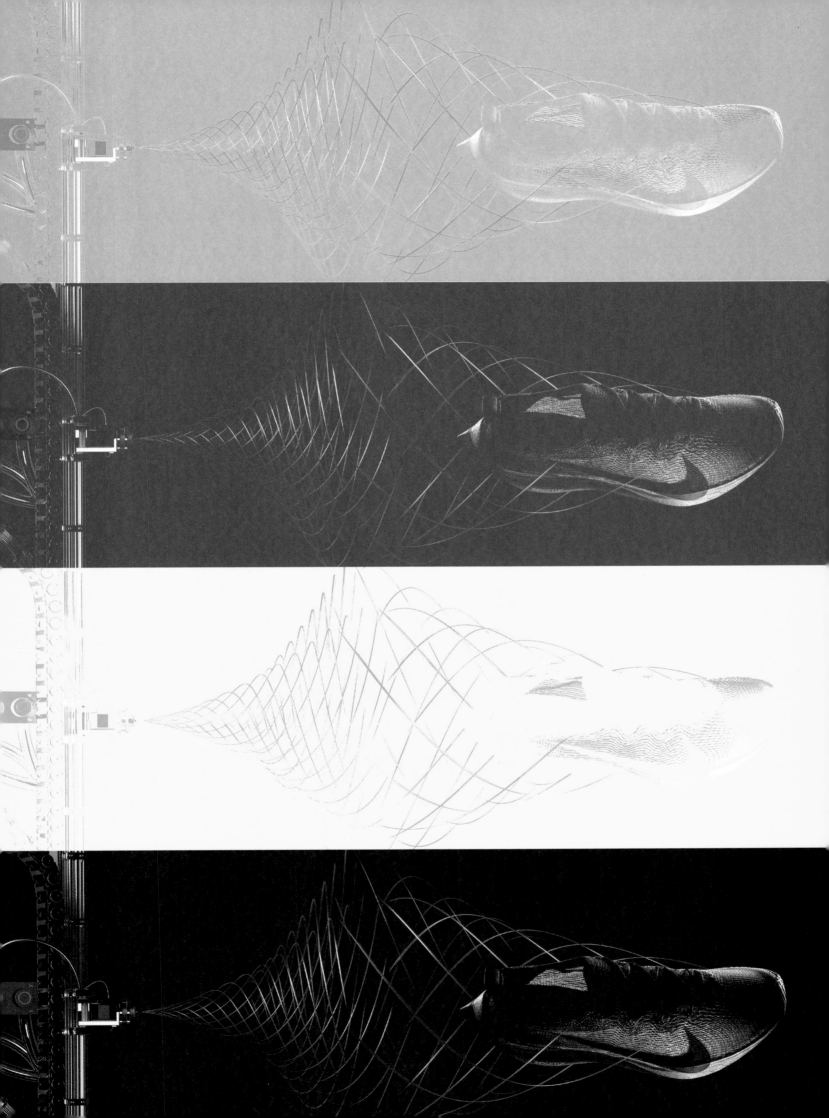

50% RECYCLED LEATHER FIBER

40% LIGHTER

5×MORE ABRASION RESISTANT

| Flyleather Cortez | White / Light Silver-White | 2017 |

As Nike continues to couple sustainability with growth, the company necessarily audits heritage materials with hefty environmental impact, such as leather. Derided for its inefficiency and toxicity, traditional leather manufacturing produces myriad scraps. As of 2017 Nike repurposes this waste, combining it with synthetic fibers and a fabric infrastructure to create Flyleather. Made with at least 50 percent recycled leather fiber, the composite textile derives from a powerful hydro process that fuses the individual components into a single textile that replicates premium, full-grain leather. In addition to mitigating waste, Flyleather uses less water and has a lower carbon footprint than conventional leather. It is also lighter and more durable and, because it is produced on a roll, improves cutting efficiency.

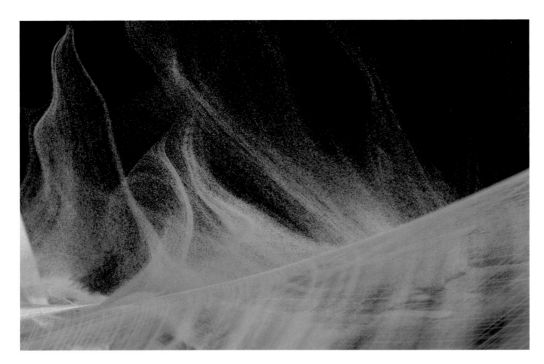

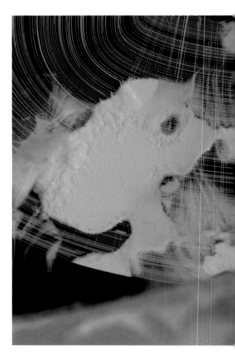

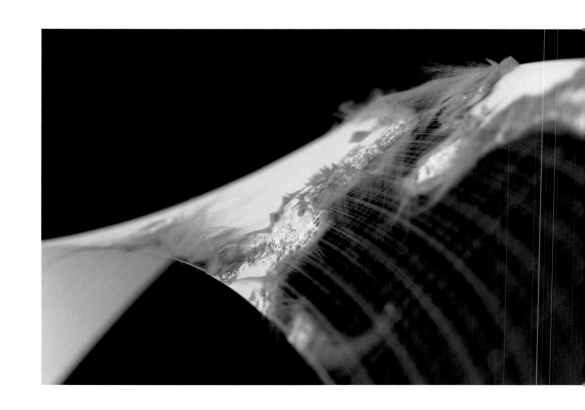

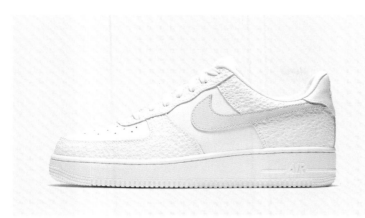

Flyleather Air Force 1 SE and outsole	White/Rose Gold/Metallic Gold	2017

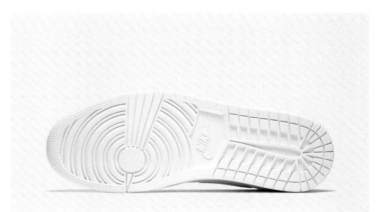

Flyleather Jordan 1 SE and outsole	White/Rose Gold/Metallic Gold	2017

Flyleather Air Max 90 SE and outsole	White/Rose Gold/Metallic Gold	2017

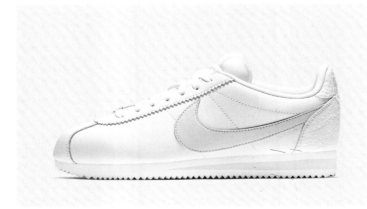
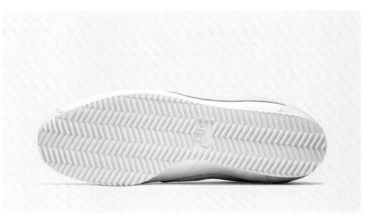

Flyleather Cortez SE and outsole	White/Rose Gold/Metallic Gold	2017

Space Hippie 03 and outsole	Grey/Total Crimson-Chambray Blue	2020

After nearly thirty years of seismic innovations traversing sustainability and performance, Nike articulated its combined circular-design learnings with the introduction of its 2019 Move to Zero initiative. Characterized as the company's "journey toward zero carbon and zero waste," Move to Zero explicitly aspires to help protect the future of sport via clearly defined metrics and ideals aimed at mitigating climate change. Fewer than six months later, the company manifested its progress with Space Hippie. The four-piece footwear collection takes its name and ethos from explorative space missions, where resources are finite and ingenuity is essential. Specifically, its uppers feature Flyknit yarns spun from at least 85 percent rPoly, which is derived from recycled plastic water bottles, T-shirts, and yarn scraps. Its cushioning repurposes factory scraps from the production of the Zoom Vaporfly 4% while its Crater Foam tooling uses 15 percent Grind rubber combined with 100 percent-recycled foam materials. The ensuing designs boast Nike's lowest carbon footprint scores to date.

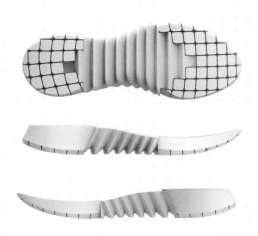

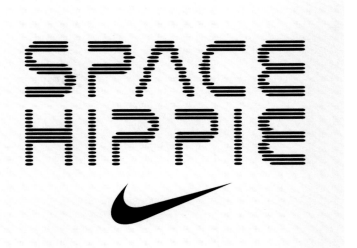

Space Hippie tooling exploration	2018

Space Hippie logo exploration	2019

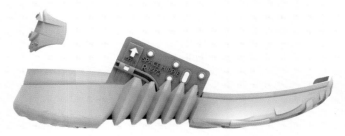

Space Hippie tooling	2019

Space Hippie 03 design exploration	2018

Space Hippie 03 prototype	2018

| Space Hippie 01 | Grey/Total Crimson-Chambray Blue | 2020 |

| Space Hippie 02 | Grey/Total Crimson-Chambray Blue | 2020 |

TRANS HUMANISM
RELIABILITY

ZØRMIBEL SPACE
HIPPIE

HIPPIE

HIPPIE

SPACE
HIPPIE

SPACE HIPPIE

SPACE HIPPIE

SPACE HIPPIE   NIKE

CRATER FOAM   SPACE WASTE YARN   ZOOMX ECO   2020 SUSTAINABILITY MISSION

NIKE TRASH TRANSFORMED

NIKE FROM WASTE TO WEAR

NIKE SPACE HIPPIE 01 02 03

 SPACE HIPPIE

 NIKE SPACE HIPPIE 01 02 03

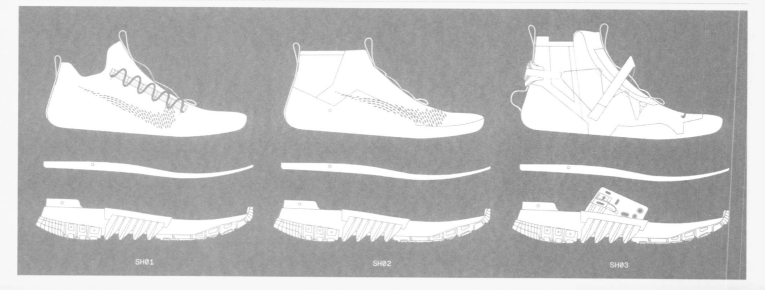

SH01   SH02   SH03

NIKE INC. Radical Design Division. All Rights Reserved.® 2018

NIKE INC.   Radical Design Division. All Rights Reserved.® 2018

NIKE INC.   Radical Design Division. All Rights Reserved.® 2018

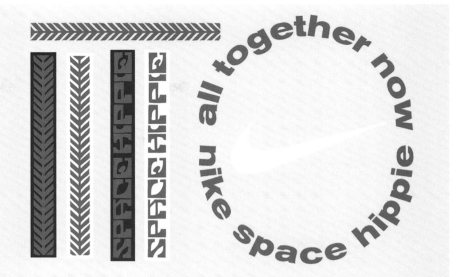

✦ Space Hippie
color swatches

space cadmium yellow This swatch is to be used in achieving a visual match in any medium of reproduction including inks, paints, dyes or other pigments when Space Cadmium Yellow is specified.	**space cadmium yellow** This swatch is to be used in achieving a visual match in any medium of reproduction including inks, paints, dyes or other pigments when Space Cadmium Yellow is specified.	**space cadmium yellow** This swatch is to be used in achieving a visual match in any medium of reproduction including inks, paints, dyes or other pigments when Space Cadmium Yellow is specified.	**space cadmium yellow** This swatch is to be used in achieving a visual match in any medium of reproduction including inks, paints, dyes or other pigments when Space Cadmium Yellow is specified.
space cadmium yellow This swatch is to be used in achieving a visual match in any medium of reproduction including inks, paints, dyes or other pigments when Space Cadmium Yellow is specified.	**space cadmium yellow** This swatch is to be used in achieving a visual match in any medium of reproduction including inks, paints, dyes or other pigments when Space Cadmium Yellow is specified.	**space cadmium yellow** This swatch is to be used in achieving a visual match in any medium of reproduction including inks, paints, dyes or other pigments when Space Cadmium Yellow is specified.	**space cadmium yellow** This swatch is to be used in achieving a visual match in any medium of reproduction including inks, paints, dyes or other pigments when Space Cadmium Yellow is specified.
space cadmium yellow This swatch is to be used in achieving a visual match in any medium of reproduction including inks, paints, dyes or other pigments when Space Cadmium Yellow is specified.	**space cadmium yellow** This swatch is to be used in achieving a visual match in any medium of reproduction including inks, paints, dyes or other pigments when Space Cadmium Yellow is specified.	**space cadmium yellow** This swatch is to be used in achieving a visual match in any medium of reproduction including inks, paints, dyes or other pigments when Space Cadmium Yellow is specified.	**space cadmium yellow** This swatch is to be used in achieving a visual match in any medium of reproduction including inks, paints, dyes or other pigments when Space Cadmium Yellow is specified.
space cadmium yellow This swatch is to be used in achieving a visual match in any medium of reproduction including inks, paints, dyes or other pigments when Space Cadmium Yellow is specified.	**space cadmium yellow** This swatch is to be used in achieving a visual match in any medium of reproduction including inks, paints, dyes or other pigments when Space Cadmium Yellow is specified.	**space cadmium yellow** This swatch is to be used in achieving a visual match in any medium of reproduction including inks, paints, dyes or other pigments when Space Cadmium Yellow is specified.	**space cadmium yellow** This swatch is to be used in achieving a visual match in any medium of reproduction including inks, paints, dyes or other pigments when Space Cadmium Yellow is specified.

✦ Accent
color swatches

base blue This swatch is to be used in achieving a visual match in any medium of reproduction including inks, paints, dyes or other pigments when Base Blue is specified.	**base blue** This swatch is to be used in achieving a visual match in any medium of reproduction including inks, paints, dyes or other pigments when Base Blue is specified.	**base blue** This swatch is to be used in achieving a visual match in any medium of reproduction including inks, paints, dyes or other pigments when Base Blue is specified.	**base blue** This swatch is to be used in achieving a visual match in any medium of reproduction including inks, paints, dyes or other pigments when Base Blue is specified.
alarm orange This swatch is to be used in achieving a visual match in any medium of reproduction including inks, paints, dyes or other pigments when Alarm Orange is specified.	**alarm orange** This swatch is to be used in achieving a visual match in any medium of reproduction including inks, paints, dyes or other pigments when Alarm Orange is specified.	**alarm orange** This swatch is to be used in achieving a visual match in any medium of reproduction including inks, paints, dyes or other pigments when Alarm Orange is specified.	**alarm orange** This swatch is to be used in achieving a visual match in any medium of reproduction including inks, paints, dyes or other pigments when Alarm Orange is specified.
base green This swatch is to be used in achieving a visual match in any medium of reproduction including inks, paints, dyes or other pigments when Base Green is specified.	**base green** This swatch is to be used in achieving a visual match in any medium of reproduction including inks, paints, dyes or other pigments when Base Green is specified.	**base green** This swatch is to be used in achieving a visual match in any medium of reproduction including inks, paints, dyes or other pigments when Base Green is specified.	**base green** This swatch is to be used in achieving a visual match in any medium of reproduction including inks, paints, dyes or other pigments when Base Green is specified.
flat white This swatch is to be used in achieving a visual match in any medium of reproduction including inks, paints, dyes or other pigments when Flat White is specified.	**flat white** This swatch is to be used in achieving a visual match in any medium of reproduction including inks, paints, dyes or other pigments when Flat White is specified.	**flat white** This swatch is to be used in achieving a visual match in any medium of reproduction including inks, paints, dyes or other pigments when Flat White is specified.	**flat white** This swatch is to be used in achieving a visual match in any medium of reproduction including inks, paints, dyes or other pigments when Flat White is specified.
black hole This swatch is to be used in achieving a visual match in any medium of reproduction including inks, paints, dyes or other pigments when Black Hole is specified.	**black hole** This swatch is to be used in achieving a visual match in any medium of reproduction including inks, paints, dyes or other pigments when Black Hole is specified.	**black hole** This swatch is to be used in achieving a visual match in any medium of reproduction including inks, paints, dyes or other pigments when Black Hole is specified.	**black hole** This swatch is to be used in achieving a visual match in any medium of reproduction including inks, paints, dyes or other pigments when Black Hole is specified.

The [Early] Nike Space Hippie Catalog.
Restricted Distribution. Internal Only

space hippie

[Nike] Space Hippie
ARTICLES

Nike's New Radicals
Section 3

space hippie is from nike's radical design tradition.

"You cannot change how someone thinks, but you can give them a tool to use which will lead them to think differently."

Buckminster Fuller

The [Early] Nike Space Hippie Catalog.
Restricted Distribution. Internal Only

space hippie

[Nike] Space Hippie
ARTICLES

Nike's New Radicals
Section 3

The Space Hippie Mission:

+ Fundamentally rewire the way we think about responsible production and consumption.

+ Radically transform thinking within Nike, the footwear industry, and the world at large.

+ Encourage divergent thinking, even when that thinking challenges existing Nike practices and accepted norms.

spacehippie

spacehippie

all together now * nike space hippie program *   2.1

Grind and manufacturing waste used for the Space Hippie Collection	c.2019

Space Hippie Collection	2020

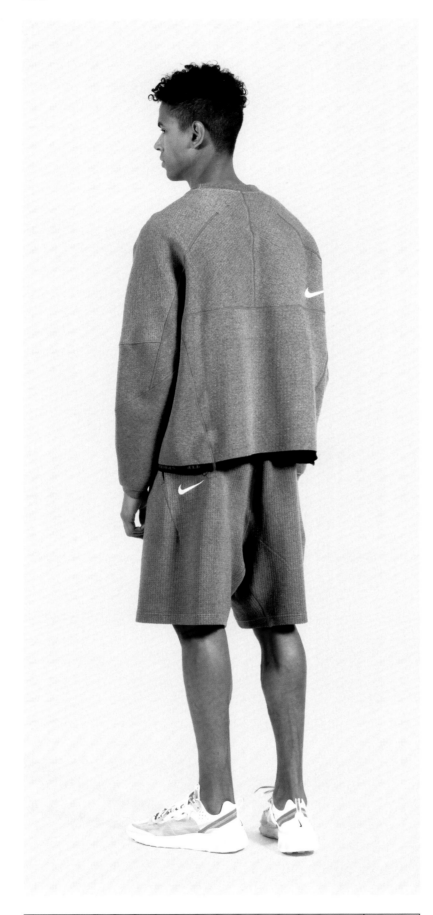

| Move to Zero* T-shirt | 2020 |

| Move to Zero* Collection | 2020 |

| Team USA Medal Stand Collection | 2020–1 |

At the same time Nike introduced its futuristic Space Hippie designs, it debuted the Team USA Medal Stand Collection for the 2020 Summer Games in 2021. Similarly grounded in cradle-to-cradle sustainability principles, the collection's jacket reimagines the iconic Windrunner in 100 percent recycled polyester, with waste-reducing knit panels. The pants are constructed of the same recycled nylon, lined with 100 percent recycled polyester mesh. Drawstring tips, zipper pulls, and logos are molded from Grind, and the collection's Air VaporMax footwear contains at least 50 percent recycled content by weight. Nike's 2020 Move to Zero* Collection adopts these same tenets; it reimagines classic Nike silhouettes using a blend of recycled polyester and sustainable cotton, and employs an innovative dyeing technology.

*Nike's journey toward zero carbon and zero waste to help protect the future of sport.

CRAFTING COLOR

Color, like sport, is a universal language. Red makes hearts race, while blue pacifies minds. Where yellow turns heads, black stealthily creeps. Each hue possesses its own scientifically documented powers, as well as deeply personal associations. At Nike, these empirical and anecdotal nuances are individually scrutinized and judiciously weighed by the company's Color Design team, which is tasked with creating seasonal color palettes that will distinguish the next six months of Nike designs. The team's specialized designers—whose backgrounds span architecture, graphic design, fine art, industrial design, fashion design, and trend research—begin their process more than two years before their work arrives in-store. Relying upon observation and experimentation, they embark on global research trips, examine the natural world, and obsess over the sports world. They test cutting-edge technologies and get their hands dirty at the dye lab in Blue Ribbon Studio, Nike's in-house craft workshop. Uniting their findings and respective expertise with the latest color theories and technologies—as well as current political, social, and cultural undercurrents—they simultaneously anticipate and shape the chromatic future. Once they outline a foundational seasonal palette, the designers create three-dimensional color bundles to methodically balance hue, texture, proportionality, and finish. Each color is then translated into an exclusive Nike color standard and assigned a proprietary name (such as Whisper Pink, Mean Green, Sport Spice, or Wolf Grey) that allows for the company to match the color—material to material and season to season—now or a decade down the line when a shoe might be reissued.

Eventually these swatches join Nike's Materials and Color Libraries. Here, they reside alongside thousands of other entries, ranging from trademark Nike Orange to high-visibility hues expressly adapted to the digital era. Even more recent additions reveal the kaleidoscopic results of innovative methods of make (such as waterless dyes, laser printing, and materials upcycling) that hint at Nike's ongoing expedition of 3-D quantum craft—an augmented landscape with the potential to dramatically evolve both our perception and conception of color.

Hyper Punch	2014

Volt	2012

Space Hippie	2020

Flyprint	2017

Nike's strategic use of color is well documented throughout the company's history—from the 1984 red-and-black Air Jordan I shoes that were banned for their rule-breaking hues to the gold flash of Michael Johnson's 1996 spikes to the disruptive introduction of Volt in the summer of 2012. The striking fluorescent yellow, which Nike used to color every track-and-field and medal-stand shoe, flouted convention dictating that footwear reflect national hues. In addition to being considered the most visible color to the human eye, Volt made Nike athletes feel and look faster, and unified them across all nations and sports. The vivid shade also alerted fans to the company's newest technology, Flyknit. In 2014 Nike applied a similar color theory to its football boots ahead of the World Cup, employing Hyper Punch, a custom fluorescent pink color specifically designed to pop against a green pitch and contrast team uniforms, catching the eyes of viewers watching the event on television.

Four years later a new technology further upped Nike's color game. Flyprint, the company's first 3-D-printed textile upper, enabled designers to generate unprecedented color effects and novel finishes, including the lenticular shimmer seen on the technology's debut shoe, the Zoom Vaporfly Elite Flyprint for Eliud Kipchoge. Inspired by the runner's home country, the design's colorway recalled the clay roads, grasslands, and forestry of Kipchoge's training environment in Kenya.

Nike's pursuit of advanced manufacturing methods continues to evolve its product palette, as demonstrated by Crater Foam, which debuted with the 2020 Space Hippie footwear collection. The foam features Grind granules—created from recycled surplus manufacturing materials—which define each midsole as uniquely polychromatic. While the introduction of chance into Nike's color process radically deviates from the practice of meticulously matching threads to drawstrings, it similarly communicates the company's commitment to help protect the future of sport.

Color swatches used to map out seasonal color palettes (top) and Nike color standards used as source materials for palette building (bottom)

The Nike Color Design team's creation of three-dimensional color bundles exemplifies the craft-driven, hands-on process that combines with state-of-the-art digital applications to inform forward-looking work. Starting with a season's theoretical palette, which pairs external and internal insights with experience and intuition, the team participates in collaborative workshops that put the proposed spectrum to practical test. Mixing found materials—from scavenged package labels and dried plants to vintage buttons and industrial rubber gloves—with textiles from Nike's existing Color and Materials Libraries, the designers discern which hues should form the core of the palette and which should serve as accents. The process also allows them to extrapolate the spectrum to serve all footwear, apparel, and equipment needs, resulting in a seasonal color "toolbox" of nearly two hundred hues that communicates a cohesive chromatic vision.

Knitted yarn loops (top) and a collection of found fabrics, hand dyed by the Color Design team (bottom)

Tropical Twist/Green Glow/Sesame/Terra Blush/Solar Flare

Dark Raisin/Ashen Slate/Crimson Bliss/Bright Mango/Green Strike

University Gold/Light Zitron/Sail/White/Green Strike/Neptune Green

Fuchsia Glow/Fuel Orange/Rugged Orange

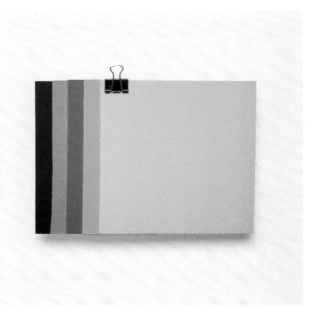

Blackened Blue/Ashen Slate/Chile Red/Cyber/Crimson Bliss

Black/Desert Dust/Sail/Opti Yellow/Bright Citron/Light Zitron

Dark Sulfur/Grain/Martian Sunrise/Orange Pearl/Pale Ivory

Purple Pulse/Deep Royal Blue/Black/Cyber/Turf Orange/Bucktan/Smoke Grey

Lime Glow/Galactic Jade/Sesame/Green Glow/Light Arctic Pink/Purple Nebula

Ashen Slate/Particle Grey/Black/Blackened Blue/Light Photo Blue/Hyper Royal

Hyper Pink/Hyper Crimson/Game Royal/Green Strike/Smoke Grey/Velvet Brown

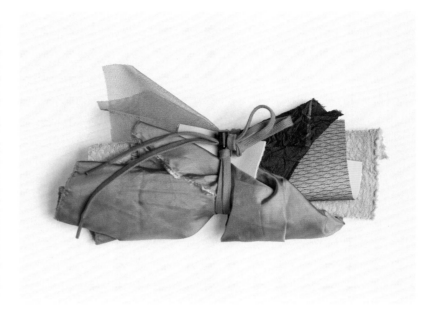

Midnight Navy/Grand Purple/Psychic Blue/Citron Pulse/Fauna Brown/Light Sienna/Purple Pulse/Steam

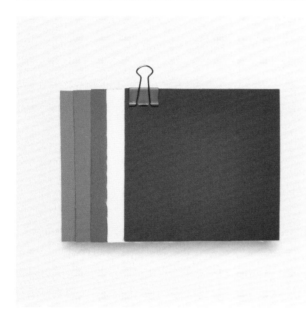

Orange/Aquamarine/Signal Blue/White/Iron Grey

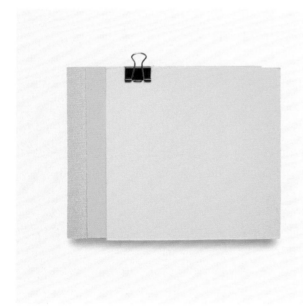

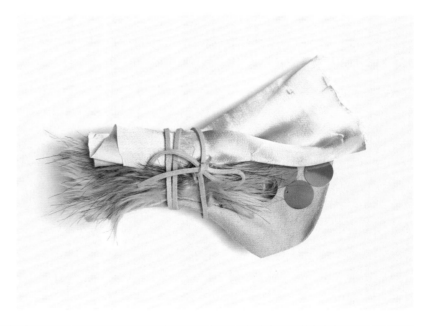

Sesame/Fuel Orange/Arctic Orange

Black/Green Abyss/Light Photo Blue/Cyber/Blackened Blue

Mahogany/Barely Volt/Concord/Turf Orange/Indigo Haze

College Grey/Pearl White/Turf Orange/Laser Orange/Baroque Brown/Rugged Orange

Green Strike/Cyber/Barely Volt/Indigo Haze

On a Sunday morning in 1971, Bill Bowerman leaped up from the breakfast table and changed history. He grabbed the waffle iron his wife Barbara had used to make their meal, brought the still-warm appliance to his workshop, and quickly mixed up a batch of urethane and poured it into the machine. In his haste, he forgot to apply a nonstick coating, and the machine never opened or made waffles again, but the idea for a new kind of rubber sole—one that would more effectively grip the track and adapt to whatever surface it was being used on—was born. Some thirty years later, John Hoke, Nike's chief design officer, went to visit Bowerman with some colleagues and found himself standing in that very same workshop, helping to repair an old shelf. Bowerman had bent an old license plate into a bracket, which had finally succumbed to decades of use. As Hoke took it down and unfolded it back into shape, he noticed it read Nike-R and asked the retired coach what it meant. "It stands for Nike Research," Bowerman replied. "Never forget that we research athletes, and all that research converts into innovation." For Hoke, who kept the plate as a treasured memento, it remains a powerful invocation of the company's true north.

"Ultimately, if we're not solving problems, making people better, creating more access to sport and more access to courage and confidence, we're not fulfilling the promise and destiny that this founder had for us," says Hoke. "From day one, innovation was a commitment, not a guarantee. We were committing to learning and to listening. But it never guaranteed success or a product or platform or any of the stuff we say today. It was about establishing a restless curiosity and drive to continuously improve."

Now for almost fifty years, Nike has explored, developed, refined, and redefined the processes necessary to institutionalize sports research and innovation. The new LeBron James Building and Nike Sport Research Laboratory (NSRL) is a testament to these efforts; it will undoubtedly be one of the most sophisticated sports research facilities ever built, allowing for Nike's researchers to collect and analyze fantastic amounts of data from all manner of activities and angles. The goal is, of course, to transform that data into actionable insights—and the team suspects that new ideas will emerge, as they have in the past, from being able to analyze human bodies and performance in ever more sophisticated ways. But despite the significant investment and dedication of resources, there is no guarantee of what those insights will be or where they may lead the business. There is only the recognition and extension of a process that—beginning with Bowerman—has brought this company this far: to always listen to the voice of the athlete. That process isn't always clear-cut. As Thomas Clarke, PhD, Nike's president of Innovation, notes, "You have to create an environment where it's OK to fail, which I think allows people to throw themselves more vigorously into things that will eventually succeed." In other words, innovation at Nike isn't a fixed destination; it's the journey to get there. Where that journey takes the company next is by no means certain, but there are hints of where the path may lead.

One direction, dubbed Quantum Craft by Hoke and his colleagues, recognizes the strides offered by computational design to boost athletic performance and drive new aesthetics. "When Bill was tinkering," says Hoke, "it was hand drawing and it took months to get something done. Now, we set the parameters, input the data, simultaneously run a billion algorithms, and, a minute later, get something back. Ultimately, I think it sets the designers and innovators free to really open the aperture and explore what's possible." While the digital tool set becomes ever more advanced, Nike's design leadership is aware that the human dimension on the other side of the screen must also be nurtured. Blue Ribbon Studio (BRS), the company's on-site experimental arts-and-crafts workshop, offers design teams ample opportunities to summon their creativity through hands-on learning and exploration. Different activities such as screenprinting, sewing, and even gardening, encourage nonlinear thinking and offer a counterpoint to the dominant software and hardware tools of the trade. For Hoke, Quantum Craft lies in the nebulous and fertile space between the two: "It's the power of imagination, fueled by calculus."

For a company that produces millions of products per year, improving the way in which those products are produced has become a critical focus. Above all, Nike is interested in protecting the future of sports for coming generations—and rightfully recognizes that vast changes in method of make, manufacturing, and service will be needed to ensure that promise. Projects such as Space Hippie point to all that can be achieved right now, but behind the scenes the company is laser-focused on finding new ways to eliminate waste, adhesives, dyes, and cross-linked materials that defy recycling and reuse. "What if we said that all of the molecules in the world that Nike's entitled to use forever are already in existence in the sum total of our shirts and shoes? You don't get any more," says Michael Donaghu, vice president of Innovation. He continues, "It becomes a physics problem. What an amazing constraint!"

These moonshot directives have led design and innovation teams to explore unique avenues for alternative materials, applications and manufacturing methods. As the company wrestles with the notion of circularity at scale, the ultimate ambition is not only to do less harm but to actually help heal the world around you. "What if when you're done with your product," Hoke muses, "you put it in the ground and you bury it because it decomposes, or you send it back to us because it's fertilizer for the next thing we're growing?"

A less transactional, more deeply realized relationship with the customer is also on the horizon. While the earliest Nikes were imprinted with a label that read "engineered and built to the exact specifications of championship athletes around the world," tomorrow's Nikes could be built to your exact specifications and adjusted to your needs. The seeds have been planted with programs such as Nike By You and Adapt, but Hoke and his colleagues envision a far more robust capability that draws on hardware, software, service, and community components to offer customers entirely new genres of products and experiences. With the goal of encouraging more people to engage in sports, Nike envisions a world where its products could ultimately help each of us overcome our biological limitations. It won't only take new methods of manufacturing and design but also a forever-wired cloud intelligence that's monitoring, coaching, enhancing, and augmenting our performance in the moment. Already with the Adapt platform, design and innovation teams are investigating a user's response to the haptic dialogue created when the shoe's laces tighten. "We learned that opening and closing actually created squeezing, and squeezing created the potential of a Morse code," says Hoke. With that notion as a launching point, he muses about the potential for creating a new kind of sensory vocabulary that could be used for everything from wayfinding on a run around town to real-time corrective guidance or haptic coaching during a match.

Given Nike's relentless forward march, some of these speculations may come to fruition within the next few years, while others may remain on the proverbial drawing board for years to come. Uncertainty and risk are at the heart of any R&D-driven business—and Nike, which relies on its innovation engine to serve the business and create the future, is no exception. While robust scenario planning can help to mitigate those risks, it almost goes without saying that 2020 has stretched the imagination of even the most imaginative scenario planner. Years of work put in for what was to have been a banner year for sporting events have been cast into uncertainty as the global pandemic caused by a novel coronavirus has upended the lives of billions around the globe. A world without such events would have sounded like fodder for a dystopian sci-fi plot some months previously but quickly became just one striking facet of a rapidly evolving new normal. Instead of cheering on athletes as they competed to qualify for games, teams at Nike contemplated the concept of sports without spectators. The company's agile pivot to training and home fitness—not to mention converting its Air MI manufacturing facility to produce a TPU face shield—shows that even in crisis Nike's spirit is indefatigable. "One of the things we're really centered on is this protection of the future of sport—really knowing what's at stake," says Hoke. "How can we be more thoughtful about the choices that we make as creatives and the problems that we solve as designers? How do we make sure that more people can play generations from now? As long as there are humans that are participating in sports, those sports and those activities will present problems for us to solve—and it's this endless possibility of 'What next? What can we go do?'" With the 2020 pandemic, these questions have only taken on greater meaning and more immediacy.

While there are no easy answers to be had, it's likely that whatever direction Nike takes, it will be rooted in its core beliefs. "We will just continue this notion of what I think sports has always been about," says Hoke, "which is people coming together to challenge, to push, and to observe each other, and to participate with each other. That's a community, and I feel like we as a company get to use that as a platform and build these communities deeper and deeper and wider and wider. If that can help us to remain human and connected to ourselves and our fellow man, I think that's great."

For the first fifty years of its existence, Nike has helped athletes run faster, jump higher, cut quicker, and, most of all, win. "There's a purity to that," notes Clarke, "but as the company evolves, you've got a lot of people that want to feel better in all aspects of well-being—not just competing but living." With that expansive notion at hand, and a mandate to explore and address the interrelated set of problems scaling from global climate change to the molecules under your feet, the Nike of today will likely be unrecognizable fifty years from now (except, surely, for the Swoosh). But to anyone paying attention, this should come as no surprise. The company was built on the premise that today's record will fall tomorrow. For the people responsible for the future of design and innovation at Nike, making the impossible possible isn't a constraint; it's a commitment.

Phaidon Press Limited
2 Cooperage Yard
London E15 2QR

phaidon.com

Phaidon Press Inc.
65 Bleecker Street
New York, NY 10012

First published 2020
Reprinted 2021 (three times), 2023
© 2020 Phaidon Press Limited

ISBN 978 1 83866 051 2

Commissioning Editor	Emilia Terragni
Project Editor	Robyn Taylor
Production Controllers	Nerissa Dominguez Vales, Sue Medlicott
Design	Maximage
Typefaces	Signs, Maxitype Antique, Optimo
Text Contributor	Erin Dixon

Picture Credits

Unless otherwise noted, all images are courtesy and copyright © Nike, Inc.

Lance Accord 130 (b), 131 (left column: second from top, bl; right column: second from top); Christopher Anderson cover image, 12, 17; Christopher Anderson and Finn Taylor 18, 21, 22, 23; Phillip T. Annand and Jacob Rochester 295–6; Andrea Bastoni 146, 201 (ml, bl), 202 (tl); Pictured: Sebastian Coe and Dan Norton 43 (mr, br); Clayton Cotterell 28–9; Harry De Zitter 120–1; James Ewing 207 (t); Marcus Fischer 300, 304–11; Pablo Franco 128 (t; second row: r); Niclas Gillis (dir.), Dorian Grinspan (creative director), James Casebere (photographer) 148–9; Paula Greif and Peter Kagan 116–17; Cindy Grey 128 (third row: l); Rick Guest 240; Harry Hall 34 (tl, tr); Genevieve Hanson 206 (br), 210 (t); Hart Lëshkina 287; Haw-lin 86 (t, m); Pictured: John Hayes and Jamie Larsen 44 (ml); I LOVE DUST 252–3; Stefan Klapko 152–3; Paola Kudacki 243; Benjamin Lennox 86 (bl, br); Adeline Lulo, model: Jasmine Santiago 154 (first row: l); Adeline Lulo, models: Jasmine Santiago and Laura Ciriaco 154 (second row: l); The Malloy Brothers 124; Mark McCambridge 22 (second row: l), 24; Megaforce 134–5; Alex Menendez via AP 129 (b); Hanna Moon 181; Fabien Montique 184; Jamie Morgan 201 (tr), 202 (mr); Katsuhide Morimoto 201 (tl, mr), 202 (br); Harri Peccinotti 144; Ralphy Ramos 154 (third row: mr); Austin Cary Rhodes 147; Pictured: Jim Ryun 44 (tl); Arto Saari 128 (second row: l); Cheril Sanchez, model: Yaris Sanchez 154 (third row: ml); Martin Schoeller 129 (t); Mario Sorrenti 211; Pete Stone 114 (tr); Emma Summerton 199; Elvin Tavarez, model: Rayly Aquino 154 (first row: r); Misha Taylor 128 (third row: ml); Nick Thornton and Warren Du Preez 187; Ryan Unruh 214 (ml, mr, b), 213, 215–20; intervention page #29; Alberto Vargas, model: Jose Estévez 154 (second row: mr); Juan Veloz, model: Monica "Chede" Soriano 154 (second row: ml, r; third row: r); Lauren Ward and Alex Kweskin 299; Vanessa Wityak 136; John Woo 150–1

CCA 2017

Every reasonable effort has been made to acknowledge the ownership of copyright for photographs included in this volume. Any errors that may have occurred are inadvertent, and will be corrected in subsequent editions provided notification is sent in writing to the publisher.

Acknowledgments

Without dreamers, rebels, mavericks, contrarians, underdogs, agitators, instigators, misfits, risk-takers, and rule-breakers, this book would not exist. Their disruptive exploits inspired its conception and creation, and their relentless commitment to manifesting ever-more-crazy dreams fuels Nike's foundational mission: to continuously evolve the legacy of Nike innovation ignited in 1972 by Bill Bowerman and Phil Knight. This unruly heritage, which began on a track in Oregon, now stretches around the globe thanks to the dedication of Nike employees, collaborators, and storytellers—past and present—including the intrepid Phaidon team that produced this book. Their collective efforts not only bring innovation and inspiration to every athlete in the world, but crucially they also embolden tomorrow's innovators. Finally, our breakneck momentum and no-finish-line mentality would be impossible to maintain without the athletes who constantly demand more: superior products, groundbreaking innovations, and constant progress. Thank you all for unapologetically stepping out of your lanes.

First and foremost Phaidon would like to thank Demetria White and Jeremiah Morse for welcoming us into the world of Nike, for their incredible insight, stories, hospitality, patience, and dedication, and for making us feel like part of the family. Special thanks also to DNA for allowing us access to the wealth of knowledge, passion, and history that exists within the archive, as well as to Bertrand Bordenave, Jeanne Huang, Nigel Powell, and the full Nike team: to all the inspiring designers, innovators, athletes, communications staff, and many others for taking the time to share your experiences and showing us the importance of the people behind the process. In addition, we wish to thank author Sam Grawe for his complete commitment to the project and for helping to craft the vision for what it has become; Erin Dixon for her insightful, thoughtful, and informative writing; and also the book's designers David Keshavjee, Julien Tavelli, and Daniel Haettenschwiller of Maximage for bringing everything together into the perfect form with huge enthusiasm and skill. Last but not least, we would like to thank all others who contributed to the project: Paul Au, Theresa Bebbington, Jane Birch, Vanessa Bird, Cameron Briggs, Nerissa Dominguez Vales, Quinn Faino, Trevor McIrvin, Sue Medlicott, Laine Morreau, João Mota, Belle Place, and Gemma Robinson.